Readers' Advisory Service

in the Public Library

THIRD EDITION

JOYCE G. SARICKS

American Library Association
Chicago   2005

Design and composition by ALA Editions in Janson Text and Helvetica using QuarkXPress 5.0 on a PC platform.

Printed on 50-pound white offset, a pH-neutral stock, and bound in 10-point cover stock by McNaughton & Gunn.

The paper used in this publication meets the minimum requirements of American National Standard for Information Sciences—Permanence of Paper for Printed Library Materials, ANSI Z39.48-1992. ♾

Library of Congress Cataloging-in-Publication Data

Saricks, Joyce G.
    Readers' advisory service in the public library / Joyce G. Saricks.—3rd ed.
        p.   cm.
    Includes bibliographical references and indexes.
    ISBN 0-8389-0897-7
    1. Readers' advisory services—United States. 2. Public libraries—Reference services—United States. 3. Fiction in libraries—United States. I. Title.
    Z711.55.S27 2005
    025.5'4—dc22   2004029271

Printed in the United States of America

09   08   07   06   05   5   4   3   2   1

For Bren and Meg,
who continue to tolerate their mother's obsession.

And especially for Chris,
who is always ready to read and to play and
who has shared a love of books from the beginning.

CONTENTS

FIGURES

PREFACE

In the years since the second edition of *Readers' Advisory Service in the Public Library* was published, in 1997, the library profession has once again experienced a dramatic increase in interest in this topic as well as in the way it is taught in library schools and practiced in public libraries across the country. The impact of the World Wide Web on library service in general and readers' advisory in particular, changes in practices, increased availability of tools, expanded knowledge of and interest in the topic, and questions from librarians convinced me that practitioners and educators would welcome an updated and expanded edition.

In this edition, I have added material in several areas. In response to increased interest in readers' advisory for nonfiction readers, I have expanded the original definition of *readers' advisory* to include materials for leisure readers of fiction and nonfiction. A brief discussion of nonfiction readers' advisory is also included. The chapter on readers' advisory reference sources has been dramatically revised to reflect the domination of online tools. I have also expanded the explanation of *appeal* with more examples, a vocabulary of appeal terms, and a discussion of how readers' advisors use reviews to discover appeal. More material on marketing—to library users and administration—acknowledges the growing importance of that aspect of our work. There are also additional bibliographies and appendixes; the Popular Fiction List is joined by a Popular Nonfiction List and examples of fiction and nonfiction Sure Bets with an explanation of their audience and appeal. Throughout the text, I have tried to include more examples to illustrate the concepts.

The philosophy behind this revision remains consistent with that of the first two editions. The aim is to introduce the user to the materials, skills, and philosophy of readers' advisory service. Rather than being prescriptive, this book offers suggestions of techniques, and all material included supports a nonjudgmental, patron-oriented, skill-based readers' advisory service. As did the first two editions, this revision offers topics for discussion, techniques to be modified to fit an individual library's service needs, and a philosophical basis for creating and adapting readers' advisory service.

ACKNOWLEDGMENTS

I wish to acknowledge the continuing support of the Downers Grove Public Library in promoting readers' advisory, especially Library Director Christopher Bowen, who has pushed us to continue growing and expanding our service, and the Library Board of Directors, who both use and support the service. The current Readers' Advisory Staff—Heather Booth, Debbie Deady, Sheila Guenzer, Marianne Trautvetter, Nana Oakey-Campana, Sue O'Brien, and Terri Williams—have not only challenged and inspired me; they have also read and reacted to drafts of this manuscript. For their dedication, willingness to try anything (and make it work!), faith in the goals of readers' advisory, friendship, and love of books and reading and the pleasure of sharing these, I am grateful.

Special thanks go to the tireless and dedicated readers of this manuscript: Heather Booth, Sue O'Brien, Georgine Olson, Chris Saricks, Duncan Smith, Cathleen Towey, Lynne Welch, David Wright, and Neal Wyatt. They worked with very short deadlines, and several went beyond anything I could have hoped, offering extensive comments to improve the manuscript. All their meticulous readings and creative suggestions have been greatly valued and appreciated, but special thanks go to Georgine as well as to Sue-Ellen Beauregard for their excellent suggestions for the Popular Nonfiction List.

Finally, my heartfelt thanks to ALA Editions' Laura Pelehach and Eloise L. Kinney for their gracious assistance and suggestions.

1

A History
and Introduction

Providing readers' advisory service in public libraries is not a new idea. Organized programs have been documented since the 1920s, although their role in libraries and the philosophy on which they are based have changed dramatically over the years. In this chapter I define readers' advisory, discuss why it is important for libraries to provide this service, and consider readers' advisory for nonficion as well as fiction readers. I also present a historical overview of past programs and the philosophy behind them, describing how current programs differ from their forerunners and fit into public libraries today.

Redefining Readers' Advisory Service for Adults

Readers' advisory service, as discussed in this book, is a patron-centered library service for adult leisure readers. A successful readers' advisory service is one in which knowledgeable, nonjudgmental staff help fiction and nonfiction readers with their leisure-reading needs. (Although this book will not address working with younger readers or with patrons seeking audio and video selections for their leisure time, I believe that those areas also fall within the purview of readers' advisory, which advocates, in its purest form, that staff help readers with all library collections that support leisure-time pursuits.) The public library as an institution has always championed and encouraged reading for information as well as for pleasure. Readers' advisors and proponents of the service subscribe wholeheartedly to the philosophy that reading has intrinsic value. Books that support this belief and address the importance of reading in the lives of adults are being published in increasing numbers.[1] Readers' advisors understand that readers are best served by a library that provides both appropriate materials and a knowledgeable staff. This belief was confirmed in a survey by St. Louis Public Library where users "placed the highest value on staff assistance . . . the ability of well-trained staff to provide accurate answers and recommendations as to 'the next best book.'"[2] Needless to say, this service must be supported, encouraged, and cherished by the library administration in order to prosper.

Previous editions of this book have focused on fiction-reading interests exclusively. This more specialized emphasis resulted in part from the fact that our collection at the Downers Grove Public Library was limited to fiction and literature (the Dewey 800s), and our work concentrated on readers using those collections. In addition, the first edition was written at a time when fiction-reading interests and the needs of fiction readers were substantially ignored by the library profession. Public libraries concentrated their time, energy, and money on facts and information, the nonfiction collection. Librarians were trained to help in the pursuit of these worthy questions; fiction readers were left to their own devices.

Times have changed. The impact of the World Wide Web on the library's reference function has forced librarians and administrators to rethink their priorities and services. As more and more potential patrons rely on the Web for answers to the reference questions that were once the mainstay of Adult Services departments, librarians, who see their circulation statistics and reference questions decreasing, are beginning to look seriously at other ways to market their collections and services. For many libraries, this has meant an increased interest in developing readers' advisory services. Until recently, there was so little information available on library service to leisure readers, especially nonfiction readers, that it is fairly easy to understand the emphasis on readers' advisory for fiction, particularly genre fiction. While we never meant to deny that similar techniques could be applied to leisure readers of nonfiction, we never specifically addressed nonfiction. That omission is rectified in this edition.

The Importance of Readers' Advisory Service in Libraries

According to the 2003 Harris poll, reading remains the favorite leisure activity for Americans.[3] Even though a 2004 National

Endowment for the Arts study reports a decline in reading, still more than half the population reported having read literature—defined as a novel, short story, play, or poetry—in the past year.[4] While libraries today offer a growing array of services for patrons, we still remain the only agency that provides free access to books, in print and audio formats. Despite increased emphasis on technology and electronic access to information, at the beginning of the twenty-first century, libraries continue to be repositories of books. During this time of technological advances, librarians are discovering that while technology provides libraries with tools that facilitate our access to information and help us better serve our patrons, many of our users meet their information needs in other ways. Adults, both men and women, come to libraries for more than stock quotations, health information, and how-to guidance; they also come to us for stories that challenge, inspire, or take them away when the world becomes too much.[5] Studies show that more than 90 percent of users come to the library to check out books and videos.[6] These are readers and viewers who come to libraries seeking material for their leisure time, and advisory staff should be provided to assist them.

Traditional public library statistical data specific to leisure reading, such as high circulation figures, are difficult to discover, and, to my knowledge, there are no national research projects based on circulation data or wide-ranging user studies for public library leisure reading combining fiction and nonfiction. On the other hand, in the states that collect fiction versus nonfiction statistics, fiction circulation tends to be about 60 percent of the total adult circulation.[7] Individual libraries have statistics that support the popularity of fiction in their institutions, but no large-scale compilation exists at this time. Ascertaining circulation totals for leisure reading of nonfiction will be even more difficult.

Despite the lack of extensive circulation data, there are powerful, pragmatic reasons for a library to provide readers' advisory service for its patrons as well as a considerable amount of anecdotal evidence of the popularity of leisure-reading titles. Concerning the latter, most practicing librarians will attest to the increasing number of patrons interested in reading fiction and popular nonfiction. One indicator of this popularity, which has been discussed extensively in the current library literature, is the pressure placed on public libraries to provide "enough" copies of best sellers. Libraries spend a sizable portion of their budgets on selecting, purchasing, processing, housing, shelving, and generally maintaining their popular fiction and nonfiction collections. Given this high patron demand and significant budgeting commitment, libraries need to address the concerns of their leisure readers more directly. If the public library as a whole is to be perceived not merely as a self-service institution in which users are expected to make choices with only minimal assistance, it follows that libraries need to provide trained, knowledgeable staff to work with leisure readers as well as with those seeking help with information requests.

Another compelling argument in favor of providing readers' advisory service arises from the organization of both the fiction and nonfiction collections, which by their very natures create some special problems that require trained assistance. For instance, patrons who walk into the library in the mood for light, quick, escapist books are confronted by thousands of fiction books organized alphabetically by author and nonfiction arranged by an even more obscure cataloging system. This arrangement can be daunting, not to mention frustrating. The organization of these collections is a major barrier for many readers; often, finding the specific kind of leisure-reading book they want is nearly impossible. Even when readers have the title of a book they have enjoyed, how can they find a similar book? The readers' advisor provides this vital link between the library's leisure-reading material and readers.

History of Readers' Advisory Services

Providing readers' advisory service for both fiction and nonfiction is not a new idea. By reviewing its origins, we can identify the underlying principles and practices that form the basis of present-day readers' advisory service. Although the roots of readers' advisory reach back into the nineteenth century, this service first flourished in public libraries in the United States in the 1920s through the 1940s.[8] Robert Ellis Lee, in his study, *Continuing Education for Adults through the American Public Library, 1833–1964*, describes three phases in the development of reader guidance, or readers' advisory, between 1922 and 1940.[9] The first phase, from 1922 to 1926, saw structured readers' advisory service begun in seven urban public libraries: Chicago, Cincinnati, Cleveland, Detroit, Indianapolis, Milwaukee, and Portland, Oregon. Reader guidance, covering both fiction and nonfiction, was a special and specialized service that was provided separately from other library services. Advisors met with patrons in private interviews, often in offices set aside for that purpose, to determine an appropriate reading plan. The advisors then prepared "individualized reading courses for persons who wished to read systematically to meet the practical needs of daily living."[10]

During the second phase, from 1927 to 1935, both the effectiveness and the scope of the service were increased. It was also during this period that the Adult Education Roundtable was formed and first met at the 1927 American Library Association (ALA) Annual Conference. In addition, public libraries featured ALA's Reading with a Purpose courses, which consisted of books and "annotated lists of books on special topics."[11]

By 1935, forty-four libraries provided a readers' advisory service. Jennie M. Flexner, of the New York Public Library, which initiated its readers' advisory service in 1929, published numerous articles and two books about that library's program. These studies provide useful insights into the kind of work being done at that time. Readers were interviewed extensively by librarians about their reading interests, both to aid in developing individualized lists and to ascertain patrons' reading levels. While this approach sounds very similar to that used in present-day readers' advisory interviews, the judgmental suppositions made about patrons then are in direct contrast to today's attitude. For example, the patron who named *Atlantic Monthly* as a magazine read regularly was felt to have better reading skills than one who read the *Saturday Evening Post* or *Time*.[12] After the interview, an annotated reading list was prepared and then mailed to the reader, who would seek out the books in the local branch library.

The growth of the idea of readers' advisory in public libraries during this second phase was attributed to three causes: "(1) the increased number of professional workers in public libraries; (2) the increased idleness and leisure caused by the Depression . . . ; and (3) the beginning of systematic research relating to problems of adult reading."[13] The studies of adult reading and readability that were carried out during this time provided a basis for the techniques librarians used in linking book selection with "the reading interests, habits, and abilities of adults" and thus made readers' advisory services more effective.[14]

The third phase, from 1936 to 1940, saw the broadening of readers' advisory within libraries. Subject specialists worked with readers' advisors in formulating reading lists. While this development indicated an expansion of the readers' advisory service, it also pointed out the extensive reading background required by librarians in preparing individualized, annotated book lists. As the demand for the service increased, providing these lists became more difficult.

During this time, more than thirty articles describing aspects of readers' advisory services appeared in professional journals, in addition to several full-length books. One study, *Helping the Reader toward Self-Education*, identified seventy reader types and classed them by occupation, race, sex, and personality traits.[15] Ranging from The Timid and Inferior-Feeling Person, The Low-Brow, and Tenement Dwellers to The Ambitious Person and the Sophisticated Woman, each type was listed with three to four book titles considered appropriate reading suggestions. For instance, The Unskilled Worker was advised to read Steinbeck's *Of Mice and Men*; for The Coward, Conrad's *Lord Jim* was suggested; The Criminal in the Making was advised to read Dreiser's *An American Tragedy*. We can only marvel at the presumption involved in making such judgments about the reader's character and then persuading each type to read and benefit from the chosen titles. This moralistic, didactic tone contrasts strikingly with that of the present. It seems amazing to readers' advisors today that librarians of the past could comfortably make the assumption that their reading suggestions would result in dramatic self-improvement in the readers. For those wishing to read further about this and other studies on the history of readers' advisory service, see the bibliography of historical sources at the end of this book.

World War II and the accompanying reduction in leisure time dramatically decreased requests for readers' advisory service, and some libraries discontinued it.[16] By 1949, readers' advisory was clearly "going out of fashion."[17] However, a Reading Guidance Institute held at the University of Wisconsin Library School in 1965 indicated continued, although perhaps peripheral, interest in the subject.[18]

The underlying concern of librarians involved in these earlier readers' advisory services was the role of the public library in adult continuing education. Librarians saw readers' advisory service as a means of helping adults meet their need for further learning. In the words of Lee Regan, "What was stressed in these early efforts was (1) the unique opportunity which libraries offered for continuous, informal adult education; and (2) the friendly and close relationship which reader's advisers formed with patrons."[19]

"Friendly and close" though the relationship between librarian and patron might have been, the approach was clearly didactic. The aim of the readers' advisory service was to move readers toward classic works, to outline a plan of reading that would be educational, not recreational. Saddled with this worthy but formidable goal of providing materials for adult continuing education and expected to fulfill almost a tutorial role with patrons, readers' advisors who subscribed to this philosophy found that the work involved in providing this service eventually became too burdensome. Librarians were unable to meet the demands for so many individually prepared and extensive reading lists. Out of necessity, the lists became more standardized, and some of the individual contact was lost.[20]

Despite differences between readers' advisory of the past and present, both in purpose and in attitude, some threads can be traced linking the early services to current practice. First, readers' advisors then and now have acknowledged the difficulty in discovering what it is that patrons are seeking when they ask for reading suggestions. An expertise in interviewing in order to discover patron interests and to match them with appropriate authors and titles continues to be vital to the process. Second, readers' advisors, past and present, need a general knowledge of fiction and nonfiction collections, an ability to recognize the quality of the books they suggest, and the ability to describe books well, both orally and in writing. Finally, present-day readers' advisors concur with their historical predecessors about the importance of the personal relationship between librarian and reader, even if these librarians would disagree about the nature of that relationship. In their 1934 study of the readers' advisory service at the New York Public Library, Flexner and Edge discuss, in terms with which we can all agree, What is a readers' advisor?[21] Such a librarian has, among other things, "a wide acquaintance with the insides of books," the ability to discuss individual books with readers, and the ability "to share his enthusiasm over certain books."[22] In short, a readers' advisor, past and present, is "a librarian at the disposal of the reader, trying to make easier and more satisfying the connection between the reader and books."[23]

Readers' Advisory Today

Librarians today find themselves in the midst of a readers' advisory renaissance. Interest in and enthusiasm for providing readers' advisory in public libraries have grown enormously in the last twenty years. Readers' advisors, and other librarians interested in programs related to the fiction collection, once sought in vain for relevant programs at national conferences; now we find them in increasing numbers, especially at conferences sponsored by the Public Library Association (PLA). In 2004, PLA in Seattle offered a Readers' Advisory/Author track with eleven programs specifically related to readers' advisory, a program on virtual readers' advisory, talk tables, and a preconference. The Collection Development and Evaluation Section of ALA's Reference and User Services Association (RUSA/CODES) established a readers' advisory committee in 1994. Since its inception, the committee has presented programs on readers' advisory at each annual conference and published two bibliographies of readers' advisory resources as well as a study of readers' advisory education.

Many state conferences, too, have offered programs for librarians interested in readers' advisory. In addition, library systems and individual libraries have focused on readers' advisory with extensive training programs provided by in-house staff as well as outside experts. All of this speaks to a growing professional recognition of the importance of readers' advisory in our public libraries and of the necessity of training for staff who provide this service.

Research in this field continues to grow as well. Both scholarly and practical articles appear in increasing numbers in library literature. (See the selected bibliography of such resources at the end of this book.) In addition, in the last few years, Neal-Schuman has published scholarly compilations of research in readers' advisory, as have Haworth Press and Libraries Unlimited.[24] Even the Library of Congress, in conjunction with OCLC, is working to improve subject access to works of fiction by expanding the range of subject headings assigned to adult fiction titles.

Organizations of readers' advisory librarians have also flourished. An example of this type of group is the Adult Reading Round Table (ARRT) in Illinois, with more than two hundred members. It recently celebrated twenty years of providing quality programs to Chicago-area readers' advisors. This group presents three readers' advisory programs yearly: a genre/literature program, a nuts-and-bolts (how-to) program, and a small group discussion for which, for example, each participant might bring and discuss a book on a specific topic. This group also produces a newsletter three times yearly and an annotated book list each year. In addition, members may participate in a two-year genre study, led by a member of the organization. Librarians should seek out others interested in readers' advisory service and form such groups, not only for the continuing education value of the meetings but also for the opportunities this activity provides to interact with others. From the meetings and the contacts members make, they develop a network of librarians with whom they can discuss books and reading interests, readers' advisory philosophy, and patron questions as well as foster further commitment to providing quality readers' advisory service.

Readers' advisory practices in the twenty-first century have also changed significantly from their pedagogical origins. The relationship between readers and librarians is now much less didactic. By and large, public library patrons are interested primarily in talking to librarians about their leisure-reading interests. Rather than "elevating the masses," readers' advisors strive to be knowledgeable about fiction and nonfiction—particularly that which is popular in their libraries—and to respond with perception and insight to the reading interests of their patrons.

Qualifications for readers' advisors and staffing requirements for a department are also seen in a different light today. Although in the past entire departments were devoted solely to readers' advisory, only a few libraries have that luxury today. Readers' advisory can be done on some level wherever there are people who care about reading and who want to help others find reading materials of interest to them. A readers' advisory service can be part of a reference or a circulation department's activities. Readers' advisors need not have professional library degrees; my own experience, as well as new research, confirms that trained paraprofessionals can be excellent readers' advisors.[25]

Expanding the Scope of Readers' Advisory

Readers' advisory has become an accepted and established service in many American public libraries, and it will continue to evolve to meet the needs of users and to incorporate technological advances. Accustomed as they are to going from the readers' interests to book suggestions, readers' advisors have always had to be flexible in their approach and attitude, capable of meeting new challenges as they arise. These skills will serve them well as readers' advisory approaches new challenges.

Nonfiction Readers' Advisory

The underlying element that links fiction and nonfiction and their leisure readers is "story." Duncan Smith, creator and product manager of EBSCO's NoveList, has written and spoken eloquently on this topic over the years and has inspired a generation of readers and readers' advisors with his thoughtful reminders of the importance of story in all our lives.[26] No matter how we designate the "readable," "creative," or "popular" nonfiction that attracts leisure readers, whether we call it "narrative nonfiction" or something else, we know that readers recognize and seek it and that we, as public service staff and readers' advisors, need to learn to as well. As Melanie Deutsch remarked as a panel member in the nonfiction readers' advisory presentation at the PLA Conference on February 26, 2004, "Patrons don't worry about Dewey when they're looking for a good book to read."[27] Nor do they necessarily look exclusively to fiction or nonfiction; they seek a story that meets their interests and mood at that moment. In fact, many libraries further expand readers' advisory services to meet all adult "story" needs, whether in audio, video, or fiction and nonfiction books.

What we lack at the time of this writing are the tools that help us provide readers' advisory service for nonfiction. As is the case with fiction genres, neither Dewey decimal numbers nor other classification schemes get to the heart of the issue: linking books that provide similar satisfactions to readers. Before readers' advisory for nonfiction readers comes into its own in our libraries, we will need a nonfiction version of *Genreflecting*, the classic genre-based guide to fiction, a tool that can provide needed background for readers' advisors and readers. What are the nonfiction genres? Surely they are broader than mere Dewey numbers. In a presentation as part of Chicago Public Library's Scholar-in-Residence program, in May 2003, Kathleen de la Peña McCook speculated that these genres might follow the pattern of cable television channels.[28] Genres might include Biography and Memoir, History, Discovery, Animals, Travel, Food, Home Improvement, Gardening, Arts and Entertainment, True Crime, and much more. Any librarian who works with nonfiction and readers will immediately see the possibilities.

For these nonfiction genres we will likely need a Popular Nonfiction List, similar to our Popular Fiction List, which identifies authors popular at our libraries. (A prototypical list is included in appendix 2.) Constructing such a resource requires staff to consider what nonfiction genres and authors are popular in their library, and, once completed, this list will provide an excellent training tool, a starting place for readers' advisors to become familiar with popular genres and authors. Eventually specialized reference sources, perhaps a nonfiction version of EBSCO's NoveList, will provide extensive background information on the popular nonfiction genres, just as they have for fiction, and web resources will also incorporate and support nonfiction readers' advisory activities.

Beyond the Book Format

While the profession is considering expanding the scope of readers' advisory to include nonfiction, we should not forget format. For many readers, listening to audiobooks provides the same satisfactions as holding a book in hand and turning the pages. Travelers—be they commuters, farmers, long-haul drivers, or vacationers—have made audiobook collections the black hole of many libraries' budgets; we seem never to have enough books in that format to satisfy readers. Story, once again, constitutes the draw for listeners, and although some patrons have informational needs that are met by our audio collections, most still are simply looking for a narrative, fiction or nonfiction, to transport them.

With audiobooks there are additional considerations, such as the questions of abridged versus unabridged and the quality of both the production and the narration, which we consider as we work with readers. As with some books, both fiction and nonfiction, for which we might encourage readers to "give it one hundred pages before you give up," it sometimes takes a little time to "fall into" the story in audiobooks. We always encourage listeners to try at least one tape or disc before deciding a title does not suit them. In addition, audiobook publishers' catalogs provide an excellent source of book titles that work well for nonfiction readers' advisory. These publishers seem to have an eye—and an ear—for titles that appeal to leisure readers.

Providing Readers' Advisory

The two keys to providing readers' advisory in any library setting, regardless of library size or staffing, are commitment to meeting the leisure-reading interests of readers and a responsive attitude toward readers, no matter what they enjoy reading. Although anyone who cares about books and reading can suggest books, a library that claims to offer a readers' advisory service has an obligation to provide knowledgeable staff as well as to make an ongoing commitment of time and library resources to developing the service.

In addition to the desire to make a "connection between the reader and books," attributes of readers' advisors include a willingness to read widely, knowledge of the interests of the library's patrons, and a familiarity with popular authors, titles, and genres. Readers' advisors of today commit time and effort to providing this service, a great deal of it spent in reading and study. Time also must be set aside to master the techniques of the readers' advisory interview, to learn to talk about books with readers, to gain familiarity with a range of popular fiction and nonfiction, and to create tools to help readers' advisors assist readers. These subjects will be covered in the following chapters.

Before discussing specific readers' advisory techniques, let's define some important terms—that will be used in a nontraditional way—to prevent confusion about their meaning and intention. First, the term *appeal* refers to those elements in a book, whether definable or just understood, that make readers enjoy the book. *Similar authors* and *readalikes* mean a group of authors whose works share elements that appeal to the same readers. When discussing fiction and nonfiction, the term *genre* means any sizable group of authors or specific titles that have similar characteristics and appeal; these are books written to a particular specific pattern. The term *good books* will be used in this book as a form of shorthand to mean fiction and nonfiction titles that are enjoyable to read and in which the writing meets a recognized quality standard. Admittedly, this may be an unstated and rather nebulous standard, but it is one most professionals use, if perhaps intuitively, to judge quality.

In summary, when we compare the philosophy of readers' advisory past and present, we can see that it is primarily the libraries' attitude toward the reader that has changed. Readers' advisors in the 1920s and 1930s saw themselves as educators; they *knew* what was good for readers and led them in specific directions. Readers' advisors today see themselves as *links* between readers and books, just as reference librarians are the connection between users and informational materials. Libraries already allocate resources—both time and money—to developing and maintaining their popular reading collections; such expenditures justify a similar commitment of staff to make the collections as accessible as possible to readers, as the St. Louis cost-benefit study above demonstrated. In the next chapter, we examine reference resources that aid readers' advisors in providing this service.

Notes

1. For example, Sven Birkerts, *The Gutenberg Elegies: The Fate of Reading in an Electronic Age* (Boston: Faber, 1994); Robert Cole, *The Call of Stories: Teaching and the Moral Imagination* (Boston: Houghton, 1989); Anne Fadiman, *Ex-Libris: Confessions of a Common Reader* (New York: Farrar, Strauss & Giroux, 1998); Steven Gilbar, *Reading in Bed: Personal Essays on the Glories of Reading* (New York: Godine, 1995); Azar Nafisi, *Reading Lolita in Tehran: A Memoir in Books* (New York: Random, 2003); Sara Nelson, *So Many Books, So Little Time* (New York: Putnam, 2003); Nancy Pearl, *Book Lust: Recommended Reading for Every Mood, Moment and Reason* (Seattle: Sasquatch, 2003); Daniel Pennac, *Better Than Life* (Toronto: Coach House, 1994); Noel Perrin, *A Reader's Delight* (Hanover, N.H.: Univ. Pr. of New England, 1988); and Lynne Sharon Schwartz, *Ruined by Reading: A Life in Books* (Boston: Beacon, 1996).
2. Glen E. Holt, "Proving Your Library's Worth: A Test Case," *Library Journal* 123 (November 1, 1998): 42–44.
3. Humphrey Taylor, "Large Decline since 1995 in Favorite Activities Which Require Physical Exercise," Harris Poll #72, December 1, 2003. Available from info@harrisinteractive.com.
4. Bruce Weber, "Fewer Noses Stuck in Books in America, Survey Finds," *New York Times*, July 8, 2004, C1.
5. In *Adventure, Mystery, and Romance: Formula Stories as Art and Popular Culture* (Chicago: Univ. of Chicago Pr., 1976), author John G. Cawelti discusses in depth the importance and role of formulaic literature in our lives.

6. "Public Unaware of Librarians' Education," *American Libraries* 32 (May 2001): 10.
7. Ken Shearer, *The Readers' Advisor's Companion*, ed. Kenneth D. Shearer and Robert Burgin (Westport, Conn.: Libraries Unlimited, 2001), xv.
8. For a more extensive history of readers' advisory, see Bill Crowley, "A History of Readers' Advisory Service in the Public Library," in *Nonfiction Readers' Advisory*, ed. Robert Burgin (Westport, Conn.: Libraries Unlimited, 2004).
9. Robert Ellis Lee, *Continuing Education for Adults through the American Public Library, 1833–1964* (Chicago: American Library Assn., 1966), 57–60.
10. Ibid., 57.
11. Lee Regan, "Status of Reader's Advisory Service," *RQ* 12 (spring 1973): 227.
12. Jennie M. Flexner and Byron C. Hopkins, *Readers' Advisers at Work: A Survey of Development in the New York Public Library* (New York: American Assn. for Adult Education, 1941), 21.
13. Lee, *Continuing Education*, 58.
14. Ibid., 59.
15. John Chancellor, Miriam D. Tompkins, and Hazel I. Medway, *Helping the Reader toward Self-Education* (Chicago: American Library Assn., 1938).
16. Lee, *Continuing Education*, 60.
17. Regan, "Status," 230.
18. Ibid.
19. Ibid., 227.
20. Ibid., 229.
21. Jennie M. Flexner and Sigrid A. Edge, *A Readers' Advisory Service* (New York: American Assn. for Adult Education, 1934), 50–57.
22. Ibid., 53.
23. Ibid., 51.
24. Kathleen de la Peña McCook and Gary O. Rolstad, eds., *Developing Readers' Advisory Services: Concepts and Commitments* (New York: Neal-Schuman, 1993); Kenneth D. Shearer, ed., *Guiding the Reader to the Next Book* (New York: Neal-Schuman, 1996); Georgine N. Olson, ed., *Fiction Acquisition/Fiction Management: Education and Training* (New York: Haworth, 1998); Bill Katz, ed., *Readers, Reading and Librarians* (New York: Haworth, 2001); Shearer, *The Readers' Advisor's Companion*; and Burgin, ed., *Nonfiction Readers' Advisory*.
25. Research in North Carolina confirms that there is no evidence that professionals provide better readers' advisory service than do paraprofessionals. See Kenneth D. Shearer and Pauletta B. Bracy, "Readers' Advisory Services: A Response to the Call for More Research," *RQ* 33 (summer 1994): 457.
26. Duncan Smith, "True Stories: Portraits of Four Nonfiction Readers," in *Nonfiction Readers' Advisory*.
27. Melanie Deutsch, "Just the Facts, Ma'am: Investigating Nonfiction Readers' Advisory" (program presented at the Public Library Association Tenth National Conference, Seattle, Wash., February 24–28, 2004).
28. Kathleen de la Peña McCook, "Readers' Advisory for Nonfiction" (discussion, Chicago Public Library, May 22, 2003).

2   Reference Sources

Every readers' advisory department should rely on its collection of reference sources. In this chapter, I consider first how to use these sources before enumerating the features readers' advisors seek in reference sources. Then I look at specific readers' advisory resources, both electronic and print, and examine those features that make them particularly useful. Next, this chapter surveys additional reference sources, not necessarily designed for readers' advisors, and discusses their use. Unfortunately, since there are no reference resources aimed at readers' advisory for leisure readers of nonfiction at this point, I cannot consider specific nonfiction resources. (However, readers will see that many general resources may be used for both fiction and nonfiction queries.) This chapter next describes a Popular Fiction List—a checklist of authors and genres popular in the Downers Grove Public Library—that was developed for use as a reference source and offers ideas for creating a Popular Nonfiction List (see also appendix 2). In discussing how and why our library created the fiction list, as well as in sharing our experiences in using it, I explain how any library can devise its own lists to reflect its collection and patron reading interests. The final section discusses the collaborative nature of readers' advisory and the importance of staff and colleagues as an often overlooked but valuable resource.

Incorporating Reference Resources into the Readers' Advisory Interview

Although reference sources are the backbone of the reference interaction, checked to discover the information the patron seeks and then cited as the source of those facts, they are not always as easy to incorporate into the readers' advisory interview, which resembles more a conversation than an actual interview. Introducing book or web resources into this conversation is not always easy. When polled about their use of resources in the readers' advisory interview, librarians reported three difficulties.[1] First, readers do not expect us to turn to resources; they frankly expect us to have read everything and to be able to make suggestions for their reading pleasure from our vast knowledge of books. One librarian reported the sense that patrons felt they were being passed off to reference books rather than receiving the personal service we pride ourselves on. Another issue involves training. We cannot simply offer a book or an electronic resource that we are unfamiliar with; learning what to find in these resources and discovering the best way to use them—and for which questions—should be part of our job. Finally, these resources need to be placed near the desk, so we remember to use them. They should also be in an area that patrons are comfortable entering, since we all know how much pleasure many readers derive from browsing these resources, both print and electronic.

An important research study shows that we have not done a very good job of incorporating tools into our readers' advisory conversations. Anne K. May, Elizabeth Olesh, Catherine Patricia Lackner, and Anne Weinlich Miltenberg, master's candidates at Queens College Graduate School of Library and Information Studies, conducted a survey of readers' advisory transactions in Nassau County (N.Y.). In addition to employing other ineffective interview techniques, in 80 percent of the transactions staff offered suggestions from their own reading, even when their reading bore no resemblance to the type of book requested.[2] Even though readers' advisory reference tools were readily available, they drew from their personal reading rather than consulting sources. That profoundly disturbing outcome should cause us all to think. Having the resources is not enough; we must also use them as we work with readers to ensure that we provide the best possible service. It is not enough simply to provide and refer patrons to readers' advisory reference tools, no matter how good they are. Librarians must become familiar with their content and learn to integrate these tools into their readers' advisory transactions in order to take advantage of all these tools offer. With that in mind, we should consider what to look for in these resources.

Evaluating Readers' Advisory Reference Sources

When we started doing readers' advisory at the Downers Grove Public Library in 1983, we had two reference resources: *Fiction Catalog* and *Genreflecting*. In contrast, today librarians are faced with the wealth of print and electronic (free and fee) resources; we now have an embarrassment of riches from which to choose. With print and fee-based electronic resources, we are limited by budget constraints, as we are in any other area of the reference collection. How many resources and which ones we purchase will depend on our own library's budget, collection, and—most important—the needs and interests of our readers. Certainly, these criteria should also dictate our choices of sites to link to on our library web pages as well, because a list of too many sites can be as off-putting to a user as no list at all. This section outlines the features to look for in print and electronic reference tools for readers' advisory; these are summarized in figure 2.1.

Figure 2.1 ▨ **What to Look for in Reference Sources for Readers' Advisory**

1. Access points/indexes
2. Plot summaries
3. Evaluative material about books
   Characteristics of the author's works
   Best or most representative titles
   Where to start new readers
4. Point of view from which written
5. Added value
   Information on the appeal of the author
   Subgenres as well as genres
   Readalikes

When we examine a potential readers' advisory reference book or electronic resource, we look first at the type of access provided to its contents. In print resources, any index is better than no index, but I firmly believe that author and title access in resource books should be made mandatory by an act of Congress. Note any books that give access beyond author and title—especially useful are access by pseudonym, character name, and subject. For example, check Mystery resources for access by detective or main character, by country, by subject (e.g., lawyers, doctors, antiques, universities), and by type (e.g., police procedural, amateur sleuth).

Full-text searching adds an extra level to the value of electronic resources. Using "Find" from the Windows Edit Menu allows librarians and other users to search a web page for particular names and topics. On other electronic resources, search menus may be more or less helpful, depending on whether users are limited to specific search terms in drop-down menus (used in *What Do I Read Next?* below) or whether they can do less structured Boolean searches (as in EBSCO's NoveList below). Because of their inherent searching flexibility, web resources are almost always superior in terms of this ability.

Treasure any resource that gives plot summaries. These can help readers decide if they have already read a particular book or whether they might be interested in reading it. Many book and web resources offer reviews of books, and these allow readers and librarians to judge the content of the book in question. Chapter 3 includes techniques for reading reviews with an eye for a book's appeal to readers. Both annotations and reviews can be useful for readers' advisory reference.

It is worth taking notice whether a reference source discusses authors' styles or the characteristics of authors' works. Just reading through these descriptions will help us become familiar with those authors—even ones we have not read—and help us in describing those authors specifically and authors in general. In addition, if comparisons are made between authors, and similarities and differences are pointed out, we have a real find. This type of information can be enormously helpful when we and the patron are on the trail of similar authors. For example, the readalike articles in EBSCO's NoveList offer both essays on an author's appeal and annotated suggestions of similar authors. (See the sample readalike article in appendix 4.)

A reference tool that offers an opinion on an author's best or most representative work gives us a title to suggest when we are starting a reader on a new author. We also watch for resources that include core collections or reading lists, as they provide a place to begin the study of a genre and serve also as a resource guide for collection development.

Often, it is the attitude of the contributors that makes one reference resource more helpful than another to readers' advisors. Reference sources written and compiled by people who love books and reading and thus write from the reader's point of view should be prized. From this type of source, the readers' advisor gains an appreciation for a title or genre as well as the enthusiasm of readers of that title or genre. Sources that offer literary critiques can be off-putting to those who are looking for ideas for leisure reading and are better suited to those involved in literary research and study.

Some reference tools have features that provide added value for readers' advisory librarians. While we can often discover information about appeal from the author descriptions, books that make the appeal more explicit are a real find. If the book talks about genres, does it also give characteristics of subgenres as well? And does it discuss how authors write across these and how the genres and subgenres blend? That kind of information can be very useful when we are learning about an unfamiliar genre. Finally, resources that offer lists of readalike authors are helpful, but the best give us enough information so we can easily tell why an author is like another. (See chapter 5 for a detailed discussion of this technique.)

As we examine our collections of readers' advisory resources, we should think about whether they have the characteristics in the checklist above. Consider, too, what kinds of questions each tool answers best. Would one help series readers by providing books in order? Is another easy to use to identify a character in a Mystery or other genre or subgenre? Can we get "recommended" reading suggestions from a specific source? Does another tell us where to start a reader in a series? Which tools provide book discussion questions and material about the authors and books? At the same time, we should also think about how we would use them with readers. What special features might we use to introduce an interested reader to this book or electronic resource? Does it have a special index? Or an easy-to-use search strategy? Does the material included fill a special niche—for readers who like a particular type of book or tone? Examining tools with these techniques in mind helps us as we look for useful resources that we can also share with readers.

Electronic and Print Resources for Readers' Advisors

The world of readers' advisory reference publishing has changed dramatically since 1989, when the first edition of this book was published. Not only has the availability of commercial and free electronic resources grown beyond our wildest imaginings but the wealth of print resources also speaks to the popularity of and demand for tools to help readers' advisors. As computers become ubiquitous at library public service desks, we increasingly take advantage of the currency and scope of web resources. Librarians and readers alike, at the library and from their homes, access the library's links to fee-based electronic products as well as free Internet resources for fiction fans.

Electronic Readers' Advisory Resources

Fiction_L

The most important web-based resource for readers' advisors at this time is Fiction_L, an electronic mailing list developed by Roberta S. Johnson and the Reader's Services staff of the Morton Grove (Ill.) Public Library in 1995 and hosted within Morton Grove's Webrary.[3] Despite its title, the focus of this electronic mailing list is not exclusively fiction but "all aspects of reader's advisory for children, young adults and adults, including non-fiction materials." Although Fiction_L was developed for and by librarians dealing with fiction collections and requests related to those collections, readers worldwide are welcome to join the discussion.

That it also serves as a clearinghouse for queries makes Fiction_L invaluable as a reference tool. Readers' advisors from across the country, and indeed around the world, post questions from staff and patrons. Very few librarians, seeking a particular author or title when a patron has offered only a sketchy description, fail to receive one or more answers from colleagues, and these generally appear within minutes of posting. Questions about readalike authors—authors whose appeal is similar to that of a reader's favorite—are common, as are requests for lists of titles on a particular subject or ideas for displays or book lists. A comment from one reader inspires another librarian, and enthusiastic responses fill the list. The success of this resource underscores the collaborative nature of readers' advisory and reinforces that, although an individual cannot read everything, someone else may have read just what we are looking for, and we are all willing to share the fruits of our reading and knowledge.

While it serves as an excellent "ready reference" source, Fiction_L is much more. For its nearly 2,500 subscribers around the world it provides a forum for sharing information on readers' advisory tools, techniques, problems, and solutions. This makes it an excellent resource for the small, isolated, or one-person library. Devoted to a wide range of readers' advisory topics, Fiction_L is a source of material useful to librarians, book discussion leaders, and others with an interest specifically in readers' advisory and more generally in books and reading. Popular topics discussed on Fiction_L include genre study, bibliographies, training, audiobooks, book discussion groups, print and electronic resources, and readalikes for popular authors.

As with any mailing list, Fiction_L is only as good as the subscribers who use it. The more specific we are when posting our questions and the more details we provide to our colleagues, the better answers we get. For example, if we want readalikes for a particular author, we get more accurate suggestions if we explain thoroughly what the patron likes about that author. It is not enough to post a request asking for readalikes for V. C. Andrews, nor is it good practice. We need to add what it is that our reader likes about Andrews; then advisors can respond with authors who will more likely share the characteristics the reader enjoys in Andrews's books.

Fiction_L has evolved into the best kind of resource for readers' advisors: a free and far-reaching vehicle for sharing information of value to colleagues; for asking general and specific questions about tools, techniques, and the philosophy of readers' advisory; for promoting conversations about books and reading around the world. With searchable archives and lists of compiled book lists from the questions asked and answered, it offers a wealth of information for both novice and experienced readers' advisors. Subscription information and archives are available at the Webrary link.

EBSCO's NoveList

EBSCO's NoveList, reviewed as "a reader's paradise and a reference librarian's dream" and available in more than half of all public libraries in the United States, sets the standard for commercial readers' advisory databases.[4] Developed by readers' advisor Duncan Smith and available since 1994, EBSCO's NoveList was originally aimed at adult fiction readers. It now serves fiction readers of all ages and includes additional information for school librarians and media specialists. This resource, like many others online, is constantly evolving and offering new enhancements.

At this writing EBSCO's NoveList offers author, title, subject, and full-text access to annotations and reviews of more than 120,000 books. Entries for adult fiction titles provide book reviews from *Booklist*, *Library Journal*, *School Library Journal*, *Rendezvous*, and *Publishers' Weekly*, with occasional excerpts from *Magill's Book Reviews*; original subject headings from Hennepin County and NoveList's catalogers; links to author websites; awards; and more. NoveList allows searching by author, title, series name, plot (subject terms chosen from a specific list or simply names, plot actions, time periods, and locations), and Boolean searches, which comb the entire record for the requested terms.

Extra features, fully searchable and outlined on the Search page, set NoveList apart. Under "Browse Lists," one can search "Best" lists of award winners and recommended titles, explore lists by genre and subgenre, and examine the full list of authors, titles, series name, and subjects. In the section "Read about Popular Titles and Topics," one can explore biographies of young adult authors; readalike articles with essays on an author's appeal and matches of similar authors; book discussion guides for adult and young adult authors, offering background material and questions with extensive answers in addition to suggested further reading; booktalks for children and young adults; feature articles on a wide and increasing range of subjects of interest to children and adults; and the "For Staff Only" section.

The "For Staff Only" section includes an array of resources for readers' advisory staff, including the Adult Reading Round Table Genre Fiction List, a self-evaluative bibliography; professional articles of note; and an extensive readers' advisory training course, since staff training is a priority for creator and product manager Smith. The "Learning Center" section of the site provides instructions on using NoveList, helpful tips, and a general guide to exploring the data within.

What's Next

Another extremely useful web resource, What's Next, is provided free online by the Kent District Library System in Michigan.[5] This wonderful tool furnishes quick access to books in series, listed in publication order. We have satisfied many readers by simply printing out the list so that they can go to the shelves and find the next book in the series. Although it does not include any information about the series—beyond author, series title, and book titles—it quickly and easily provides just the information that we so often need working with patrons. Since it is a web resource, it can also be updated efficiently whenever authors add another title or a new series. For those who prefer, the library also sells a print version of the database.

What Do I Read Next?

This tool, described in more detail below with print resources, is also available in an electronic format. This version includes the data from all editions of the books, except for the overview essays. Lists of award winners, best sellers, and pathfinders provided by major public libraries are also accessible and link users to full title entries. As in the book version, lists of similar and recommended authors are also retrievable. Rather awkward pull-down menus listing search terms limit this tool's usefulness online.

Print Readers' Advisory Resources

There are currently two main publishers of hard copy resources for readers' advisors, Libraries Unlimited, now part of Greenwood Publishing, and ALA Editions. Libraries Unlimited publishes *Genreflecting* and the subsequent series of guides on specific genres following the pattern Betty Rosenberg initiated in 1982: a definition of the genre and subgenres along with lists of authors, usually including titles, that fit within that category. More recent editions also include more about working with fans of the genre and information about websites and other reference materials of interest. The ALA Editions titles offer background on various genres from the perspective of appeal and why readers read that genre. These also focus more on practical readers' advisory techniques related to the genre: the readers' advisory interview, working with readers in libraries, and helpful lists of authors and titles worth knowing. Both series provide useful genre overviews, background, and important authors and titles for new and experienced readers' advisors. For extensive lists of authors and titles, consult the Genreflecting Advisory series; for in-depth information on the appeal of the genre and typical authors and titles, consult the ALA Readers' Advisory series.

Genreflecting

Betty Rosenberg taught a library school course called "Reading Interests" that was designed to help future librarians understand "common readers" and their tastes. Her book, *Genreflecting*, grew out of the syllabus for that course. Diana Tixier Herald joined Rosenberg as coauthor of the third edition in 1991. Since Rosenberg's death in 1993, Herald has taken on sole responsibility for *Genreflecting*; the fifth edition of this pioneering work was published in 2000.[6]

After an introduction on the nature of genre fiction and its relationship to readers, libraries, and publishing, a chapter is devoted to each of eight genres: Adventure, Crime, Fantasy, Historical, Horror, Romance, Science Fiction, and Western. Each chapter includes three sections: "Themes and Types," "Topics," and "D's Picks" (suggested reading in that genre). At the start of each chapter, Herald offers a concise overview of each individual genre as well as a short discussion of how readers' advisors work with fans of this genre. Then the "Themes and Types" section follows with descriptions of individual subgenres and authors and titles to become familiar with, many with brief annotations. The numerous subdivisions make this book an invaluable reference for students, readers, and readers' advisors. The second section of each genre chapter, "Topics," includes a wide variety of interesting and useful information. Here, Herald includes lists of classic authors, "bests" within the genre, anthologies, bibliographies, histories, criticism, encyclopedias, films, book clubs, manuals, awards, online resources, and more, followed by the third section, a list of titles in the genre that are among her personal favorites.

Beyond its useful genre definitions and examples of genre fiction, what makes *Genreflecting* a classic readers' advisory reference tool is the attitude Rosenberg established in the first edition, in 1982. The first edition's epigraph, "Rosenberg's First Law of Reading: Never apologize for your reading tastes," sets the tone for the book and has appeared in each subsequent edition. Rosenberg was, and Herald is, a reader, and their remarks come from the viewpoint of readers who enjoy genre fiction, not necessarily from that of librarians or readers' advisors. Rosenberg wrote in the introduction to the first edition, "Genre fiction is not to be taken seriously and analyzed to death. It should be written about by those who enjoy it."[7] Rosenberg's approach to each genre, carried on by Herald, is nonjudgmental; she simply addresses the pattern within the genre and discusses its appeal to readers. She also counteracts some people's disdain for the tastes of the "common readers," for their perception of genre fiction as the bottom rung of the fiction ladder. She unabashedly advocates reading for pleasure and attempts, in this book, to give librarians an understanding of genre fiction so that they can provide assistance to other readers who enjoy it. Under Rosenberg's tutelage, reading and enjoying genre fiction become virtues, not closet vices. Herald has maintained this tone in subsequent editions.

It was Rosenberg's attitude that initially made *Genreflecting* such a useful tool for us. The book came as a godsend when we were just starting our readers' advisory department. Rosenberg put us on the right track by giving us a basic understanding of different genres so that we could talk with readers with a real appreciation for their interest and a commitment to serving them.

For both novice and experienced readers' advisors, *Genreflecting* is a "must" read. It is a remarkable reference book that provides a framework for learning more about genres, an extensive list of authors and titles to suggest to interested readers, and an example of the attitude that inspires and sustains readers' advisors. Although *Genreflecting* is certainly useful and comprehensive, Herald herself admonishes, "It should be used as an introduction in need of continual supplementation."[8] *Genreflecting* provides a broad and firm foundation for the readers' advisor, but it is only a starting place. As we readers' advisors read more within and about genres, we sometimes find that we want to refine *Genreflecting*'s classification of authors within genres, and we will discover others to add. We stretch our own understanding of and our ability to discriminate among themes and subgenres as we compare our own lists to those in *Genreflecting*. While *Genreflecting* is a good starting place for developing a thorough understanding of genre fiction, readers' advisors must watch for and note changes in the genres and add new authors and subgenres as they appear. This is one of the problems with print publications: their lists are often out of date before they even arrive in libraries. For this reason web updates are invaluable. Libraries Unlimited maintains a web page, http://www.genreflecting.com, on which Herald and other authors of titles in the series add new titles to keep their books more up-to-date.

Other titles in the Genreflecting Advisory series that are useful for readers' advisors working with adults include the following: *Romance Fiction: A Guide to the Genre*, by Kristin Ramsdell; *Fluent in Fantasy: A Guide to Reading Interests*, by Diana Tixier Herald; *Now Read This: A Guide to Mainstream Fiction, 1978–1998*, and *Now Read This 2: A Guide to Mainstream Fiction, 1990–2001*, by Nancy Pearl; *Hooked on Horror: A Guide to Reading Interests in Horror Fiction*, 2nd ed., by Anthony J. Fonseca and June Michele Pulliam; *Blood, Bedlam, Bullets, and Bad Guys: A Reader's Guide to Adventure/ Suspense Fiction*, by Michael Gannon; *Christian Fiction: A Guide to the Genre*, by John Mort; *Strictly Science Fiction: A Guide to Reading Interests*, by Diana Tixier Herald and Bonnie Kunzel; and *Make Mine a Mystery: A Reader's Guide to Mystery and Detective Fiction*, by Gary Warren Niebuhr.[9]

ALA Readers' Advisory Series

The *Readers' Advisory Guide to Genre Fiction*, by this author, performs the *Genreflecting* role for ALA Editions.[10] It describes fifteen fiction genres: Adventure, Fantasy, Gentle Reads, Historical Fiction, Horror, Literary Fiction, Mysteries, Psychological Suspense, Romance, Romantic Suspense, Science Fiction, Suspense, Thrillers, Westerns, and Women's Lives and Relationships. Each chapter offers a definition of the genre, characteristics of the genre and its appeal to readers, benchmark or key authors for the genre and subgenres, tips on preparing to work with readers and for the readers' advisory interview, reference sources, and lists of suggested authors for introducing readers of other genres to this genre and for leading fans of one genre to other genres they might enjoy. Sure Bets (described in detail in chapter 5 of this book and discussed in appendix 3) are included for each genre. Appendixes offer general tips for the readers' advisory interview, an overview of readers' advisory reference sources, and the Five-Book Challenge, a list of five important authors and titles in each genre that would provide a reader, librarian, or patron with a better understanding of the genre. A general index includes authors, editors, titles, subjects, and series.

Like *Genreflecting*, this book and others in the series are written by fans of genre fiction, people who understand the pleasure readers find in these titles. Here, too, the approach is nonjudgmental, highlighting what fans appreciate in the genres they love, and the enthusiastic tone invites readers to discover and appreciate the qualities of the genre being discussed. Rather than the longer lists of authors in *Genreflecting*, *The Readers' Advisory Guide to Genre Fiction* emphasizes the appeal of the genre and offers a few representative authors to help readers' advisors gain an understanding of typical characteristics of the genres. The focus is more on the way readers' advisors learn to think about and thus understand popular fiction. As such, it complements *Genreflecting*. Together, the *Readers' Advisory Guide to Genre Fiction* and *Genreflecting* offer readers' advisors an in-depth look at popular fiction. And both, along with the other titles in each series, are good books to share with other readers, as they provide endless browsing pleasure and reading suggestions.

Other titles in ALA's Readers' Advisory series follow a similar pattern and include background information on the genres and working with readers as well as lists of important authors and titles, often grouped by subgenre or theme. These titles include *The Short Story Readers' Advisory: A Guide to the Best*, by Brad Hooper; *The Romance Readers' Advisory: The Librarian's Guide to Love in the Stacks*, by Ann Bouricius; *The Mystery Readers' Advisory: The Librarian's Clues to Murder and Mayhem*, by John Charles, Joanna Morrison, and Candace Clark; *Science Fiction and Fantasy Readers' Advisory: The Librarian's Guide to Cyborgs, Aliens, and Sorcerers*, by Derek M. Buker; and *The Horror Readers' Advisory: The Librarian's Guide to Vampires, Killer Tomatoes, and Haunted Houses*, by Becky Siegel Spratford and Tammy Hennigh Clausen.[11]

What Do I Read Next?

Another series that demonstrates the type of reference work particularly useful for readers' advisory reference is Gale's *What Do I Read Next?*[12] Begun in 1990, the print volumes in this series highlight the year's publications in

Fantasy, Historical, Horror, Inspirational, Mystery, Popular Fiction, Science Fiction, Romance, and Western. An introductory essay to the genre highlights trends in the previous year. Within each genre section, entries provide the following information: authors, title, subgenre, names of important characters, time period, locale, a brief plot summary, review citations, a list of selected titles by that author, and a list of similar authors and titles recommended for readers who enjoyed each book. As mentioned earlier, good indexes are invaluable in readers' advisory reference books. Each volume has a wide range of useful indexes, accessing series, time period, locale, genre (with subgenres), character name, character descriptor (e.g., librarian), author, and title. In addition to the biannual multigenre volumes and occasional single-genre volumes, Gale also offers a fee-based web version of this source, described briefly above.

Other Resources of Interest to Readers' Advisors

The reference tools discussed above were designed for readers' advisors, but a search of our book collections and an Internet search for book and genre-related websites will reveal a number of useful titles and sites that were designed for other purposes but can be used profitably by readers' advisors and fans of leisure reading. Many satisfied patrons and librarians have benefited from these and other print and electronic resources.

Because websites seem to appear and disappear at an alarming rate, only a few established sites are highlighted here. Posting a query on Fiction_L will quickly provide a list of the hottest sites to explore and share with readers.

Amazon.com and Barnesandnoble.com

The electronic bookstores Amazon.com and Barnesandnoble.com dominate book selling on the Web, and their flexible search engines often make them our first choice in trying to decipher a reader's confused version of a book title. Both sites provide their own version of readalikes, but these lists seem more based on what was purchased by readers rather than what authors actually appeal to fans of another title. Explore them as possibilities rather than offering them to readers as perfect matches. Both also offer book reviews and, more importantly, reader comments. These often reveal the range of a book's appeal, and the librarian who has time to explore them in depth will come away with an excellent sense of the way a particular book appeals to readers. Both offer useful lists of best-selling books within genres and cover fiction and nonfiction titles. Barnesandnoble.com has also added a section called "Meet the Authors" where it provides fascinating tidbits about the life and writing of a growing number of authors, as well as similar authors, and, in many cases, information on where to start in reading an author. Amazon.com offers book discussion guides as well as annotated (sometimes quite comprehensively) lists by readers who recommend read-alikes or genre favorites. These enhancements can offer useful tips for readers' advisors exploring a particular author and style.

Library Web Pages and Web Links

Many public libraries have readers' advisory and book-related pages on their library websites. Not only do they often provide links to book-related sites on the World Wide Web, they also offer numerous book lists and bookmarks as well as other guides to fiction collections and authors. An exciting new feature on some library web pages is virtual readers' advisory, which, using the same technology available for virtual reference, promotes 24/7 access to trained staff who offer book suggestions and assist with other readers' advisory queries. As I write this, such programs are still in their infancy, but this is likely to be a growing trend in the next few years. Of particular interest is Cleveland Public Library's Read This Now (http://www .readthisnow.org/chat/), which includes live chat with "genre geniuses," reader's resources, and Book Tracker, an online way to keep track of what you have read. This is the kind of program to watch.

Several excellent library web pages include the following: Johnson County (Kans.) Library's Readers' Advisory Page (http://www.jocolibrary .org/index.asp?DisplayPageID=431); Reader's Club, at the Public Library of Charlotte and Mecklenburg County (N.C.) (http://www.readersclub.org/ default.asp); Reader's Services, at Morton Grove Public Library (Ill.) (http:// www.webrary.org/rs/rsmenu.html); Bookweb, at Williamsburg Regional Library (Va.) (http://www.wrl.org/bookweb/); and Waterboro (Maine) Public Library (http://www.waterborolibrary.org). Note that these include many features—links to other sites, databases of librarians' reviews, book lists and bookmarks, and online readers' advisory forms through which they solicit information about readers' interests and provide lists of reading suggestions.

Fiction Catalog

Fiction Catalog remains a useful readers' advisory resource, especially for older authors and titles, although both print and online versions have been surpassed by excellent coverage and indexing in many newer publications.[13] Still, it is a standard resource in many libraries and useful as a selection and weeding guide, reference tool, and source of suggestions for readers. The print version of *Fiction Catalog* is issued as a hardbound book every five years, with four annual paper supplements. The fourteenth edition lists almost six thousand titles of classic and contemporary works of adult fiction, including novelettes and composite works. The new editions are not cumulative, although many titles reappear in subsequent editions. The reason for this is that titles to be included in each edition are selected by a panel of librarians from public library systems. These librarians receive a list of possible titles, seek a consensus from other librarians in their systems, and vote for the ones they believe should be included. They need not have read the books, nor do they need to consider whether titles have been listed in previous editions or supplements.

Fiction Catalog is divided into two sections: a main entry section and an index of titles and subjects. The main section is arranged alphabetically by author, then title. Information about editions and ISBNs for in-print books, number of pages, and sequels (where appropriate) are all part of the bibliographic data. Each entry includes a descriptive summary and an excerpt from critical remarks, usually from a review. Readers usually find that the summary gives enough information to let them decide whether they have read or want to read a particular book. *Fiction Catalog* is definitely a book we can put in patrons' hands; with a brief introduction, they can use this reference tool very satisfactorily on their own. The title and subject index provides subject and genre access to the individual book descriptions in the main section and includes a wide variety of subjects. Among the many subjects listed are geographic places, historical periods and events, people, lifestyles (e.g., SOCIETY NOVELS, POVERTY, FARM LIFE), genre, and literary types (e.g., DIALECT STORIES, STREAM OF CONSCIOUSNESS, PARODIES). There are numerous *see* and *see also* references to direct the user.

Discovering Useful Resources

How do we find reference sources useful for readers' advisory? With the features listed in figure 2.1 in mind, scour your library's shelves and search the Internet for book- and author-related websites. We were surprised to see that we already owned several very useful print sources, but we were unaware of their scope until we started looking for background material on genres and authors from the point of view of readers' advisory service. One of our best finds was *The Traveler's Reading Guide: Ready-Made Reading Lists for the Armchair Traveler*.[14] Although it is now sadly out of print, we discovered it at a time when it was difficult to find fiction set in specific states in the United States and around the world. This met that need nicely, and we had to buy extra copies for the circulating collection, because readers loved to take it home and peruse the entries. Now, of course, there are other sources that readily provide this information. We have found that it is best to keep these resources close to the public service desk and to bookmark the websites and perhaps link to them from our library web page. That way we can more easily introduce readers to these resources as well as use them for ready reference. Genre readers love to discover resources that explore their particular reading passion; we find them poring over these books and websites, making lists of authors and titles they want to try.

For more comprehensive lists of readers' advisory resources, consult the extensive bibliographies produced by the American Library Association's Readers' Advisory Committee, which is part of the Reference Users Services Association/Collection Development and Evaluation Section (RUSA/Codes). In 1996, they prepared an initial list of resources, published in *RQ*.[15] An update of that list of resources was published in the summer 2004 *RUSQ*.[16] This list is divided into two sections—"Core Collections" and "Expanded Collections"—and includes information on ways in which each source is useful to readers' advisors. A second list, covering free web-based resources, is scheduled to appear in *RUSQ* in 2005. And, as noted above, queries posted on Fiction_L, the readers' advisory mailing list, can also help readers' advisors discover the latest and best print and electronic resources.

It is wonderful to consider the abundance of readers' advisory reference tools, yet this wealth can also create problems. First, the number of resources can be overwhelming. As we do with reference resources, we need to make sensible decisions about the kinds of books and electronic resources we need. Links to two-dozen websites from our library home page are of little value if neither we nor our patrons know how to use them to best advantage. Just because an Internet site is free or inexpensive does not necessarily mean it has value for readers' advisory work. We need to learn to apply evaluative standards to Internet as well as book resources.

We also need to master the intricacies of these resources and learn to share them with readers. As the May study, described above, points out, we often fail to use the resources that are readily available. It is not enough simply to provide and refer patrons to readers' advisory reference tools, no matter how good they are. Librarians must become familiar with their content and learn to integrate these tools into their readers' advisory transactions in order to take advantage of all these tools offer.

Although both book and electronic resources are certainly intriguing and useful, they are simply tools or, as EBSCO's NoveList's Duncan Smith likes to say, added memory.[17] They free staff from the difficulty of desperately trying to remember every author and title. They allow us to be facilitators—to act as guides to the collection—by expanding our memories and knowledge of popular fiction and by helping us retrieve information readily. They can be helpful memory joggers, places to go when our minds go blank. They give us an added edge and another resource to use in working with patrons.

In addition, these sources help establish in the minds of patrons, and sometimes administrators, the fact that questions about fiction reading are legitimate and important and that resources exist to help answer such questions. We collect these memory-enhancing tools, not only to legitimatize our work but also to make research into unfamiliar authors, genres, and subjects more practical and rewarding. On the other hand, resources alone will never replace the human readers' advisor. Books and electronic sources will never be able to interpret the quirk of the eyebrow or other body language we learn to recognize and respond to as we talk with patrons about books.

Popular Fiction and Nonfiction Lists

Although many librarians read fiction and nonfiction, it is the rare librarian indeed who has time to read extensively and can advise knowledgeably in all the genres patrons request. That is why we have found it useful to develop a list of areas, including representative authors, that are popular at our library. This kind of homegrown reference tool is an excellent supplement to reference resources. It pulls together basic and frequently requested information into an easy-to-use resource that helps staff as they are expanding their own understanding of genre fiction and as they work with patrons. Such a list also does double duty by serving as a reading plan for readers' advisors, as discussed in chapter 5, and for training staff, as noted in chapter 7. The protypical Popular Nonfiction List in appendix 2 fills the same role as the Popular Fiction List described in detail below. It should be evaluated in the same way and serve as a starting point in creating your own list.

It may be easiest to illustrate the value of having a list of popular genres and authors by describing the Popular Fiction List we created. The copy included in appendix 1 is the summer 2004 version of our list, the first of which was developed in 1983. Originally, our list consisted of twelve genres with 12 authors in each. Twelve is by no means a magic number, so choose a number you are comfortable with. Although our latest version still includes 144 authors, the equivalent of 12 authors in twelve genres, there are, in fact, fourteen genres—ten genres with 12 authors each and four genres with 6 authors. This adaptation reflects changes in the popularity of some genres with publishers and readers.

Before you decide how many and which authors to include, you may wish to read the section on "Designing a Reading Plan," in chapter 5, which explores the list's role as a training tool and reading plan. The decision to use the list in this way may affect which genres and how many authors you include. No matter what you decide, we recommend that some standard genres at least be included: Fantasy, Horror, Mystery/Detective, Romance, Science Fiction, and Thriller. The others you choose should be based on your needs, situation, clientele, and collection.

Over time, our list has undergone many changes in both the genres and the authors included. At one point we expanded the list to thirteen genres with the addition of Women's Lives and Relationships. This was not a step that we took lightly. Over the past several years, we have experienced a growing interest in novels by women that explore women's lives and their relationships. We first met the need through several very successful annotated book lists, but we finally decided to add this group of authors as a separate genre. Novels by these authors feature female protagonists. They focus on relationships—with family, friends, and lovers—and portray women trying to make sense of their lives. A range of popular authors, such as Danielle Steel, Barbara Delinsky, and Barbara Kingsolver, exemplify these characteristics.

The Gentle Reads category also fills a niche need in our community. These are authors who write novels that contain no explicit sex or violence and that endorse traditional values. Many readers describe just this kind of book to us, and we find it very useful to have a list of authors we can suggest without hesitation or reservation. Gentle Reads, more than any other genre group on the list, present difficulties for staff and patrons alike. Classic author Miss Read may be the traditional benchmark, but some readers of this genre find her too gentle; they may prefer an author such as Jeanne Ray, who takes them outside the quiet village setting but still evokes the same gentle "feel." Although fiction published by Christian publishing houses would certainly fit here, our readers are seeking Gentle Reads, not necessarily Christian Fiction, so our list includes only the representative authors we have identified that meet the Gentle Reads needs of our readers. Your library's list of Gentle Reads authors may be quite different from ours.

Another nonstandard category we include is Literary Fiction. Originally called In a Class by Themselves, and then Literate Fiction, this group of authors writes complex, literate, multilayered novels that wrestle with universal dilemmas. That pattern is evident in the works of all the authors on our list, from Richard Russo to Alice Hoffman. These are the authors we often suggest to readers who seek award-winning writers.

Crime/Caper first appeared on the 1993 version of our list. These writers—Carl Hiaasen, James Ellroy, and Elmore Leonard, for example—share elements with many authors on the Mystery and Suspense genre lists but are not necessarily writers of those genres. Social and moral issues are frequently the themes of these authors; in addition, criminal investigation, hard-edged details of crimes, and flawed heroes characterize these popular authors and their books. The tone of these books may be darker, as in Ellroy's titles, or black humor may dominate, as in Hiaasen's and Leonard's.

Although it is important to include genres popular in your library, these should be true, definable genres, in which specific elements characterize the pattern followed by the books. In developing a list of popular genres, there is always the temptation to create genres from groups of authors who are really linked in other ways, perhaps by subject or even gender, rather than genre. African American authors, for example, do not constitute a separate genre, since books by these authors are not written to a particular, identifiable pattern, as by definition genre fiction always is. Pulitzer Prize winner Toni Morrison and Mystery writer Eleanor Taylor Bland are both African American writers, but each has her own following of fans, and their books differ dramatically. If Bland or other African American Mystery writers are popular, they belong on the Mystery genre list, not on a separate list that merely groups authors by race or gender. Creating a book list that reflects the range of African American authors is a better way to meet interest and demand for books by these authors. On the other hand, there may be many more African American authors or writers of Christian Fiction, spread through the genres, on a library's list in a community where these writers are extremely popular.

Although a library can use a list someone else developed, it will not serve your staff and patrons as well as one you develop yourselves. Creating this kind of list as a departmental training exercise is discussed in chapter 7. You can certainly construct your own list from scratch, but it may be easier to start with our list, included in appendix 1, and tear it apart. Simply start with a genre you know to be popular in your library and consider each of the authors, deleting those not popular and adding others who are, following the suggestions detailed below. You will notice that the list in appendix 1 consists only of genres and authors, not titles. Discovering typical titles by each author is part of the training process as we develop a reading plan based on genres and authors on this list.

The first step in constructing your own list, whether fiction or nonfiction, is to choose genres that reflect the interests of your readers and the authors available in your collection. As mentioned above, there are several traditional choices that any such list should include, but any additional choices—which genres and how many additional genres—should reflect your library's situation. Not every community needs Crime/Caper or Gentle Reads, for instance, but there is bound to be something special that your readers request and with which you and your staff need to be familiar.

In creating any list of popular fiction, we need to do some preliminary information gathering. The first step is to determine which genres and authors our library patrons are reading. Several simple survey techniques may be used to give an indication of fiction reading patterns. You might try keeping track of all your readers' advisory interactions for a few months. We simply kept a sheet of paper at our service desk and indicated any author or genre that was specifically requested by a patron. By examining the list at the end of that period, we could see which genres and authors were in demand. Additionally, surveying the staff who work with fiction readers, perhaps asking them which frequently requested authors seem to be too popular ever to be found on the shelves, is another way to identify authors and genres that are popular among readers. Circulation staff can often identify authors and genres that circulate heavily. Shelvers are often an overlooked source of information; if they are assigned to shelve particular sections of the alphabet or individual genre sections, they have a good sense of which authors they shelve most frequently. By surveying the books that are returned and noting those that are put on reserve, we can obtain even more information. These informal surveys should provide enough information to use in choosing which genres and authors to include in the Popular Fiction List.

More formal and time-consuming methods of obtaining information also exist. A carefully conducted reader survey, using a well-thought-out questionnaire, would certainly furnish useful data and would undoubtedly add to the findings obtained from the more informal sources. Weeding the fiction collection is another activity that can provide useful information about patrons' reading habits. A very good indication of our readers' tastes may be obtained by checking circulation figures during weeding and noting the authors who have gone out both frequently and recently. Regular small-scale weeding is also an excellent way to acquaint the readers' advisory staff with the collection in general and with specific authors and titles that are popular in our libraries and avoids the onus and expense of large-scale weeding projects.

Next, we need to select representative authors from our collections within each genre we choose. In addition to the survey techniques described above, we might also search reference books and reviews to find key authors in a genre. Here are five simple guidelines to follow in choosing fiction authors to include.

1. The authors need to have written more than one or two books in the genre. I strongly discourage including an author who has written only a few books. If we include such an author, we limit the usefulness of our list. For example, even though *The Devil Wears Prada*, by Lauren Weisberger, and *The Curious Incident of the Dog in the Night Time*, by Mark Haddon, were extremely popular with readers, we would not consider them for this list, because they are both first novels.[18]

2. Several titles by each author should be available in our collection. It is little help if an author has written twenty books but our library has only one or two of them. Interlibrary loan is a possible source for additional titles once a reader is hooked, but as much as possible, this list should provide instant gratification. Books should be immediately available for readers whenever they are in the library.

3. To be useful, these lists should not be just a specialist's idea of the "best" in a genre. Originally our list included both classic and popular authors. Several years ago, as a training exercise, we sought to change that emphasis and include only the authors most popular with our readers. We also limited the list to living authors. Our concern was that it was too easy to fill the list with classic authors who no one reads anymore, except perhaps students completing assignments. Although our list now reflects popular authors more accurately, it must be supplemented with classic authors when we use it to gain background in a genre. For example, when we began our study of the Mystery genre, we felt we needed to review classic authors as well as currently popular ones. In our early reading we paired Agatha Christie with Robert Barnard, Dorothy L. Sayers with P. D. James,

and classic Private Investigator Mysteries by Raymond Chandler and Dashiell Hammett with those of Robert B. Parker. If your list, like ours, emphasizes currently popular authors, you will need to devise ways to gain familiarity with classic authors as well in order to understand a genre or to advise a reader who has read "everything" by newer authors.

4. Strive for a balanced grouping of authors and try to include those who represent diverse aspects of the genres we know to be popular among our readers. A Mystery/Detective list, for example, would not be as useful if it included only writers of Police Procedurals.

5. Be careful of authors who write in more than one genre. Unless our collections are physically divided by genres to some extent, a reader tracking down an author of Thrillers may pick up the same author's Mysteries or Westerns by mistake and be disappointed, not to mention confused. Include such authors if you feel they are too important to overlook, but caution users of your list that the authors write in more than one genre.

Not every popular author can be slotted into a genre on this list. If several very popular authors seem not to fit into existing genres on the list, they should be examined carefully to see if they share elements that make them a genre of their own.

You may, as we do, get questions about your list, such as, Why is this prominent author not included? The answer may be that you simply did not think of him or her. However, it is also possible that author is not popular in our library. The point of the list is to include a range of authors that our patrons enjoy reading, not authors we think they *ought* to read.

The popularity of the individual genres on this list can give us an idea of genres for which there is a ready-made audience for annotated book lists. For example, if you have a hard time limiting a genre to a set number, you may have identified a topic that would make a popular book list. The two projects complement each other. The genre lists give us a start with a core group of possible authors, while our work on the book lists may uncover authors who deserve inclusion in this core list. The popularity of and demand for Legal Thrillers, for example, would likely be better met by an annotated book list, which reflects the range of this subgenre, than by a list of authors of Legal Thrillers on a Popular Fiction List, which readers are not as likely to see and use.

One last caution: Do not aim for the ultimate list; it is better to have a partial list, even if it is just in draft form and not available for patron perusal, than to strive for the perfect resource. Expect to revise the list regularly to reflect your own expanding knowledge of popular fiction as well as changes in your patrons' reading tastes. Since this list can be an important reference tool, do not let your thinking about a genre progress too far beyond your list; update it regularly to keep the list current and useful.

Although you will not want to think about updating the list before you have written a first draft, updating the list by reevaluating both the genres and the authors included is another important activity. Ours has changed dramatically since its creation in 1983, with genres and authors added and deleted to reflect changes in reading interests at our library. Readers' advisors can discuss which authors are still being requested and should stay on the list, which should be deleted, and which newly popular authors should be added. (Once you have set a comfortable number of authors within a genre, it is best to hold to that number. It is easy to keep adding new authors without deleting others, but adhering to a set number makes you more conscious of which authors really belong on the list.)

The Popular Fiction List became a lifeline for our staff when we first started working closely with fiction readers. We developed it, quite simply, out of desperation. Early on, we found that the simple fact that we had a list of popular authors to refer to and share with readers made us much more comfortable in talking with readers about genres. If the patrons said they read Romances, we had a list readily available of possible authors to suggest, even though the range of subgenres included meant that not all Romance readers would necessarily enjoy all the authors. Still, it was a list to hold in hand, to give us some measure of confidence as we began working with readers. The list's manageable size also meant that when a patron mentioned a name we knew to be on the list, we could usually place it in a genre and mention other authors in that genre. Since the list contained only authors whose books we owned, we were likely to find books on the shelf for the patron. The psychological benefit of having a list of names, classified by genre, to share with readers was impossible to calculate. We worried a lot less about drawing a blank and not being able to find any books to give patrons because, if all else failed, we always had the Popular Fiction List as a backup source of 144 popular authors. In addition, because we knew these to be popular authors at our library, this list has always provided a supplemental source when the patron just wanted a good read. With the list, we had popular authors we could start reading and sharing with other readers.

A Popular Fiction List, then, can be an important readers' advisory resource. It can help give staff confidence in talking with readers about a genre as well as providing a reading list of popular and representative authors. A well-constructed list can be a valuable guide to help readers' advisory staff become more familiar with popular genres. This feature is discussed more fully in chapter 5 in the section "Designing a Reading Plan."

Staff as a Resource

Readers' advisors rely extensively on staff and staff-created resources. Chapter 6 discusses the bookmarks and annotated book lists that staff create. These become useful reference tools for all staff, not just those who write them. In addition, they become resources—guides to aspects of the collection—for patrons as well.

The Popular Fiction and Popular Nonfiction Lists are another source that, once created, allow staff to become a resource and share their knowledge of particular authors and specific genres. These lists of popular authors should be posted in the readers' advisory staff area, and all advisors should develop the habit of initialing authors' names as they read. Knowing which staff member is well read in a particular genre alerts other staff to a resource person whom they may consult when they want to increase their own knowledge of that genre or when they have a patron who wants to talk with another fan. An initialed list also serves as a gauge that indicates how staff individually, and the readers' advisory staff in general, are growing in their knowledge of popular genre authors.

Finally, readers' advisory staff should remember that all library staff, including those who do not specifically do readers' advisory, can be excellent resources for tips about both fiction and nonfiction books. All readers who are willing to share information on the books they have read or heard about add to our store of knowledge about books—and readers. In this era of straitened circumstances, with its emphasis on expensive electronic access to materials and information, it is easy to forget that one of our most useful reference sources is the knowledge of our staff and fellow readers. Readers' advisors are readers who enjoy sharing their knowledge and love of books—with fellow staff members and patrons alike. Talking about books, sharing what we are reading, is one of the easiest ways to tap this resource. Strategies and techniques throughout this book rely on the collaborative nature of readers' advisory and sharing information about books and authors, both informally through conversation and more formally through written annotations. Readers' advisory work is about making connections—among authors and their books, among readers and staff and the books they share, and with colleagues and all who read and share their pleasure in the books they enjoy. Sharing information is the linchpin of readers' advisory work, and we all need to work on ways to do this consistently and effectively. Chapter 7, on training, discusses sharing information more fully, but it is too important—and too often neglected—not to be emphasized here as well.

In summary, reference sources are the backbone of a readers' advisory department, but they are only as good as the staff who use them. It is therefore important for librarians to understand what elements make reference sources specifically useful for readers' advisory work and to familiarize ourselves with the materials we now own as well as to purchase and develop others to enhance our ability to work with readers. Once we have resources, we must also integrate them into our readers' advisory interactions so that patrons can also discover the reading pleasures derived from using these tools as well.

Reference sources—paper, electronic, and human—are a good starting point for both new and experienced readers' advisors. These resources provide information that readers' advisors can use to become familiar with authors, titles, and types of fiction. Thus, they are important both as reference tools for answering questions and as training materials. They also increase our comfort level on the desk, as we know that we can go to these to look for answers to the questions we receive. Making readers' advisory reference sources available and using them with patrons validate the readers' advisory requests patrons make and emphasize the fact that we are treating these questions as seriously as any other reference question. Reference sources are only one facet of readers' advisory, one type of tool we can become familiar with and rely on. In the next chapter, I consider in detail the nature of a book's appeal, how readers' advisors identify this elusive quality, and how to use it in working with readers.

Notes

1. Joyce G. Saricks, "Best Tools for Advisors," in *The Readers' Advisor's Companion*, ed. Kenneth D. Shearer and Robert Burgin (Englewood, Colo.: Libraries Unlimited, 2001), 173–74.
2. Anne K. May and others, "Readers' Advisory Service: Explorations of the Transaction," in *The Readers' Advisor's Companion*, ed. Kenneth D. Shearer and Robert Burgin (Englewood, Colo.: Libraries Unlimited, 2001), 135.
3. Fiction_L (Morton Grove, Ill.: Morton Grove Public Library, 1995). Available from http://www.webrary.org/rs/FLmenu.html.
4. EBSCO's NoveList: Web-Based Resource (Ipswich, Mass.: EBSCO, 1994). Available from http://www.epnet.com; and review by Cheryl LaGuardia, *Library Journal* 124, no. 13 (August 1999): 152.

5. What's Next (a list of books in series), (Grand Rapids, Mich.: Kent District Library, 2000). Available from http://www.kdl.org/libcat/whatsnext.asp.
6. Diana Tixier Herald, *Genreflecting: A Guide to Reading Interests in Genre Fiction*, 5th ed. (Englewood, Colo.: Libraries Unlimited, 2000).
7. Ibid., xviii.
8. Ibid., xxvi.
9. Kristin Ramsdell, *Romance Fiction: A Guide to the Genre* (Englewood, Colo.: Libraries Unlimited, 1999); Diana Tixier Herald, *Fluent in Fantasy: A Guide to Reading Interests* (Englewood, Colo.: Libraries Unlimited, 1999); Nancy Pearl, *Now Read This: A Guide to Mainstream Fiction, 1978–1998* (Englewood, Colo.: Libraries Unlimited, 1999) and *Now Read This 2: A Guide to Mainstream Fiction, 1990–2001* (Englewood, Colo.: Libraries Unlimited, 2002); Anthony J. Fonseca and June Michele Pulliam, *Hooked on Horror: A Guide to Reading Interests in Horror Fiction*, 2nd ed. (Westport, Conn.: Libraries Unlimited, 2003); Michael Gannon, *Blood, Bedlam, Bullets, and Bad Guys: A Reader's Guide to Adventure/Suspense Fiction* (Westport, Conn.: Libraries Unlimited, 2004); John Mort, *Christian Fiction: A Guide to the Genre* (Englewood, Colo.: Libraries Unlimited, 2002); Diana Tixier Herald and Bonnie Kunzel, *Strictly Science Fiction: A Guide to Reading Interests* (Englewood, Colo.: Libraries Unlimited, 2002); and Gary Warren Niebuhr, *Make Mine a Mystery: A Reader's Guide to Mystery and Detective Fiction* (Westport, Conn.: Libraries Unlimited, 2003).
10. Joyce G. Saricks, *Readers' Advisory Guide to Genre Fiction* (Chicago: American Library Assn., 2001).
11. Brad Hooper, *The Short Story Readers' Advisory: A Guide to the Best* (Chicago: American Library Assn., 2000); Ann Bouricius, *The Romance Readers' Advisory: The Librarian's Guide to Love in the Stacks* (Chicago: American Library Assn., 2000); John Charles, Joanna Morrison, and Candace Clark, *The Mystery Readers' Advisory: The Librarian's Clues to Murder and Mayhem* (Chicago: American Library Assn., 2002); Derek M. Buker, *Science Fiction and Fantasy Readers' Advisory: The Librarian's Guide to Cyborgs, Aliens, and Sorcerers* (Chicago: American Library Assn., 2002); and Becky Siegel Spratford and Tammy Hennigh Clausen, *The Horror Readers' Advisory: The Librarian's Guide to Vampires, Killer Tomatoes, and Haunted Houses* (Chicago: American Library Assn., 2004).
12. Neil Barron and others, eds., *What Do I Read Next? A Reader's Guide to Current Genre Fiction* (Detroit: Gale, 1990–); available from http://www.galenet.com.
13. *Fiction Catalog*, 14th ed. (New York: Wilson, 2001); also available from http://www.hwwilson.com.
14. Maggy Simony, *The Traveler's Reading Guide: Ready-Made Reading Lists for the Armchair Traveler* (New York: Facts on File, 1992).
15. Readers' Advisory Committee, Collection Development Section, RUSA, "Readers' Advisory Reference Tools: A Suggested List of Fiction Sources for All Libraries," *RQ* 36 (winter 1996): 206–29.
16. Ibid., "Recommended Readers' Advisory Tools," *RUSQ* 43 (summer 2004): 294–305.
17. Duncan Smith, "Readers' Advisory Goes Electronic" (paper presented at Public Library Association Sixth National Conference, March 26–30, 1996).
18. Lauren Weisberger, *The Devil Wears Prada* (New York: Doubleday, 2003); Mark Haddon, *The Curious Incident of the Dog in the Night Time* (New York: Doubleday, 2003).

3   Articulating a Book's Appeal

When the readers' advisory staff began reading popular fiction, writing annotations, and talking with fiction readers, we saw that some books seemed to fit together—seemed to appeal to the same readers—and we became more and more interested in discovering the reason why this was so. This chapter addresses more specifically the issue of how we actually ascertain an individual book's appeal and connect different books to each other. It examines the crucial elements that help us define and describe a book's appeal—pacing, characterization, story line, and frame—and discusses how a readers' advisor looks at books to discover their appeal. First, however, we need to discuss why this way of thinking about books is so important in readers' advisory work.

From the beginning of our work with fiction readers, we saw that an understanding of appeal is the keystone of successful readers' advisory work. Years of working with fiction readers and training readers' advisors have confirmed this early experience. We have found that most readers are usually not looking for a book on a certain subject. They want a book with a particular "feel." As we work with readers in libraries, drawing on both fiction and nonfiction collections, it very quickly becomes clear that we need to understand both subject headings and appeal characteristics if we really want to serve readers. The last chapter highlighted the importance of discovering reference resources that provide subject access to fiction. However, none of these reference tools for fiction and nonfiction addresses appeal, the feel of a book, and its effect on readers.

What exactly do we mean when we talk about appeal, and how do appeal elements differ from subject headings? The meaning may be clearer if the second question is answered first. Consider the different ways we might describe a book: by basic plot, subject descriptors, and then appeal. In *The Flanders Panel*, Arturo Pérez-Reverte writes of a young art restorer in Madrid who discovers clues to a murder in the medieval painting of a chess game that she has been employed to clean.[1] As she investigates, she becomes embroiled in a present-day murder case that oddly parallels the medieval one. Subject headings accumulated from six OCLC Worldcat entries cover a range of topics, including ART, FLEMISH—FICTION, WOMEN ART HISTORI-ANS, CHESS—FICTION, ART, SPAIN—FICTION, CHESS PROBLEMS—FICTION, MYSTERY FICTION OR DETECTIVE AND MYSTERY STORIES, AND MADRID (SPAIN)—FICTION. Subject headings on EBSCO's NoveList include the fol-lowing: MYSTERY STORIES, SPANISH—TRANSLATIONS INTO ENGLISH; SPANISH FICTION—TWENTIETH CENTURY—TRANSLATIONS INTO ENGLISH; WOMEN ART RESTORER-DETECTIVES—MADRID, SPAIN; CHESS; PAINTING, RENAIS-SANCE (EUROPE).

When we consider the way in which this book appeals to readers, how-ever, we also think in terms of pacing, characterization, story line, and atmosphere as well as style. We add to this skeleton the sense that the story is *densely written* and that the profusion of *detail*—about medieval art, the process of restoration, the clues presented in the painting, the implications of the painting's chess game, the mysteries in past and present—may slow the pacing but create an *engrossing* story. The book presents an *intricate and engaging* plot, full of *intriguing* puzzles and *layers* of meaning, as present events begin to parallel those in the past. Characters are more *quirky* than sympathetic, but we readers are pulled into the tale and into the minds of the characters. They surprise us as they react to plot complications. This is also a *dark, moody* tale, *suspenseful*, as tension builds to the unmasking of the murderer, and the author writes in a *sophisticated, elegant* style.

Unless readers are actively seeking titles within given subject headings, they need a clear and thoughtful plot summary that includes a basic descrip-tion as well as phrases such as the italicized appeal elements to help them decide whether this is a novel for them. We do, of course, find readers seek-ing novels that feature chess or art or that are translations of foreign fiction, but the subject headings alone give no indication of the tone of a novel or of the manner in which its author handles these subjects. Nor does the plot summary alone; readers' advisors and readers need a combination of these elements. Appeal elements describe more accurately the "feel" of a book. They take us beyond the bare bones provided by subject descriptors or a straightforward plot summary; they enhance these, and, in combination with them, they reveal more of the book's essence.

If we consider how we interact with readers when we talk about books, we realize immediately that we naturally share books using appeal to expand on subject headings or basic plot summaries. We may talk about the black humor in Carl Hiaasen's offbeat Crime novels set in southern Florida; the elegant, evocative prose that characterizes Ann Patchett's work; or the blend of danger and the sometimes horrific quotidian details of survival, stranded in the Andes, in Piers Paul Read's *Alive: The Story of the Andes Survivors*.[2] Although subject headings may address aspects of these descriptive elements, they cannot convey the same depth of meaning. Appeal is what takes us—and readers—beyond mere subjects and plotlines. As we see in this chapter, appeal terms, added to a plot summary, open up books for readers and allow them to decide if this is a book they are in the mood to read and might enjoy. Thinking and talking in terms of appeal simply provide a formal structure to the way we naturally think about and describe books.

Now back to the first question: what exactly do we mean by appeal? The elements of books to which a reader relates constitute the appeal of a book for the reader. That sounds straightforward, and, in fact, readers and readers' advisors often recognize this appeal long before we can actually define it. As we can see from the description of Pérez-Reverte's book earlier in this chapter, we need to understand appeal to amplify what we learn about a book from subject headings and plot descriptions. As readers, as well as readers' advisors, we often develop a sixth sense about which books go together and interest the same readers—not necessarily because the books are in the same genre or deal with the same subject but because they evoke the same responses in readers; they have the same "feel."

The problem for readers' advisors becomes one of more consistently identifying this "feel" so that we can work better with readers. Although appeal may be the key to identifying what a reader enjoyed in one book and may be looking for in another, putting this appeal into words can be a challenge for readers' advisors as well as for readers. Although difficult, the process of articulating appeal is not impossible. It is natural for us to include appeal—the way a book affects us—in our descriptions, whether we are conscious of this or not.

For example, if we have just read a Legal Thriller by Steve Martini and want to describe it to a friend, we would say something about the subject of the plot. However, in our description we might also mention that the book is fast paced or a page-turner; that the author presents characters we relate

to and really care about; that there are twists in the plot, unexpected surprises, or a general building of suspense; that we might become immersed
in details of the legal process or of a curious point of law on which the plot
hinges; and, finally, that the tone is upbeat, with the underdog hero winning
in the end. More importantly for readers' advisory work, using these appeal
terms, we can describe books without giving away the plot or having to
remember too many details. We can also distinguish among books that may
be assigned the same subject headings but that have very different impacts
on the reader. If we have also read Scott Turow's Legal Thrillers, we can tell
from the description of Martini's books that they would likely not appeal to
the same readers—or not for the same reasons. Turow's are slower paced,
with the story unfolding more deliberately; there is a greater emphasis on the
finer points of characterization; the legal and social issues are treated in a more
serious fashion; and there may be an open, rather than a resolved, ending.

Calling a book a page-turner or a compelling read identifies a book's
pacing. Comments about introspective and involving first-person novels or
about quirky characters refer to *characterization* and how it affects readers.
Whenever we describe a book's plot as complex or convoluted, as combining multiple threads, or as dealing with moral or social issues from child
abuse to politics, we are reflecting *story-line* elements that describe a book's
appeal to readers. Referring to the wealth of historical detail or the interesting pieces of information about antique clothing suggests the author's attention to background detail, just as the use of adjectives like *bleak* or *upbeat*
suggests a particular atmosphere or tone, and all of these are part of the *frame*
an author constructs. These are the kinds of terms we use daily in describing
books, without thinking that we are doing anything out of the ordinary. We
are speaking as readers in the language other readers understand.

The discussions in this chapter should help crystallize this descriptive
process. Readers' advisors want to formalize the way we naturally think
about books so that it becomes easier to recognize elements of appeal more
consistently and to describe books in terms that allow readers to decide if
certain titles will meet their needs at the moment. These techniques can be
applied not only to books we have read but also to those books we have only
read about or heard of. What I suggest here is simply a more systematic
approach that capitalizes on a reader's natural inclinations in describing
books to fellow readers. The discussion of how to make this part of our routine is centered on the four basic appeal elements—pacing, characterization,
story line, and frame—which, singly and in combination, address the ways
in which books affect readers. I consider each element separately, focusing

on both the language we use to share that appeal with readers and a list of possible questions that help us identify that appeal element. Although the list may seem overwhelming at first, it is simply a compilation of memory joggers, an incomplete catalog of the ways we already think about and describe books. In our library, we also use these questions when we are making notes about books we have read, an activity discussed in detail in chapter 5.

In the discussion of each element, notice that readers' advisors do not measure books by literary and critical standards but by *readers' perceptions*. Although it is important for readers' advisors to be aware of levels of writing styles, well-developed characters, and consistent plots so that we can suggest the best books we know, we should also remember that readers themselves often tolerate a wide range of quality if other elements of appeal are present.

Each aspect of appeal is considered separately in this chapter, yet a book's appeal is really based on a combination of these elements described below. One book may have characters similar to those in another story, but the fact that the author gives it a lighter, less serious treatment can make the story appeal to a very different audience. Both Mary Stewart and T. H. White have written Arthurian fantasies, but White's madcap romp has a different appeal from Stewart's more serious, elegiac approach. The elements considered below are not the ultimate list of factors that determine a book's appeal; rather, these are a beginning, a rudimentary listing of possible elements. The more that readers' advisors work at articulating appeal, the better we become at identifying it and at asking the questions that help us effectively ascertain a book's appeal as well as the kinds of books a particular reader is in the mood to read.

Pacing

Pacing is the first element readers are aware of, albeit often unconsciously. If we talk with readers about a book's pacing, we might say it is fast paced, or a page-turner, or that the story unfolds at a more leisurely pace. The book may be densely written, which promises a more measured pace. Or we might describe it as engrossing, a book so involving we do not want to put it down. How do we discover this information? What clues do we as advisors find in the books to help us identify pacing, and how do we translate our reactions into a vocabulary to use with readers? Figure 3.1 summarizes the questions we might use to determine a book's pacing.

Figure 3.1 ▓ Questions to Consider to Identify Pacing

1. Are characters and plot quickly revealed or slowly unveiled?
2. Is there more dialogue or more description?
3. Is the book densely written?
4. Are there short sentences, short paragraphs, and short chapters or other indications of a telescoped time frame?
5. Is there a straight-line plot, or are there multiple plotlines, flashbacks, or alternating chapters related from different points of view?
6. Do characters act or react to events?
7. Is the book end oriented or open-ended?
8. What is the pattern of the pacing?

Are characters and plot quickly revealed or slowly unveiled?

How does the author move the reader along—by quickly revealing characters and actions or by slowly unveiling the book's plot and purpose? Do readers fall right into the action of the book, or does the story move at a more measured pace? When we were first offering readers' advisory at our library, we were desperately searching for more authors who wrote like Mary Higgins Clark, who was not writing quickly enough to satisfy her many fans. We came across Ruth Rendell, who also wrote fairly short novels of Suspense, often featuring women in danger. When we offered Rendell to a Clark fan, we were told in no uncertain terms that Rendell did not share the same appeal. After some discussion, we discovered that pacing made the difference between the two; Rendell's book simply did not move at the same quick pace as Clark's.

Readers often will relate to this difference and prefer to read one type of book over another. It is interesting to note that readers' preferences for one style or the other may not be something they can define, and if they are faced with a choice between a "fast-paced" or "slow-paced" book, readers will almost always choose the former. Slow pacing seems to have negative connotations. However, if each book is described invitingly, readers can more readily make choices about what they would really like to read. In the readers' advisory interview, we may offer two books in order to determine the type of pacing the reader is in the mood for at the moment. We may describe one novel as featuring nonstop action, with many plot twists, and the other book as developing more slowly, adding layer upon layer, with characters and story line unfolding as the book progresses. Given options such as these, readers can choose the type of pacing they are in the mood to read.

Is there more dialogue or more description?

Dialogue often moves the reader along more quickly, while description tends to slow the flow of the novel. Readers' advisors can usually tell if one or the other predominates simply by flipping through the book. More white space on the page generally means more dialogue, and the book can likely be read more quickly. To see this difference, riffle through the pages to compare Amanda Quick's racy Regency Romances, which feature snappy dialogue and a page-turning flow, to Sharyn McCrumb's ballad series, Mysteries in which evocative descriptions of characters and place draw the reader in and purposefully slow the pace.

Is the book densely written?

Density suggests a more elegant writing style, but it also reflects the amount of detail and description an author employs. Densely written books, in which the language is emphasized and each word is important, do not flow in the same way as books written in a more conversational style. The former may be more lyrical or poetic, and readers may choose this type of novel because they take pleasure in the beauty or elegance of the language. This is not to say that some fast-paced books are not densely, elegantly written, but faster pacing usually demands a less dense style. Denser, more lyrical writing usually slows the pacing, as it requires readers to concentrate on words as well as characters and story, even when there is a lot of dialogue. Andrea Barrett's elegant, layered Historical Adventure, *The Voyage of the Narwhal*, is a good example of denser writing.[3] In contrast, a more conversational—or even cinematic—style, such as that used by Clive Cussler in his Dirk Pitt Adventure novels, utilizes free-flowing prose that directs readers to follow action and characters rather than to read each word closely for depth of meaning. Densely written books are often described by readers as engrossing, which does not necessarily mean fast paced. These usually build in intensity and do not usually seem fast at first. Thomas Harris's classic novel of serial murder, *The Silence of the Lambs*, is a good example of a densely written book that keeps the reader turning the pages at a fast pace.[4] One way to judge whether a book is densely written or not is to consider if this is language an English teacher would get excited about.

Are there short sentences, short paragraphs, and short chapters or other indications of a compressed time frame?

Short sentences, paragraphs, and chapters also affect the flow of the novel, as they pull the reader more quickly through the story. Longer sentences, paragraphs, and chapters often reflect denser prose, usually more description, and thus slower pacing. Dan Brown's page-turning Thrillers, which combine art, religion, and science with Adventure and Mystery, exemplify the former type, with hardly a chapter longer than four pages, while P. D. James's style in her complex and elegant Mysteries, featuring longer chapters and denser prose, is an example of the second. Some authors, especially writers of Thrillers and Suspense, indicate the passage of time with date or time "stamps" at the start of each chapter. This is another device that forces readers to move quickly through the book, as they see the action telescoped within a narrow time frame. Alistair MacLean's *The Guns of Navarone*, a popular book still assigned to high school students and one that flies off displays, is a classic example of this.[5] Here, with just forty-eight hours to stop the infamous German guns, the Allied team is working against the clock as they cross the island. MacLean gives the day and time at the head of each chapter, and this device reminds readers of the urgency of the mission and keeps them turning pages quickly. Questions about these techniques can be answered easily by physically glancing at the book; we can often offer these useful observations about pacing to patrons even when we are unfamiliar with the titles in question, simply by riffling through the books.

Is there a straight-line plot, or are there multiple plotlines, flashbacks, or alternating chapters related from different points of view?

Each type of plotline can be used to speed or slow the pacing. In Mystery and Suspense novels with multiple plotlines, each thread may contain a vital clue or piece of information. Even though readers may need to concentrate more to follow the threads and see how they ultimately intertwine, they may read more quickly—or perceive the book as faster paced—because of the alternating plotlines. On the other hand, this profusion of plot and character details may complicate, and thus slow, the story. In Erik Larson's *The Devil in the White City: Murder, Magic, and Madness at the Fair That Changed America*, this compelling true story alternates between the building of the Columbian Exposition in 1893 and the exploits of serial murderer H. H. Holmes.[6] Especially if readers enjoy one thread more than another, they may read quickly or skim to return to their preferred story line.

Changing points of view may have a similar effect. This technique may slow the story as it forces readers to reacquaint themselves with the characters each time they appear, but it may also speed the flow because readers want to know what is happening, especially if one chapter ends as a cliffhanger and then the next chapter features another character or plotline. Jeffery Deaver's Lincoln Rhyme Suspense novels filled with investigations and forensic details are a good example. In these, the story and the reader's focus alternate between detective and killer, but since chapters end with readers left on the edge of their seats, they read quickly to discover the outcome. This technique also allows more depth of characterization, however, and that may force a more leisurely pace. Whatever its effect on pacing, this approach has a particular appeal to readers who appreciate the insight it gives them into characters, and if we are aware of its presence in a book, we can share that information with readers.

Do characters act or react to events?

In some books, characters are reacting to events as they occur rather than being more involved physically in the action. In the former case, the pace is often slower, more involving, more intimate. Placing characters in physical jeopardy usually speeds the action and, thus, the pacing. For example, Ruth Rendell takes us inside the minds of her characters, and we follow their thoughts as they consider their actions. In contrast, Mary Higgins Clark puts her characters in physical jeopardy and forces them to act, pulling us through the story more quickly.

Is the book end oriented or open-ended?

Readers who ask for fast-paced books are often looking for novels that are end oriented, those that focus on how the plot will be worked out—on solving the mystery, rescuing the characters from danger, finding a mate. These readers prefer a satisfying conclusion. Slower-paced novels are often open-ended, lacking total resolution. Many readers of these novels relish discovering what happens to the characters as events unfold; they relate to the characters' reactions rather than to the action, or perhaps to the working out of a particular concept or idea. Thus, if readers request other titles like Peter Høeg's haunting *Smilla's Sense of Snow*, it is useful to consider if the ambiguous ending is part of the appeal before offering something like

Martin Cruz Smith's *Gorky Park*, which may seem similar on the surface in terms of frame and characterization but which clearly provides its protagonist with a tenable resolution.[7] Books in an ongoing series present a different situation, since they include characters we follow over time. Janet Evanovich, with her Mysteries featuring bounty hunter Stephanie Plum, and Laurell K. Hamilton, with a St. Louis–based Horror series starring vampire hunter Anita Blake, write fast-paced books in series that leave key underlying plot and relationship elements to be resolved (or advanced a bit more) in the next book.

What is the pattern of the pacing?

Does the book grip the reader immediately or build in intensity? Pacing is more than how quickly or slowly one reads the book or how the action progresses. There is also a pattern to pacing. Popular authors of the last century wrote according to a pattern that is in sharp contrast to that of many of today's best selling authors. In most of Charles Dickens's novels, for example, the first one hundred pages are devoted primarily to introducing characters and setting up the story. Later the pacing increases dramatically, but the first section of the book moves slowly. Most best-selling authors today hook readers in the first few paragraphs with dramatic action or an intensely emotional experience, and this immediacy is the signature of these authors, just as the slower introduction is Dickens's usual signature.

In some genres, as well as in individual titles of fiction and nonfiction, pacing constitutes the main draw for fans. Readers of Thrillers, Suspense, and Adventure stories (both fiction and nonfiction) often choose these genres because they like books that move at breakneck speed, that pull readers in from the first few pages and keep them turning pages until the end, wondering how the story will be resolved.

Pacing, then, is determined by the reader's perception of a combination of factors, ranging from the amount of dialogue or description to the density of the writing, the way characters react, and the way the story is constructed. By understanding these elements and how they affect readers, readers' advisors can often identify clues to pacing from conversations about a book, from reviews, or from our own reading to use in describing books to readers. It is clear, too, how thoroughly these appeal elements intertwine and overlap to give an overall impression of a book. This will become more evident in our discussion of the next element of appeal, characterization.

Characterization

How do an author's characterizations affect readers? One need only look to the Mystery, Science Fiction, and Fantasy genres to see how we relate to increasingly popular series characters, whose lives we follow through a succession of novels. In nonfiction, consider the growing popularity of Biographies and Memoirs, from David G. McCullough's mammoth *John Adams* to Dava Sobel's *Galileo's Daughter: A Historical Memoir of Science, Faith, and Love*.[8] We are also intrigued by eccentric or strong secondary characters, whose presence implies depth in the level of the book's characterizations. Some readers prefer introspective characters, and others favor books with several characters whose lives and activities intertwine. Still other readers describe themselves as looking for character-centered books. The following questions, summarized in figure 3.2, aid in understanding the role of characterization in a book's appeal.

Are the characters developed over time, or are they types we recognize immediately?

How does the author present characters? In Ed McBain's 87th Precinct Police Procedurals, for example, the reader recognizes and relates to the members of the police force from the very first pages. By using recognizable stereotypes, McBain can draw the reader quickly into the story. And, although the characters may change from book to book and even within a

Figure 3.2 ▨ Questions to Consider to Identify Characterization

1. Are the characters developed over time, or are they types we recognize immediately?
2. Is the focus on a single character or on several whose lives are intertwined?
3. What is the point of view from which the story is told?
4. Is characterization the most important aspect of the book?
5. Is the reader expected to identify with the characters or observe them?
6. Are there series characters, followed through and developed over several related novels?
7. Are there memorable and important secondary characters?

book, they remain readily identifiable—though not exaggerated—types. Other authors present characters who grow and change during the course of a novel. Anne Tyler's characters, in contrast to those of McBain, reveal their natures over time. We learn to know them only a little at a time and our vision keeps changing. Fans of this type of characterization, of unique and often surprising characters, are often displeased if we suggest novels in which the characters are not developed in the same way. Asking readers to describe characters they have enjoyed—or not enjoyed—usually makes it clear which type of characters they prefer.

Is the focus on a single character or on several characters whose lives are intertwined?

If there are several characters, how important are the relationships among them? Much genre fiction relies on a single main character who dominates the novel, although most also offer well-developed secondary characters. However, novels that fit in the Women's Lives and Relationships genre often feature multiple heroines, friends whose lives and relationships intertwine, and the chapters highlight these characters singly and together, as their lives intersect. Lee Smith's *The Last Girls* tells of a reunion of college friends, traveling down the Mississippi as they did thirty-five years earlier, reminiscing and scattering the ashes of their deceased friend.[9] The depth of characterization and interrelationship that this technique allows produce a cast of finely nuanced characters.

What is the point of view from which the story is told?

First-person narration is usually quite intimate, taking the reader inside the main character's thoughts. Many Private Investigator Mysteries are first-person narrations, with the reader seeing all that the protagonist sees and acting as a sounding board for the detective's mental conjectures. Sue Grafton's private investigator, Kinsey Millhone, is a good example of this point of view, and her mental ruminations add to our understanding of her character and her cases. Historical Fiction offers other examples. There is an obvious difference between Robert Graves's *I, Claudius*, with its rather jumbled first-person account of actions and reactions, and Colleen McCullough's series covering the history of ancient Rome.[10] The latter employs third person and a straightforward, detail-laden historical explication of events. Both offer sound historical detail, but the difference in point of view creates two unique books. It is important to be aware of this difference because, in our experience, some readers react strongly to narrative voice, either preferring or disliking the intimacy of first person.

Point of view is more than just narrative voice, however. More important, readers' advisors need to discover the answer to the questions, Whose story is this? and How is the point of view integral in shaping the story? Some genres are dependent on point of view. Romantic Suspense, according to our readers, has to be written from the threatened heroine's point of view, whether in first or third person, or the story simply does not have the same appeal for them. In many novels of serial murder, readers expect to get the point of view of both the killer and the detective. Seeing both points of view gives readers a sense of omniscience and the ability to perceive possible outcomes; they know who is evil and what he is planning, but they also have an idea when he will strike. This element separates these novels from Horror books, in which the reader does not always know the evil and expects to be jarred at irregular intervals as the unexpected occurs. For this reason, Horror novels generally do not appeal in the same way to readers who are fans of serial murder novels.

Is characterization the most important aspect of the book?

Are the characters more important than the plot, setting, or atmosphere? Readers often describe themselves as enjoying character-centered novels, by which they usually mean books in which characters—their inner lives, thoughts, actions, and reactions—are the most important element. The author's energy is directed primarily toward character development. Michael Shaara's *The Killer Angels*, which analyzes the Battle of Gettysburg through the eyes of its participants and reveals as much about the people as the battle, is a classic example.[11] Since character development and pacing usually work at odds with each other, books described as character centered are generally not perceived as fast paced. Fascinating characters and their relationships also fill Kaye Gibbons's novels of Women's Lives and Relationships. These intelligent, spirited women, ranging in age from eleven to seventy, dominate the novels. Their reflective, interior, nostalgic stories unfold at a leisurely pace, and there is often not much action. The pleasure for her fans is in exploring the characters and their lives.

However, we all know readers who are fans of particular series or other genre titles who tell us they read these authors and series because they love the characters, or find them extraordinarily interesting, or otherwise relate to them and their plights. Does that make these character-centered novels? The answer is that they are not character centered in the same way as more literary novels are. Readers like these characters and thus consider the book character centered. If a reader likes Mary Higgins Clark's books because she finds the characters so intriguing, she adheres to a different definition of "character centered" and applies different standards than does the reader of Gibbons, and we would certainly offer books that reflect her definition rather than more literary titles.

There is a distinct difference between books that concentrate on the characterizations, as do Gibbons's novels, where there may be little action in the plot and the focus is on language and depth of character development in a single book, and those that feature series characters or characters to whom the reader readily relates. In Gibbons's books, readers are more likely relating to what the characters think and experience; in Clark's or other genre titles, readers are generally more interested in what is happening to the character. In many genre series (for example, Elizabeth Peters's Amelia Peabody/Radcliffe Emerson Mysteries, which follow the couple and their son through decades of Egyptian history at the turn of the twentieth century, and Lois McMaster Bujold's Miles Vorkosigan Science Fiction series, which tracks his exploits through the universe), the characterizations are indeed an important appeal, as series characters develop over time and readers want to follow events in their lives. However, Mystery, Science Fiction, Fantasy, or Suspense series are not character centered in the same way as Literary Fiction. We understand the difference between the appeal of these contrasting types of characters, and we ask readers to give us an example of the character-centered books they love before offering one type or the other. Readers' advisors should always follow the reader's definition of appeal or genre classification rather than to try to provide the "correct" information. For these fans of character-centered genre fiction, we would not be suggesting literary authors but rather authors who treat characters in the same fashion as the ones these readers enjoy.

Is the reader expected to identify with the characters or observe them?

Are we drawn into the characters' lives, with the action experienced through their eyes, or distanced from them, with the story related to the readers? In the former case, readers receive a more intimate picture; in the latter, readers are more distanced from the characters, observing rather than participating in their stories. Are characters sympathetically or objectively portrayed? Some characters are meant to be sympathized with (R. F. Delderfield's Englishmen, for example, or the heroine in a Romance), while with others, such as those in the Psychological Suspense novels by Ruth Rendell/Barbara Vine or the Skolian Empire Science Fiction novels by Catherine Asaro, for example, the reader is more comfortable observing their actions from a safe distance rather than participating in their lives. The characters may be interesting but not necessarily sympathetic or likable.

Are there series characters, followed through and developed over several related novels?

Many readers enjoy series and look for all books in which a series character appears; reading the new book in that series is just like visiting old friends. The Mystery, Science Fiction, and Fantasy genres offer a wealth of series characters, many of whom readers follow for decades, becoming intimately involved in their lives and interests as well as in their cases, worlds, and quests. Even Literary Fiction has a place for series characters. Consider, for example, John Updike's Rabbit novels, each of which reflects a decade of contemporary life and opinions from the 1950s to the 1980s. In Anne Tyler's novels, characters do not reappear, but each novel features characters with similarly quirky natures.

Are there memorable and important secondary characters?

Since they may help define the tone and atmosphere of the book, secondary characters can be as important as the protagonists who define its viewpoint. Recurring secondary characters provide interesting plotlines that keep series fresh. They reveal information about the main characters from a different vantage point. Many are so well developed and interesting in their own right that they attract readers who follow them as closely as the protagonist in a series. Where, for example, would Sherlock Holmes be without Dr. Watson, Nero Wolfe without Archie Goodwin, or Eve Dallas without Roarke, in J. D. Robb's ongoing futuristic detective series? In fact, secondary characters can add to the overall appeal of a series or of a single title that features strong characterization. Both their role in the story and their interaction with the protagonist add an extra dimension to many works of fiction. Some readers follow series for the pleasure they find in the range of well-developed secondary characters who appear regularly. Anne Perry's great-aunt Vespasia in the Inspector and Charlotte Pitt Mysteries comes immediately to mind, as does the wacky crew from Janet Evanovich's Stephanie Plum series, the loyal crew and allies who aid and abet Lois McMaster Bujold's Miles Vorkosigan, and the increasingly complex cadre of love interests in Laurell K. Hamilton's Anita Blake series. We try to watch for elements of personal appeal, ranging from the romantic to the zany, among protagonists and secondary characters, as these elements are often exactly what some readers tell us they are looking for; they add to the charm and appeal of a book as well.

Although these may seem a lot of questions to be aware of in considering characterization, the answers to them are readily found in reviews, on book jackets, and in conversations with readers, as well as in the books we actually read. Fans can effortlessly describe the kinds of characters they enjoy, often more easily than they can remember or describe a plot. Simply asking a question such as "Did it take you a while to know the characters, or did they seem familiar right away?" gives us insight into the nature of the characterization in a book a reader has read. Or when talking with a Mystery reader, asking her to describe her favorite detective offers a clear picture of the kind of Mystery the reader enjoys.

Readers who read primarily for well-developed characters find much to appreciate in the Literary Fiction genre and certainly in Biography, Memoirs, and even History, where the character's life takes center stage. However, we should not forget that for some readers, good characterizations mean genre novels in series, in which they get to know the characters very well. Offering both types and describing one as more literary and the other as a popular series allow the readers to make a choice based on current interest and mood.

Story Line

When we think about story line and describe it to other readers, we go beyond mere plot summary. Books may be violent or sensational (James Patterson's novels of Suspense, such as *Along Came a Spider*, and Richard Preston's *The Hot Zone*) or gentle (Doris Kearns Goodwin's *Wait Till Next Year: A Memoir* and Jan Karon's inspirational tales of small-town life), issue oriented (Barbara Ehrenreich's *Nickel and Dimed: On (Not) Getting By in America* or Orson Scott Card's provocative Science Fiction classic *Ender's Game*) or action oriented (Patrick Robinson's Military

Thrillers or Jon Krakauer's *Into Thin Air: A Personal Account of the Mount Everest Disaster*), or investigative (Jonathan Kellerman's Mystery series featuring Alex Delaware or Ann Rule's exploration of True Crime cases).[12] We describe books as family centered, inspirational, tragic, or racy, relying on a vocabulary designed to reflect the impact of the story line on the feel of the book. Figure 3.3 lists useful questions to consider with readers or when reading ourselves.

Does the story emphasize people or does it highlight situations and events?

When we talked about characterization above, we asked whether the characterizations were the most important element of the work. Although readers are less likely to say they read for plot than for characters, readers expect a good story that is, according to their personal standards, well told. Within this story the reader enjoys, are the people the focus, or do the action and events drive the story? Shane stands out as the hero and the focal point of Jack Schaefer's classic Western, but most readers probably do not choose it for the character study of the Western hero.[13] They read *Shane* to experience the classic tale of the lone man who rides into a community, effects justice, and leaves. It is the story, translated into this particular setting, that draws the reader. On the other hand, Tracy Chevalier's Historical novels, such as *Girl with a Pearl Earring*, demand vibrant and detailed settings, but the focus is on the characters caught in these times.[14] Simply asking readers to describe the book they enjoyed and then listening carefully for these kinds of distinctions enable us to tell whether they prefer story lines that emphasize characters or ones that focus more on events and action. In the same

---

Figure 3.3 ▨ Questions to Consider to Identify Story Line

1. Does the story emphasize people, or does it highlight situations and events?
2. What is the author's intention in regard to story line?
3. Is the focus of the story more interior and psychological or exterior and action oriented?
4. Does the story take place on more than one level?

way, when we describe the plots of actual books from this standpoint, readers often realize that they are more interested in one aspect than the other.

What is the author's intention in regard to story line?

What is the author's treatment of the subject? Is this serious drama or soap opera, or is it a little of both? Both Elizabeth Berg and Danielle Steel write about women and the problems they face in their lives. While both deal with serious issues, they treat them very differently, and it is unlikely that Steel readers would appreciate Berg's weightier approach or that Berg's fans would find Steel's treatment satisfactory. Is the author's intent comedy or satire, or is it to take a more serious look at a moral or social issue? A writer such as Carl Hiaasen may deal with serious and provocative issues, yet his satiric approach to contemporary Florida culture is dramatically different from that of Nobel laureate Toni Morrison, who addresses issues from a much more serious perspective. Each type of writing has a particular appeal and a loyal audience, so it is important to recognize the differences between them, whether the reader is interested in fiction or nonfiction.

Is the focus of the story more interior and psychological or exterior and action oriented?

The Thriller genre offers a clear-cut example of the distinction between interior, psychological writing and exterior, action-oriented writing. Although he certainly includes action as his books reach their conclusion, Legal Thriller writer Scott Turow, who has been compared to Dostoyevsky, takes readers inside his characters, and this interior, more cerebral focus stays with the readers. On the other hand, readers are more likely to recall the external action in novels by Lisa Scottoline, even if her characters have introspective moments. We might designate the former as character-centered novels and the latter as plot-centered novels. Again, given the choice, with each author offered invitingly, readers can decide which type they are in the mood to read.

Does the story take place on more than one level?

While some readers prefer a straight-line plot with few distractions, others look for more complex tales, fiction and nonfiction, which may involve parallel stories or stories in which layers of meaning are built or peeled away.

The Flanders Panel, discussed above, offers parallel puzzles in the past—concerning the medieval painting—and in the present, as someone is clearly re-creating the historical crime. *The Book Nobody Read: Chasing the Revolutions of Nicolaus Copernicus*, by Owen Gingerich, describes the author's search for copies of Copernicus's famous *De revolutionibus*.[15] One story line tells Copernicus's story and presents a fascinating history of sixteenth-century Western science, while another presents Gingerich's quest to identify, locate, and view copies and offers a contemporary tale of academic rivalries and politics that parallels the historical.

As is the case with the previous appeal elements, the issues in identifying story line are more difficult to explain than to discover in actual conversations with readers or in our own reading of books and reviews. In addition, story-line elements intertwine with the other appeal elements. Whether a book unfolds in layers or follows a straight-line plot affects the pacing, as does an emphasis on interior versus exterior action, with the latter likely leading to a faster-paced story. A story line that focuses on people, rather than the action or setting, hearkens back to elements of characterization, discussed above.

We can also generalize that some genres emphasize story over other appeals, although this is not necessarily true with every author and title within the genre. Science Fiction, for example, is speculative fiction, usually set in the future, that explores moral, social, intellectual, philosophical, and ethical questions. It may be action oriented or more philosophical, but the story, with these provocative issues, takes precedence over pacing, characterization, and even background or frame. Mysteries are also plot centered. They are puzzles, even though the characters are important. Adventure (with its emphasis on action and on a mission to be undertaken) and Psychological Fiction (with its elaborately constructed plots relying on mental twists, surprises, and layers of meaning) also focus on story line. In our nonfiction collections many genres, including History, Adventure, Survival, Travel, True Crime, and Nature, may feature story line over other appeal factors.

Frame

Although pacing may often be the initial element readers use to select the books they are in the mood to read, the frame—setting, atmosphere, background, and tone—may be the most pervasive. When we describe this element, we speak in terms of the tone of the book, which may be bleak, suspenseful, or upbeat. The feel of the book might be humorous, magical, or romantic. The atmosphere may seem foreboding, menacing, uplifting, or more generally evocative. These adjectives reflect tone and alert the reader to the overall impression a book gives.

The easiest aspect of frame to identify may be setting, although by *setting* I do not mean mere geography but something more. Anyone who reads Mysteries, for example, knows that there is more than one type of Mystery set in the South; unless a reader wants only Mysteries set in the South, no matter what, similar geographic settings do not necessarily mean that the books will have the same feel and appeal. For example, Rita Mae Brown's lighthearted Virginia-based Mrs. Murphy series stars a cat who communicates with a host of animals and helps her owner, small-town postmistress Mary Minor "Harry" Harristeen, solve murders. In contrast, James W. Hall writes the dark and disturbing Thorn series, set in the Florida Keys. Both share a geographic setting in the South but reflect distinct moods and probably do not share readers. Setting as an element of appeal really means background and tone, not geographic place.

Frame can also mean the type of detail provided in the book. In novels that portray the lives of the "rich and famous," such as those by Jackie Collins and new writers Lauren Weisberger (*The Devil Wears Prada*) and Plum Sykes (*Bergdorf Blondes*), it is not simply the location that is important to many readers.[16] Rather, the descriptive details—especially the author's emphasis on elegant clothing, stylish decor, brand names, and gourmet dinners—draw readers. If they do not find these descriptive elements in a rich-and-famous novel, some readers tell us that the book is not quite right, although they often may not understand why. This setting is a kind of atmosphere or tone that pervades the book, a feeling we get from reading it. To identify this atmosphere, we ask ourselves the questions summarized in figure 3.4.

Figure 3.4 ▓ Questions to Consider to Identify Frame

1. Is the background detailed or minimal?
2. Does the frame affect the tone or atmosphere?
3. Is there a special background frame?

Is the background detailed or minimal?

Is there a lot of information or detail—historical detail, for example? Could the book take place elsewhere without altering its effect on readers? Does the action take place in any barnyard with a rustic feel, or is it set in a barnyard on the plains of Kansas just after the Civil War, as in Jeanne Williams's *No Roof but Heaven*, rich with explicit details of both the physical structures and the times?[17] Or are the novels simply stories dropped in to a specific time, as are Amanda Quick's Regency Romances? These books give a general impression of the period, but the dialogue and story are more important than setting and might not always be true to the time period. Watch for titles in which the author gives many specific details versus those in which we are simply left with a general impression. To alert readers, some reviewers use the wonderfully evocative term *wallpaper* to describe novels, particularly those with historical settings, where the background is minimal and not integral to the story line.

Does the frame affect the tone or atmosphere?

A book's tone can make it suspenseful, light, romantic, comic, upbeat, or dark. Is the frame instrumental in creating that sense of intrigue or foreboding? What impression, or feel, does the book give? Sometimes the frame generates the atmosphere and sets the tone more gracefully and effectively than any other technique, as in Horror and Romantic Suspense novels. The description of the atmosphere, or background, can determine how readers feel about a book, and some authors use this element more effectively than characters or action to set the stage. In Nora Roberts's *Carnal Innocence*, for example, the steamy southern heat and the enveloping atmosphere of decay are so dramatically evoked that they are almost tangible.[18] They effectively set the stage for violent murder. On the other hand, the inviting, cozy tone employed by Jeanne Ray and Rosamunde Pilcher sets the stage for more comfortable tales, with events unfolding at a more leisurely pace. In both types, this frame is crucial to the success of the novel with fans.

Is there a special background frame?

Some authors create a special frame in which they set their novels, and this background interests some readers as much as the story itself. I have noticed this phenomenon particularly in conversations with readers of fiction in series. For instance, Anne McCaffrey creates a culture of dragonriders and an entire world on Pern. As in many Science Fiction and Fantasy series, this world building establishes an extensively detailed frame on which the characters and story play out. The same is true with the Mysteries of Tony Hillerman, set in the Southwest. Here, details of Indian culture and life imbue the Mysteries with a certain cachet. Many readers tell us how much they enjoy books with a distinctive ambience or sidelight—be it gardening, opera, theater, rare books, antiques, or the trendy and glamorous worlds of the rich and famous—and that they will enjoy almost any novel, regardless of subject, in which the author pays meticulous attention to the background or frame.

Frame, the setting as well as the tone or mood, dominates some books and genres. In Historical Fiction, the extensive descriptions of life during a particular period constitute a large measure of the genre's appeal. These background details also permeate the Thriller genre, in which the Legal, Medical, Scientific, Military, Financial, Espionage, or Political background and accompanying jargon permeate the novels. In the Horror genre, the distinctive atmospheric tone alerts readers to impending turmoil. Among nonfiction books, frame is often an important appeal of Travelogue books, especially those that delve beneath the surface. In fact, frame becomes an important appeal in any nonfiction book that probes beyond the ordinary and offers fascinating insights into mundane and unusual subjects alike, as in Laura Hillenbrand's *Seabiscuit: An American Legend* (horses, horse racing, the Depression years), Miles Harvey's *The Island of Lost Maps: A Story of Cartographic Crime* (theft of old maps), or William M. Bass's *Death's Acre: Inside the Legendary Forensic Lab—the Body Farm—Where the Dead Do Tell Tales* (forensic anthropology, forensic investigations of crimes).[19]

Appeal characteristics speak to the combination of elements to which readers relate. Although it is also often a factor, I have not specifically addressed the issue of writing style. When describing books by appeal, it is important to acknowledge that writing styles vary widely. Some readers want only elegantly written, critically acclaimed novels, while others desire a more conversational style. Some readers will only read books in which the writing style meets their critical standards. Other readers may read for a particular element—a subject (vampires) or genre (Legal Thrillers) or background detail (Fabergé eggs)—and these readers will read everything that meets those specific criteria, no matter what the writing style. If we are aware of the style, we might provide that information when speaking with readers or describing the book in writing, but all comments should be nonjudgmental, allowing readers to make the choice of the books they are in the mood to read. For example, we might describe an author's lyrical style or another writer's conversational tone. This holds true for nonfiction as well as for fiction; readers might have a strong interest in a certain subject but reject what we offer because they do not like the author's writing style.

To think in terms of appeal simply means to use the thought processes that already take place when we consider books, to concentrate on a book's appeal rather than solely on subject or even genre. This is a mind-set, a way to focus the impressions we have gained from reading and gleaning information about books from patron comments, book jackets, and reviews. Instead of reading for plot details, we read with an eye to the range of a book's appeal. This becomes second nature when we begin to read books this way.

Following this practice reaps several immediate benefits. First, and most important, when we describe books by their appeal, readers can more easily see which books they are in the mood to read today. Describing books by appeal allows us to offer them to readers in such a way that they can readily identify ones they might enjoy. In addition, we can recognize the type of book that will not appeal to the readers we are assisting. For example, not all English Mysteries interest the same readers. An experienced readers' advisor would probably not suggest Agatha Christie's Miss Marple Mysteries to readers who ask for more books like Sir Arthur Conan Doyle's Sherlock Holmes series. Readers' advisors quickly discover that, with respect to character, Christie's pleasant and elderly amateur, who has brought the art of detection to near perfection through seemingly innocuous gossip and idle curiosity, holds a different attraction than Conan Doyle's more reserved and intellectual sleuth. Nor could we offer the fan of Jan Karon's comfortable and charming tales of a small-town Episcopal priest the fast-paced, apocalyptic books in the Left Behind series by Tim R. LaHaye and Jerry B. Jenkins. Both may fit within the rubric of Christian or Inspirational Fiction, but they are unlikely to be thought similar by fans of one or the other. In fact, recognizing which books do not have the same appeal for readers is an easy and very useful result of employing this focus, and it makes us a true resource for readers.

Another benefit of this mind-set is that it allows us to talk intelligently about books we have not read or did not enjoy. We will never be able to read everything, and we do not personally like everything we read. However, neither fact should prevent us from sharing these books with readers who might enjoy them. Both these eventualities are discussed in more depth in chapter 4, "The Readers' Advisory Interview." It should be clear that focusing on appeal allows us to learn—without reading every book or enjoying everything we read—what makes a book popular with readers. The terminology of appeal then allows us to articulate this popularity and characterize these books more readily. Without either lowering our personal standards or denigrating a reader's taste, we can talk about nonstop action, characters we recognize from the first page, or a suspenseful atmosphere, and we can provide readers with enough clues to decide whether or not they want to read the book.

Using this technique also allows us to see the range of appeal in a book and helps us open our minds to the various ways a book might appeal to readers. Thinking in terms of appeal clarifies how the same book may appeal to readers for different reasons. For example, one reader may relish the action and adventure of Nobel Prize winner Henryk Sienkiewicz's *With Fire and Sword*, while another may read it for the sense of time (the 1640s), the place (eastern Europe), and the political and social situations it describes.[20] In fact, as Duncan Smith reflects in his essay "Valuing Fiction," every reader reads, or creates, his own version of every book he reads.[21] Readers bring their own background and experience to books; thus, they are not affected by the author's prose in identical ways. The ability to listen to what an individual reader enjoyed and to translate those comments into appeal allows us to work with a wide variety of readers without delving deeply into their reading background or personal details. Talking with fans of Dan Brown's *The Da Vinci Code* makes this point obvious.[22] Readers related to the art history or the church politics or the hero and his quest and asked for more books with that appeal. Readers' advisors need to be open to the range of possible appeals in books.

Appeal also helps us cross genres, based on what readers tell us they enjoy, and introduce readers to authors they probably would never have discovered on their own. Readers who like Mysteries that feature bumbling detectives as characters may also enjoy books featuring bumbling spies and hapless heroes of humorous Romances, not to mention humorously picaresque and eccentric characters caught in Fantasy or Science Fiction worlds beyond their imagining. Readers' advisors can open up the depth and breadth of the library's collection to readers by communicating these appeal elements in discussions about books.

Another strong argument for using appeal as the basis of readers' advisory work is that it allows us to remember and retrieve so much more about books we have read. Over the years, hundreds of participants in my readers' advisory workshops have practiced describing books only by their appeal.

The responses have been overwhelming. Librarians have found they can recall far more than they ever expected when they think about a book's appeal rather than its plot. The truly revealing part of this exercise, however, is that other members of the group, those who listened to the appeal-based descriptions, found it far easier to decide whether or not they were interested in reading the books their partners described. Our patrons deserve the same opportunity.

Appeal frees us from reliance on plot summaries and from giving mini booktalks by providing a framework on which we can attach all the information we know about an author or title—drawn from our personal reading of books, reviews, book jacket summaries—as well as what we have heard about a book or author from fans or colleagues. If we tie our readers' advisory interviews to mini booktalks and to plot summaries, we may feel compelled to talk only about books we have read and, of those, only those whose plots we remember. Relying on appeal allows us to characterize comfortably an author or a genre as well as a specific title and make suggestions for a wider range of books than we could ever read ourselves.

Unfortunately, practice with more formal booktalking techniques has programmed us to think about plot first. Thus, changing from relating plot summaries to offering appeal-based descriptions takes practice. This is not to say that plot summaries are not valuable—we certainly incorporate plot details into our appeal descriptions—but they are not as useful in isolation; they need to be enhanced with appeal. In chapter 7, "Training," I discuss the importance of talking about books with staff so that this activity becomes an integral aspect of our routine. We practice—at first in incomplete sentences—describing books by their appeal before we work on pulling the information into a cohesive whole, in the same way we used to practice summarizing plots. Knowing how useful this technique is in working with readers, how it allows us to see what it is about a book that makes it popular, to characterize even works we do not personally enjoy, and to focus on what readers tell us as they describe what they enjoy reading, we understand the importance of appeal in our readers' advisory service.

In considering a book's appeal, readers' advisors should keep two final points in mind. First, although the above explanation of a book's appeal is closely tied to genre fiction, readers and readers' advisors know that the same connection to appeal exists among all types of books, even nonfiction and novels that are not traditionally considered as fitting within a genre. All readers of fiction and nonfiction appreciate receiving suggestions of authors of the same caliber and appeal as those they enjoy. Second, our readers' advisory skills allow us to suggest a wide range of potentially interesting authors to readers, and we need to be careful not to limit what we offer. We know from our own reading choices that we are not always looking for the same kind of book, and we need to be careful that we do not characterize readers too narrowly and think of a particular patron as enjoying only Thrillers, Mysteries, or any other type of book or level of quality.

The Vocabulary of Appeal

For years we have struggled with the idea of creating a thesaurus of appeal terms, words that could be used to describe pacing, characterizations, story line, and frame in such a way that they would mean the same to every reader—and librarian—who used them. Whenever we saw or heard them, we would understand exactly what was meant. Although there do seem to be words that work this way, developing a comprehensive list has proved a daunting task. The terms included in figure 3.5 are only a preliminary list of possible words, grouped under each appeal element. These are words that suggest the appeal elements; however, as we will see in the examples from reviews and discussions of books below, there are many others. Use this list as a starting place to develop your own thesaurus of appeal terms; watch for others that work and add them to your list. We need to be aware of and learn to recognize the range of words that describe a book's appeal. When we use them in annotations or when speaking with readers, we should be certain that they are as unambiguous as possible and nonjudgmental. For example, to talk of the pacing as *slowly unfolding* is better than to say the book is slow paced. We are, after all, using these terms to describe books so that readers can choose what they are in the mood to read; we are not offering critical appraisals. Notice that almost all the listed terms are adjectives. Subject headings are nouns, but appeal terms are the adjectives that describe our reactions to books, that provide the layers of meaning, and that open up the books we share with readers.

Other words are just as suggestive; these are merely a sample of the type of words that intimate the meaning we wish to convey. Try these and others with staff and readers to discover the ones that seem to capture the sense of the book's appeal. Think about these when writing the annotations, described in chapters 5 and 6. Look for these words and similar ones when reading reviews and when listening to readers describe books that they have enjoyed or hated. We do not necessarily need a controlled vocabulary to

Figure 3.5 ▓ The Vocabulary of Appeal

Pacing

breakneck, compelling, deliberate, densely written, easy, engrossing, fast paced, leisurely paced, measured, relaxed, stately, unhurried

Characterization

detailed, distant, dramatic, eccentric, evocative, faithful, familiar, intriguing secondary (characters), introspective, lifelike, multiple points of view, quirky, realistic, recognizable, series (characters), vivid, well developed, well drawn

Story Line

action oriented, character centered, complex, domestic, episodic, explicit violence, family centered, folksy, gentle, inspirational, issue oriented, layered, literary references, multiple plotlines, mystical, mythic, open-ended, plot centered, plot twists, racy, resolved ending, rich and famous, romp, sexually explicit, steamy, strong language, thought-provoking, tragic

Frame and Tone

bittersweet, bleak, contemporary, darker (tone), detailed setting, details of [insert an area of specialized knowledge or skill], edgy, evocative, exotic, foreboding, gritty, hard edged, heartwarming, historical details, humorous, lush, magical, melodramatic, menacing, mystical, nightmare (tone), nostalgic, philosophical, political, psychological, romantic, rural, sensual, small town, stark, suspenseful, timeless, upbeat, urban

Style

austere, candid, classic, colorful, complex, concise, conversational, direct, dramatic, elaborate, elegant, extravagant, flamboyant, frank, graceful, homespun, jargon, metaphorical, natural, ornate, poetic, polished, prosaic, restrained, seemly, showy, simple, sophisticated, stark, thoughtful, unaffected, unembellished, unpretentious, unusual

---

describe appeal. However, we need to be aware of what we see, hear, and say and learn to recognize the words that suggest a book's appeal. These words give us an idea of the range of appeal and how to talk about that appeal; they open us to the possibilities. We also need to be careful to choose words that our readers will understand as well. Even *appeal* is not a word a reader will automatically use, unless we have used it earlier.

Discovering Appeal in Book Reviews

Since we will never have time to read enough books to cover all the interests of our patrons, we need to find ways to expand our knowledge of popular fiction and nonfiction. Other techniques will be discussed in chapter 5, but, as part of this discussion of appeal, it seems appropriate to point out that readers' advisors can also discover much of the appeal of a book by reading good book reviews. As we know, readers are not so much interested in the fact that a book is a Mystery or a Thriller; they want to know if it is fast paced and filled with sympathetic characters and enough suspense to keep them on the edge of their seats. Or whether it centers around an intellectual puzzle that requires painstaking investigation and an intellectual spark and stamina on the investigator's part to uncover the perpetrators. Those are the clues we need to look for, and if we are alert, we will find them in the book reviews we read. Figure 3.6 gives two sample fiction book reviews.

Phrases that indicate appeal are underlined in these two reviews of different types of Historical Fiction. Notice that each presents a wealth of information about the book and its audience.

Kathleen Hughes, in the review of Wilbur Smith's *Warlock: A Novel of Ancient Egypt*, from *Booklist* magazine, acknowledges that the popularity of this Adventure novelist, who is known for his storytelling ability, will draw readers to this novel, set in ancient Egypt. The story-line elements stand out: this is a novel that combines action and adventure with intrigue, suspense, and even romance. The frame is also important, with the exotic and detailed historical setting in ancient Egypt, filled with politics, military particulars, and mystical religious elements. Characterizations, although interesting, probably lag behind story line in importance. Even if the reviewer did not state that the novel is fast paced, one would certainly assume that from the description, with the emphasis on action and adventure.

When we read reviews, we need to think about which readers might enjoy this kind of book. Is it only for fans of Historical Fiction, or might it also appeal to someone who appreciates novels with unusual, exotic settings? Or fans of political intrigue? Or even readers of Historical Romance? Certainly we might suggest the book to any reader who appreciates a suspenseful, action-filled tale and whose pleasure will not be diminished by the historical setting and the romantic subplot.

This kind of thinking leads us on to consider whether this book reminds us of other authors and titles. Might it work for fans of J. Suzanne Frank's

Figure 3.6   ▓   Fiction Reviews

Smith, Wilbur. *Warlock: A Novel of Ancient Egypt*. New York: St. Martin's, 2001

Smith, the best-selling adventure novelist whose previous books include *River God* (1994), *Monsoon* (1999), and *Seventh Scroll* (1995), returns to the genre with this epic action tale of intrigue, suspense, and adventure set in ancient Egypt. The story follows a *mystic* Warlock, Taita, as he fights, schemes, and plots to protect the life of the young boy-pharaoh Nefer Memnon from the various factions attempting to assassinate him and take over the throne of Egypt. The young pharaoh's father has recently been killed in a similar plot, and it will take all of the Warlock's knowledge and mystical powers to keep the young boy safe until he is old enough to rule the land. Smith is an excellent storyteller, and the fast-moving action and the exciting plot will hook even those who normally don't appreciate historical fiction. Romance fans will especially love the thrilling subplot about doomed (or nearly so) yet passionate lovers. Smith is a popular author, and his many fans will be clamoring for copies of this one. Kathleen Hughes. *Booklist* 97 (March 1, 2001). Used by permission.

Shaara, Jeff. *Rise to Rebellion*. New York: Ballantine, 2001

The son of Michael Shaara, author of the classic historical novel *The Killer Angels* (1974), seems to have inherited his father's talent. The younger Shaara also writes meticulously researched and compelling historical novels. His latest brings a fresh perspective to some of the familiar figures associated with the Revolutionary War. Making excellent use of a you-are-there approach, Shaara focuses on a handful of prominent historical figures, including Benjamin Franklin, George Washington, John and Abigail Adams, and British general Thomas Gage. We witness the American colonies experiencing growth pains and an increasing desire for independence and the corresponding British insensitivity to the needs and wants of the colonists; we observe coalescing resistance to such insensitivity, verbalized best by Franklin when he says to the British public in general, "With your vast army and your great navy, you may have the *power*, but you do not have the *right*." As in all good historical fiction, Shaara's novel gives historical figures flesh-and-blood viability. At nearly 500 pages, this novel requires a major investment in reading time, yet it is an investment painlessly made for it pays profitable dividends. Brad Hooper. *Booklist* 97 (March 1, 2001). Used by permission.

Reflections in the Nile, first in a time-travel Romance series with a detailed historical setting?[23] Or for readers of P. C. Doherty's Egyptian Mysteries? Or simply for readers of fast-paced Political Thrillers, perhaps set in an exotic corner of the world and thus offering fascinating details of that world, whether modern or historical? Thinking about which readers might enjoy this book and trying to identify other authors that this reminds us of opens our minds to the possibilities. We gain far more from the review than from a simple description of the book.

Early on in the second review, we see that Jeff Shaara's book, *Rise to Rebellion*, appeals to a different audience. From the first we know that the pacing will contrast sharply with that in Smith's novel. That the novel is "meticulously researched" suggests an abundance of detail that will slow the pacing. *Booklist*'s Brad Hooper confirms that the novel will be a "major investment in reading time," yet since it is also a "compelling" read, fans will not feel their time has been wasted. Characterizations are detailed and strong. These are real people, and we see the good and bad of their characters. This "you-are-there" approach to events in American history, with historical personages populating the novel, offers a detail-rich view; we "witness" and "observe" events featuring these characters. Unlike Smith's book, this fact-filled and lengthy novel is not a page-turner, but the details and descriptions of people and events are so fascinating that fans of this style will be undaunted by the length. This type of book will appeal to a different audience than Smith's and might make a good companion piece to titles from nonfiction, such as *John Adams*, by David G. McCullough, or Sharon Kay Penman's detailed Historical novels featuring British royalty.[24]

The contrast between the two also reinforces our sense of what makes plot- versus character-centered books. With the emphasis on action, adventure, and intrigue, Smith's book is likely to appeal more to readers who enjoy a plot-centered book, where the story takes precedence, even though many will certainly appreciate the characters. Shaara's novel, on the other hand, places characters firmly within a historical context. Although the setting in time is important, the focus is on the characters within this setting, and the strong characterizations make this title a good suggestion for readers who prefer character over story and especially to fans of biography, since many here are actual historical characters.

The same thought processes can be followed when considering a book review for a nonfiction title. Gilbert Taylor's *Booklist* review of Barry Strauss's *The Battle of Salamis: The Naval Encounter That Saved Greece—and Western Civilization* (see figure 3.7) suggests several points of interest for the reader who is not tied to a "fastidious" rendition of historical events. This is for the popular reader of history, and, for such a reader, Strauss offers a "compelling" and "evocative" tale, filled with "plausible" characterizations of historical figures from almost 2,500 years ago, engaged in one of history's most important naval battles. In addition to the intellectual undercurrents—

Figure 3.7 ▨ Nonfiction Review

Strauss, Barry. *The Battle of Salamis: The Naval Encounter That Saved Greece—and Western Civilization.* **New York: Simon & Schuster, 2004**

> One of world history's most significant naval battles, the Battle of Salamis in 480 B.C.E. has as its cornerstone Herodotus, the so-called Father of History. But some modern historians derogate him as the Father of Lies. A classical historian, Strauss treats Herodotus, who wrote 50 years after the battle, as a credible source, though some details are amendable in light of sources such as the dramatist Aeschylus, who reputedly fought in the battle. However, textual exegesis is muted in Strauss' treatment. In compelling fashion, Strauss imaginatively accentuates the local geography and the experience of battle; however, he is most evocative when outlining the strategic thought of the leaders, Xerxes for the Persian Empire and Themistocles for the Hellenic alliance. Strauss' plausible characterizations of these leaders are tied not only to their political culture but also to events, such as the desertion in sea battle by Greek ships, a prospect Themistocles exploited in his famous ruse, which precipitated Salamis. A factually fastidious historian might disapprove of Strauss' license, but he creates for a popular readership both an intriguing and an explanatory narrative of the epic battle. Gilbert Taylor. *Booklist* 100 (June 2004). Used by permission.

---

how reliable is Herodotus?—one discovers that the playwright Aeschylus, a participant in the battle, plays a role in the history as well. While the reader learns about the location and battle details, he is also privy to the strategies employed by the opposing leaders. The review provides a wealth of information about the book and its audience, but it also provides enough information that readers' advisors may be able to see links to fiction titles as well, either about ancient or more modern battles.

Some reviews are even more explicit in offering suggestions of other books, authors, and genres that might appeal to readers of the reviewed title. The best reviews allow us to make mental comparisons and to see connections between the appeal of this title and others. Even reviews that are mostly plot summary offer some clues to the appeal of a particular title. All readers' advisors should read reviews, whether they actually have selection responsibilities or not. Reading reviews in professional journals as well as in the popular press makes us aware of trends in publishing and keeps us current with popular authors and titles. If we read reviews with an eye—and an ear—for the appeal, we are also more likely to remember something about the book when a reader asks us if we have read it.

Other Factors to Consider

Identifying and then describing a book's appeal takes practice. Sometimes it helps to think about what the author does best. What strikes us about the book? The page-turning pace at which we read it? The fascinating characters who stayed with us long after we finished the story? The provocative, issue-oriented story line that made us see the world in a new way? Or the elaborately detailed setting in another time and place? Considering these questions helps us to see what we appreciated most in the book, but it also makes us aware that there are other possibilities and that other readers might have identified with a different element.

We might also consider what makes the book popular. What do readers talk about in terms of this author or story? No matter what we discover in a book, we need to be aware of what other readers are saying. In appeal there are no correct answers, only impressions that we share with other readers. We consider whether characters or story seems more important. Does the reader fall into the book immediately or learn about the story at a more leisurely pace? Is there a frame, extra information to entice the reader? If this book is part of a genre, how does it fit with others, or does the appeal cross over to other genres as well?

Finally, consider what other authors or titles the book reminds us of. Every reader who enjoyed this title will be looking for something else "just like" it, so it behooves us to think ahead. Is this book similar in appeal or different from others by the same author? Thinking about what makes a book similar to another title often helps us identify the appeal. We also consider who else might enjoy reading this book and why.

Certainly, all these questions seem too much for anyone to reflect on for every book we read or read about. I would argue, however, that with practice, this way of thinking about books and the appeal becomes second nature to readers' advisors. We already unconsciously consider many of these factors as we read. Thinking about a book's appeal allows us to lead readers from books to others they might enjoy.

In summary, readers' advisory sometimes seems an inexact, unstructured, undocumented discipline, but to the extent that there is a key, a formula, appeal seems to fill that role. Unraveling a book's appeal is best compared to working with, and ultimately solving, a puzzle. Readers' advisors discover clues to appeal in the books themselves as well as in reference resources, book jackets, and reviews. Then we compare our perceptions to those of other readers—staff and patrons—and synthesize all these elements into an understanding of a book's appeal. Finally, we develop a vocabulary that builds on the way we naturally think about books and allows us to share them more easily.

Understanding the appeal of books and authors—and putting the information we glean from reading and hearing about books in a framework structured around appeal elements—allows us to offer a range of titles to readers. Since we are simply building on a natural tendency, we relate more easily to the way readers choose books and are not deterred by the feeling that there is only one perfect book that will satisfy readers each time they come to the library. Thinking in terms of appeal allows us to respond to patron tastes and moods with a range of titles that might interest them.

In my experience, the more we work with appeal and the more we allow appeal to structure our readers' advisory interviews, the more successful and satisfying these interactions become. Thinking in terms of appeal allows us to see what an author does best—character, story, pacing, or perhaps atmosphere. We can identify the feel of the book, the impressions readers take away. We can talk about books we have not read or did not like because we can readily gain information about appeal without actually reading or enjoying every book we talk about. The next chapter explores ways in which we use appeal and reference sources in working directly with readers.

Notes

1. Arturo Pérez-Reverte, *The Flanders Panel* (New York: Harcourt Brace, 1990).
2. Piers Paul Read, *Alive: The Story of the Andes Survivors* (Philadelphia: Lippincott, 1974).
3. Andrea Barrett, *The Voyage of the Narwhal* (New York: Norton, 1998).
4. Thomas Harris, *The Silence of the Lambs* (New York: St. Martin's, 1988).
5. Alistair MacLean, *The Guns of Navarone* (Garden City, N.Y.: Doubleday, 1957).
6. Erik Larson, *The Devil in the White City: Murder, Magic, and Madness at the Fair That Changed America* (New York: Crown, 2003).
7. Peter Høeg, *Smilla's Sense of Snow* (New York: Farrar, 1993); and Martin Cruz Smith, *Gorky Park* (New York: Random, 1961).
8. David G. McCullough, *John Adams* (New York: Simon & Schuster, 2001); and Dava Sobel, *Galileo's Daughter: A Historical Memoir of Science, Faith, and Love* (New York: Walker, 1999).
9. Lee Smith, *The Last Girls* (Chapel Hill, N.C.: Algonquin Books of Chapel Hill, 2002).
10. Robert Graves, *I, Claudius* (New York: Random, 1961).
11. Michael Shaara, *The Killer Angels* (New York: McKay, 1974).
12. James Patterson, *Along Came a Spider* (Boston: Little, Brown, 1993); Richard Preston, *The Hot Zone* (New York: Random, 1994); Doris Kearns Goodwin, *Wait Till Next Year: A Memoir* (New York: Simon & Schuster, 1997); Barbara Ehrenreich, *Nickel and Dimed: On (Not) Getting By in America* (New York:

Metropolitan, 2001); Orson Scott Card, *Ender's Game* (New York: T. Doherty Associates, 1985); and Jon Krakauer, *Into Thin Air: A Personal Account of the Mount Everest Disaster* (New York: Villard, 1997).

13. Jack Schaefer, *Shane* (Boston: Houghton, 1949).

14. Tracy Chevalier, *Girl with a Pearl Earring* (New York: Dutton, 2000).

15. Owen Gingerich, *The Book Nobody Read: Chasing the Revolutions of Nicolaus Copernicus* (New York: Walker, 2004).

16. Lauren Weisberger, *The Devil Wears Prada* (New York: Doubleday, 2003); Plum Sykes, *Bergdorf Blondes* (New York: Miramax, 2004).

17. Jeanne Williams, *No Roof but Heaven* (New York: St. Martin's, 1990).

18. Nora Roberts, *Carnal Innocence* (New York: Bantam, 1991).

19. Laura Hillenbrand, *Seabiscuit: An American Legend* (New York: Random, 2001); Miles Harvey, *The Island of Lost Maps: A True Story of Cartographic Crime* (New York: Random, 2000); and William M. Bass, *Death's Acre: Inside the Legendary Forensic Lab—the Body Farm—Where the Dead Do Tell Tales* (New York: Putnam, 2003).

20. Henryk Sienkiewicz, *With Fire and Sword*, W. S. Kuniczak, trans. (New York: Hippocrene, 1991).

21. Duncan Smith, "Valuing Fiction," *Booklist* 94 (March 1, 1998): 1094–95.

22. Dan Brown, *The Da Vinci Code* (New York: Doubleday, 2003).

23. J. Suzanne Frank, *Reflections in the Nile* (New York: Warner, 1997).

24. McCullough, *John Adams*.

4   The Readers' Advisory Interview

This chapter covers one of the basics of readers' advisory service: the readers' advisory interview, the conversations readers' advisors hold with readers. Although I call it an *interview*, a term with which members of the profession are more comfortable, *conversation* more aptly describes both the tenor and intent of this interaction. Below I describe this conversation and then examine the preparation and skills needed to become accomplished readers' advisors. To become proficient in conducting readers' advisory interviews, librarians must direct the way they think about books and adopt a method of thinking that becomes second nature and that can then be applied both to books they read and to those they read or hear about. Along with formalizing a way of thinking about books comes the necessity of learning to talk about books, of putting mental observations and impressions about books into words. This chapter provides suggestions for doing this as well. How this interview works, ranging from ways to open this conversation with readers to possible ways to respond to reader queries, is also discussed. Finally, I describe some special situations, drawn from my experience as a readers' advisor. Experienced readers' advisors will recognize situations they have encountered, while new readers' advisors will see situations they might eventually face and have a chance to think about how they might deal with them.

A Definition

The readers' advisory interview is actually a conversation between the advisor and the reader about books. A readers' advisor will certainly use all the same communication skills involved in reference interviewing to get readers to describe their reading tastes and what they are in the mood to read at the time. Yet, unlike a reference interview, this is not primarily a question-and-answer exchange; it is a conversation, with readers telling the readers' advisor about books and their leisure-reading tastes and the readers' advisor listening and suggesting possible titles. The measure of success for the readers' advisory interview is not whether the reader takes and reads the books the readers' advisor offers. Rather, the exchange is a success when readers perceive, based on the service they receive, that the library is a place where they can talk about books and obtain suggestions and resources to meet their reading needs. As with any good conversation, a successful readers' advisory interview is not, nor should it be, a onetime encounter. The advisor encourages readers to return and give their reactions to the books suggested, thus establishing an ongoing dialogue between readers and the readers' advisory staff.

Since the readers' advisory interview usually occurs in an open area, it is rarely a two-person encounter. Fortunately, readers are notorious eavesdroppers when they hear books being discussed. Other patrons often chime in with their impressions and suggestions of possible titles. The readers' advisor may describe several books to one patron only to have them disappear from the shelves as a soon as the readers' advisor and the patron turn their backs. Or a patron may say, "Last time I was in, you were telling another woman about a novel that took place during the Irish Potato Famine. It sounded so good that I'd like to read it." The trick, then, is to remember which book was being discussed.

Before proceeding further, I want to consider two issues that play important roles in the way we address readers' advisory inquiries. The first is the distinction between suggesting and recommending books, and the second is the question of quality, specifically the use of the phrase *well written*.

Suggesting versus Recommending

Although the distinction between *suggest* and *recommend* may seem a trivial question of semantics, our terminology preference is important. We provide far better readers' advisory service when we stop using these words interchangeably. When we talk with friends, we likely *recommend* titles we want them to read, based on our personal knowledge of their interests or perhaps because we want them to read and then discuss that particular book with us. When we work with readers in a library, we talk with them about what they might enjoy reading. We then *suggest* a range of books that might appeal to them, based on what they have said about their reading tastes, interests, and mood.

When we make this distinction, when we suggest rather than recommend, we change the focus of our patron interactions. From the advisor's standpoint, it is far less threatening to talk with a reader and suggest a range of books than to take the responsibility for recommending a title or two we think are appropriate. Readers are more comfortable returning with comments, especially negative comments, about books we have suggested than about those that come recommended. We all know how difficult it is to tell someone that we really did not like the book they insisted we would love. Suggestions establish a friendly, professional rapport between librarian and reader. They allow readers to choose whether to read a book or not, and they also allow readers the freedom to like a book or not.

Quality and "Well Written"

The manner in which we describe *quality* writing is another, more difficult, issue. We should try to avoid the phrase *well written*. The phrase means almost nothing to the reader who hears it. We may have a group of authors or titles to which we apply this term, but all readers have their own favorite books they consider well written. We have all heard readers apply *well written* to the gamut of fiction and nonfiction, no matter how critics review the writing style. For most readers the phrase *well written* is the highest accolade they can bestow on a book or writer they love. From this stems the difficulty in applying the phrase with any consistency or assurance of a common understanding of its meaning. When readers connect with a book, when it satisfies them, they view it as well written. On the other hand, a style that one reader lauds may be disparaged by another, not because of any prescribed quality standards but simply because that style does not appeal. For example, Duncan Smith suggests that readers who enjoy fast-paced, action-oriented novels may not consider a book such as Kazuo Ishiguro's *Remains of the Day*, winner of Great Britain's prestigious Booker Prize, well written because it does not meet their personal standards for a well-written, satisfying book.[1] In Ishiguro's novel, the measured pacing, as the author takes his time revealing character and story line, moves the story more slowly, and readers who prefer more action may not be satisfied, nor may they regard this as well written, no matter how many awards it has received.

When trying to indicate quality at the readers' advisory desk, I have found it far more useful and informative to talk about the way an author uses language or about an unusual or distinctive style if such comments seem relevant. We might also describe a book as an "award winner" or "critically acclaimed" if we believe a reader would relate to this information. In the readers' advisory interview, the words *well written* have become an empty, catchall phrase; unfortunately, relying on it to describe a "quality" title is a hard habit to break, as we know from experience.

To summarize, then, a readers' advisory interview is a conversation between the advisor and the reader about books. The goal is to establish the idea of a readers' advisory service in the minds of readers so they know that suggesting books and asking for suggestions are legitimate library activities. Patrons accustomed to asking reference questions at the reference desk will not necessarily assume that they may ask for reading suggestions as well. Using many of the same communication skills that reference staff use, the readers' advisor tries to get a picture of the type of books the reader enjoys, makes some suggestions—perhaps using or referring the patron to the resources described in chapter 2—and invites the reader to return. In the next section we will discuss the preparation and skills that are needed to conduct successful interviews.

Preparing for the Interview

Thinking about Books

If you are a reader, you know that sharing a good book is one of the joys of life. One of the pleasures of doing readers' advisory is just that—sharing books with people. We have all had the experience of reading a book and thinking immediately of a friend who would also enjoy reading it. While sharing books with friends is usually based on a history of mutual experiences and interests, approaching an anonymous or relatively unknown library patron and suggesting a book is quite another matter. Yet such "informal" encounters comprise almost all the book suggestions readers' advisors make in a library. It is important to understand how to share books with readers so that, with practice, a readers' advisor can talk with almost anyone about books and reading.

Preparation for the readers' advisory interview begins long before the dialogue with a patron takes place. The key to successful readers' advisory is in learning how to think about books, which is a three-phase process. First, readers' advisors begin with the book's appeal, what makes the book a "good read." Second, advisors group the book with other titles and authors who have similar appeal. Third, readers' advisors consider how authors and titles fit within a genre or area of interest.

This thought process comes more easily to some than to others. Not only can they remember almost every book they have ever read but they can talk about books in a way that makes us want to read them immediately. Fortunately for those of us who do not possess this talent naturally, there are relatively straightforward techniques that we can learn, practice, and master. In fact, if you are a reader, you probably already use them unconsciously.

The first technique—reading a book with an eye to its appeal—goes against many of our English teachers' instructions to read critically to identify themes, symbols, and so forth. Rather, the reading we do as readers' advisors in preparation for suggesting books to other readers grows naturally from our own enjoyment of books. In talking with a friend, for instance, we describe our reactions to a book by its appeal, as discussed in the previous chapter. As a readers' advisor, we simply need to expand this viewpoint, to ask, "What is it about the book that would appeal to another reader?"

When reading, readers' advisors watch for a book's best feature: characterization, frame, pacing, or story line. Sometimes more than one element stands out, but more often a single feature strikes us. For example, in a particular Thriller, the key to the book's appeal may be the strong, sympathetic hero. In another book, it may be the exotic setting or the fascinating historical detail. In still another book, the appeal may be witty dialogue or insight into problems. In describing Patricia Cornwell's or Kathy Reich's Mysteries, both of which feature a medical examiner, it is easy to identify the wealth of medical and forensic detail they contain, whether we have read their books or only heard about them. With Clive Cussler, we might focus on the adventure element and the range of background material he brings to his books. We read with the goal of discovering the appeal, identifying it, and describing—even if only mentally—what seems to be the book's best feature or features. We found this exercise to be invaluable when we began to talk about books with other readers, because focusing on the appeal made talking about books easier and more natural. We also note any of the book's unusual details: the book may provide interesting insights about antiques and the antique business, or the author may have drawn the etchings that illustrate the book. These elements are sometimes a wonderful draw for patrons, so they are worth noting.

While readers' advisors are looking for a book's best features, they should also be alert to characteristics that might limit its appeal. For example, might the amount of explicit sex or violence offend some readers? Does the author employ an unconventional style that may annoy some readers? Does the book advocate a particular political, religious, or social position? Does it address social or moral issues that some readers might find offensive? None of these characteristics should necessarily keep a readers' advisor from suggesting a particular book, however. Although certain elements may bother some readers, they may be the very features that attract others. Readers' advisors simply need to be aware of the presence of these elements. In the next section, "Talking about Books," and later, in "Special Situations," I discuss more fully how to handle those aspects that may limit a book's appeal to certain readers.

After we started identifying a book's appeal when we spoke with readers, we found ourselves moving on to the second phase: mentally grouping books with other authors and titles that have similar appeal. As I suggested in chapter 3, when we finish a book, we simply ask ourselves, What other books are like this? What other books would appeal to the reader who enjoyed this one? We think about the particular kinds of characters, story line, pacing, point of view—all of the elements that affect a book's appeal. That two books feature amateur detectives does not necessarily mean they would appeal to the same reader unless other elements work together to give the books the same feel. For example, the admirers of Lawrence Block's burglar/detective/rare-books dealer Bernie Rhodenbarr would not automatically consider Diane Mott Davidson's Goldie Bear, caterer cum sleuth, to be of the same ilk. Even though they both feature amateur detectives and are Cozy Mysteries (without explicit sex and violence), they do not necessarily share the same fans. Other factors—the character of the detective, the setting, the atmosphere, the frame—may combine to create a different readership.

It is sometimes difficult to come up with similar books and authors, even after having practiced this technique for years. However, the mental exercise of trying to think of other books with similar appeal strengthens our ability to group similar authors and titles. As we do this, we try not only to identify authors but also to articulate what makes their books similar to the book we have just read. Are the characters developed in a similar fashion? Do the clues unravel in a similar manner? Are they both fast-paced stories that the reader finds immediately engrossing? Readers' advisors should always strive to identify these similarities. We have found that, with practice, it is even possible—and extremely useful—to apply this comparative questioning technique to books for which we have read only the reviews and those that we have heard discussed by friends and patrons. Readers' advisors become attuned to clues that signal similar appeal for readers and are thus able to link books with greater ease.

The third phase in learning how to think about books—considering how a book fits within a genre—continues the practice of grouping similar authors and titles. When working with a genre, librarians often find it useful to look for dissimilar authors as well. For example, if we read Stephen King's Dark Tower series and realize that it is not like J. K. Rowling's Harry Potter books, we have made an important and useful distinction within the Fantasy genre. It is often easier, in fact, to identify like authors after eliminating those who are dissimilar. The ability to recognize that authors and titles are similar or dissimilar and the reasons why expands our understanding of the genre. We readers' advisors find ourselves creating a framework that allows us to characterize genres and to place authors within those genres.

The ability to group authors and titles also helps a readers' advisor link books in which the similarities may not be immediately obvious. For example, a fan of critically acclaimed Literary Fiction might also appreciate the quality of language and provocative story lines of John le Carré's Espionage Thrillers, P. D. James's Mysteries, and Stephen Pressfield's Historical Fiction. Having successfully identified a book's appeal, readers' advisors will find that, as readers become more comfortable with the advisor's suggestions, we can often expand readers' horizons beyond such elements as time or setting, which would seem to separate books. Helen Fielding may very well have had this sort of connection in mind when she included character names and themes from Jane Austen's *Pride and Prejudice* in *Bridget Jones's Diary*.[2] By the same token, Romance readers who enjoy the sophisticated world of the upper class as portrayed in some Contemporary Romances may also enjoy Regency Romances, even though they are set almost two hundred years earlier. Both provide a glimpse of the fashionable world of the period— clothes, language, important personages—in addition to the romance.

Even after readers' advisors have mastered this method of thinking about books—of reading for the book's appeal, grouping similar authors and titles, and linking books within a genre—one essential component still remains: *readers' advisors need a way to remember what they have read.* We all know the frustration of not having enough time to read everything we would like to read (not to mention everything library patrons believe we have read or ought to have read). It is just as disconcerting, however, not to remember the title of a wonderful book that would be just right to suggest to a particular reader or to add to a display. There are undoubtedly many solutions to this problem, and it is important to find one that suits each advisor. I like mine for its simplicity. I keep a notebook with a list of the authors and titles I have read, drawing a line between months. Adding a code letter next to each work can help to further differentiate books by genre but is not a necessity.

How could any device this simple help us remember the dozens of books we read each year? You would be surprised. Because the list is chronological and divided by month, it is possible to place a book in time among other books read, and that information alone often jogs our memory of the book. When we look at a title on our list, checking the date and the titles that appear before and after it will often bring the book vividly to mind. We can recall much of the plot, characters, and feel of the book. This is not to say that this method gives us instant recall of every book we have read, but it does give us a better chance to remember the appeal of the book. However, simply keeping a list of what we have read is not enough. We must also review the list frequently. This practice refreshes our memory and even allows us to make connections between books that we might otherwise have missed. Looking back over the list, we often realize that the book we just read is similar to something we read several years earlier. In chapter 5, I discuss a more elaborate method of recording what I have read.

To be a readers' advisor, we need to learn how to think about books. Once we have mastered the techniques of identifying a book's appeal and started keeping track of what we read, we will see the rewards in our expanding knowledge of books and how we relate to readers. Having thought through and used these techniques, readers' advisors develop a way of looking at books that allows us to evoke useful responses from patrons and to help readers define their own reading interests.

Talking about Books

As readers' advisors master the art of thinking about books, we also need to practice talking about books. As I pointed out above, the more that readers' advisors practice identifying the appeal of the books we read, the easier it becomes to recognize that appeal. In the same way, the more that advisors describe books by their appeal, the more skilled we become. Verbalizing our discoveries as we begin to read for appeal provides the acid test for some of our pet theories about books. Talking about a book's appeal with others—friends, staff, and patrons—takes readers' advisors out of the vacuum of simply reading and thinking about books. It gives us an opportunity to test our opinions about a book's appeal and to hone our interviewing skills. We readers' advisors find out quickly which approaches work and learn to refine our techniques accordingly. It is primarily through talking with others about books that readers' advisors discover which questions work in a readers' advisory interview—that is, which questions elicit responses from readers and which do not.

We begin by talking about books informally, listening to what readers say about books and sharing our impressions. While we listen to someone describe a book, we attempt to understand its appeal and group it with books we know. We find ourselves asking mentally, Who else writes that kind of book? or What other book is it like? These are the same questions we ask ourselves when we finish reading a book. If a friend liked one book and not another we thought was similar, we ask why. For example, we suggested Stephen Coonts's Military Adventures to a reader of W. E. B. Griffin. The reader came back to say these books were not exactly what he had in mind. He explained that Coonts was too technical for his taste, and what he enjoyed about Griffin were the stories. Another Military novelist, such as Joe Weber, who relies less on technical details, was a better match. Framing questions to elicit this information will be discussed later.

Informal encounters not only allow readers' advisors to test our opinions about books and authors; they can also be excellent sources of information about good reading—books to pass on to other readers. We encourage friends, colleagues, and patrons to tell us about books they have enjoyed. After all, at its best readers' advisory is a two-way conversation, involving both the giving and taking of suggestions. In a library where this atmosphere of sharing books exists, readers' advisors will find more and more patrons talking about books with each other and even suggesting titles they have enjoyed to total strangers. The amount of book sharing that goes on is amazing. However, readers' advisors need to be prepared for the consequences of this situation. We often find ourselves in a hopeless state of having more books suggested to us than we will ever be able to read!

Library staff members who think and talk about books are a great asset. In the best of all possible worlds (and libraries), talking about books, sharing what we read, is not limited to a single department. Readers' advisory work flourishes in an atmosphere in which it is not unusual for anyone and everyone to talk about books; and the more that books are discussed throughout the library, the more the people actually doing readers' advisory will benefit. When discussing books becomes an accepted and welcome part of staff interactions among librarians themselves and with patrons, the library's visibility as a resource for readers increases. Readers grow more comfortable sharing their own reading interests in such an environment.

These informal discussions with friends, patrons, and colleagues are extremely useful for validating readers' advisors' perceptions about what they read, for gleaning additional reading suggestions, and for creating an atmosphere in which books are discussed. However, they are not a substitute for regularly scheduled discussions among the readers' advisory staff. There are many ways to handle such discussions. In *The Fair Garden and the Swarm of Beasts: The Library and the Young Adult*, Margaret A. Edwards describes the process whereby she trained her new young adult librarians, prescribing a list of three hundred books for them to read and discuss with her![3] Our approach at Downers Grove Public Library, described in chapter 5, includes a much more limited directed reading plan and is less structured. In addition, the department meets monthly, and we always begin these meetings by talking about what each of us is currently reading. From this experience, we refine our ability to describe a book by its appeal, and we learn from our own attempts as well as from listening to others. We pick up additional information about books and related authors and titles from other experienced readers' advisors, and we rather effortlessly expand our familiarity with books that we can later share with patrons. We also have a chance to bring up and discuss problems, such as books for which similar authors and titles are not immediately obvious.

No matter what our individual situation, it is important to set up opportunities to talk about books with others who do readers' advisory directly or who understand how readers' advisors think and talk about books, whether in our own libraries or outside. Although there is no substitute for the opportunity to practice talking about books among colleagues in a setting away from patrons, it is also important to share books with colleagues on the desk. Readers overhear our conversations and feel more comfortable sharing their own reading interests. Of course, in every conversation outside of closed offices, we are onstage and need to remember to describe books by appeal, not by critical opinions, whether positive or negative. For further inspiration and examples of the joy of talking about books, have a look at Christopher Morley's *Parnassus on Wheels* and Helene Hanff's *84, Charing Cross Road*.[4] In fact, they are required reading for our staff, not because these works follow our suggested techniques but because they are wonderful examples of people who treasure books and can talk about them in a way that makes us want to do so too.

Setting the Stage

When we begin our shift at busy service desks, we can expect to be bombarded with a variety of information requests from patrons, ranging from business statistics to information on obscure medical disorders and beyond. One of the biggest obstacles readers' advisors face is making the almost instantaneous shift from providing specific factual information using a range of highly technical sources to serving the patron who wants a good book to read or several books for vacation reading. Making this kind of mental leap is no easy task. Strategies to deal with this situation are vital for all readers' advisors, from the newest to the most experienced.

The following warm-up exercises can help a readers' advisor prepare for the rigors of making these dramatic shifts in focus and technique. If you have practiced thinking and talking about books, you have already accomplished a great deal of this preparation. The following techniques, when part of the desk routine, require only a few minutes early in a shift and are invaluable in helping us mentally set the stage for encounters with readers.

First, when working at the service desk, check the bookshelves in the area in which most readers browse. Some libraries separate newer books from the rest of the collection, and it is often the newer books that attract patrons first. Others have special display areas where patrons congregate. Whatever the arrangement, when readers' advisors are at the public service desk, they need to know what is on these shelves because these are the books they can most easily draw on to share with readers. It is impossible to browse the entire fiction collection, but spending a few minutes previewing a manageable area not only gives you an idea of what is available that day but also starts you thinking about books, a crucial step in preparation. Look for titles in the genres or subgenres that your patrons request most often— Romantic Suspense, Cozy Mysteries, Thrillers, Romances, Travelogues, or whatever else is being asked for at the library—and start thinking about how you would describe the titles to patrons. It is especially useful to identify titles in popular genres with which you are less familiar; doing so increases your familiarity with the genre and prepares you for patrons' requests. Keep in mind some possible title suggestions for "regulars"—patrons who come in routinely on a particular day of the week or month. Nothing pleases them more than a good book they have somehow missed. If you have time, glance at a few book jacket summaries as well, to learn about unfamiliar titles.

This is a good time to check displays and add titles. In our library, we try to have several book displays highlighting subjects or types of fiction, in addition to our permanent Good Books You May Have Missed display. (Displays are discussed in more detail in chapter 6.) In this display, which features older and sometimes overlooked titles in our collection, we try to ensure that we have a range of genres represented. Filling the displays gets us into the stacks, handling books and thinking how we might share them with readers. Since these displays also serve as a lifeline of sorts when our minds go blank, it is important to know that they are well stocked and to have an idea of what books are there.

Next, check what is currently on the best-sellers lists. We post the *New York Times* best-sellers list from the weekly *New York Times Book Review* near our recent books and keep another copy at our desk. This list is especially useful because the short synopsis that accompanies each title is often just enough to jog our memory of what a particular book is about. We also check to see if copies of best sellers are on the shelf. Unless your library is far better stocked than ours, you will know that such a possibility is unlikely. The answer to this dilemma is to consider what other authors might appeal to the reader seeking a specific best seller. For example, when Nora Roberts appears on the best-sellers list, we supply a lot of other Romance and Romantic Suspense fiction, such as that written by Sandra Brown and Catherine Coulter, to readers who are waiting their turn for Roberts's new book. The same principle applies to any other best-selling authors, whether fiction or nonfiction. It is important for us to know which authors we may be asked for so that we can be prepared to suggest other possibilities when a patron requests authors and titles that are too popular to be available on the shelves. We developed our "While You Are Waiting" bookmarks, described in detail in chapter 5, to meet this need. Since they provide lists of suggestions to read while readers are on the reserve list, they effectively meet the needs of many readers.

The final warm-up suggestion involves keeping a log or notes of readers' advisory requests. In the beginning we kept such a log, which listed requests followed by the books suggested by the staff, and we checked it whenever we came on the desk. This started us thinking generally about readers' advisory requests and alerted us to currently requested authors and topics so that we could be prepared for similar questions. Keeping and referring to these questions gives us a chance to think about how we would handle them if asked.

The Readers' Advisory Interview

Most patrons do not expect to find a readers' advisory service in the library. In fact, many patrons would not consider asking for reading suggestions to be a valid request. Recent research suggests that among the top-four reasons fiction readers do not ask for assistance is that "a question about fiction (which is unimportant) would be perceived as being frivolous and waste staff time."[5] They would not hesitate to ask questions such as, "Do you have information on how to fix a broken washing machine?" or "When was the Chicago Fire?" but, curiously, asking for something for their leisure reading—a good Espionage novel or a book like Ross King's *Michelangelo and the Pope's Ceiling*—does not occur to them as being a permissible question.[6] Readers' advisors need to validate the fact that talking about books is a legitimate activity for both the librarian and the reader.

For the most part, readers' advisory interviews do not just happen. Readers' advisors cannot wait for a patron to ask about a book; instead, we must seek out patrons. We believe that librarians must be aggressive in offering this service to patrons. We use every opportunity to reinforce with our patrons the idea that the role of the readers' advisory staff is to suggest books to readers, that we know popular fiction and nonfiction, and that readers should feel free to talk with us about their reading interests. We recognize that some patrons prefer to browse on their own; although we respect their privacy, we also want to be certain that they know the service is available. They cannot use a service they do not know exists. We offer the service without being intrusive. Readers may not talk with us the first time, but they often feel safe approaching us when they return to the library. With just a few words, we have set the stage for future encounters, which often develop into long-term relationships between readers' advisory staff and readers.

Only when readers are comfortable coming to the desk and have been helped do we find substantial numbers of readers asking us directly for assistance. More often, readers come to the desk to ask about a specific author, or sometimes a genre. They may have been reading Michael Connelly and are looking for more of his titles. Or they want the new Janet Evanovich novel that just came out today. In the cases of these popular authors, once we have answered the immediate question, finding another title by Connelly or taking a reserve for the Evanovich novel, we might ask, "Do you also read T. Jefferson Parker or Robert Crais?" for the Connelly fan or "Have you discovered Jennifer Crusie or Nancy Bartholomew?" for the Evanovich reader. These are useful ways to start a readers' advisory conversation. These questions show readers that we are knowledgeable, that we can make suggestions, and that talking about books—and particularly about similar authors—is accepted behavior, the kind of request they should be comfortable making at our desk.

What about the reader who asks us for a best seller? This book is unlikely to be available for immediate checkout. In our experience, however, the majority of the people who come to the library are looking for a good, satisfying read, and the John Sandford novel of Suspense they just read about in the paper is their suggestion as a possibility to fill this need. Another author, such as James Patterson with his Alex Cross series, may be a very satisfying suggestion to tide them over while they are awaiting their turn for the Sandford. However, we should also be open to the possibility that readers may not even really want the kind of book they ask for when identifying an author on the best-sellers list. Sandford may simply be a name someone gave them, and in talking further, we may find them something else much more satisfying.

The final way readers' advisory interviews begin is when we approach browsers in the book stacks. Readers' advisory, like any other public service work in a library, cannot and should not be done solely from behind a desk; librarians need to be in the stacks with the books and the readers. Although some readers approach readers' advisors for suggestions, in most cases readers' advisors need to make the initial contact. Our staff tries to speak with every patron who comes into the fiction area. Our offer of assistance is designed to let patrons know that we are there to suggest books. In our experience, questions such as, "Is there a special book you are looking for?" or "May I suggest something to read?" are more likely to elicit a response than the question, "Can I help you?" Readers are unlikely to feel that suggesting titles and discussing their reading tastes is the kind of assistance we have in mind, although implementing some of the promotional techniques discussed in chapter 6 may make readers more aware that we value their leisure-reading questions.

When we talk with readers, we try to reinforce the idea that suggesting books is a service we routinely provide. Some additional approaches we use include "Would you like some suggestions, or are you comfortable browsing?" "Are you finding what you are looking for, or could I suggest something for you?" and simply, "May I suggest something for you to read?" We have found that these are all effective ways to alert patrons to the readers' advisory service the department provides. Patrons looking puzzled or leaving the area without a book are also often responsive to an offer of assistance. Whenever we receive repeated requests for a certain kind of book, we take advantage of this fact and incorporate it into our approach. For instance, the comment, "Looking for something light for the summer?" makes a good beginning on hot July days. We always make sure we have some titles in mind for the patron who readily agrees. If patrons say no, they often feel the need to explain: "No, I'm looking for something more like Stephen King. Do you know anyone like him?" Then we have a clue as to what to offer.

Once we have the reader's attention, we need information in order to make suggestions. Traditional questions, such as "What do you like to read?" usually do not elicit helpful information because patrons can rarely come up with a useful answer on the spur of the moment, and then they feel foolish. We have found a better approach is to request, "Tell me about a book you really enjoyed." Or, "Is there an author you consistently read?" Even asking, "Have you read anything lately that you disliked?" can start a useful exchange. Readers often find it easier to describe a book they did not enjoy, giving us valuable information that we can use in suggesting more-appropriate titles and authors. Readers are surprisingly forthcoming in describing both what they enjoy and what they do not. A patron might say, "The last book I read was too slow; nothing ever happened" or "I just didn't like the characters." Both responses provide clues that, with some rephrasing, can help patrons recognize what they do like. For example, we may reply, "What about a book with a lot of action? Maybe a Thriller or an Adventure story?"

If this approach still does not provide enough information, we ask appeal-based questions: "Do you like a book with a fast-moving plot or one that focuses more on the characters?" Offering the reader a choice allows the readers' advisor to narrow the range of possible suggestions. If the reader responds to the fast-moving plot, the next question might be, "Have you read any Mysteries or Thrillers?" as both types of books may have fast-moving plots, or at this point we might describe the features of a popular Suspense writer, such as Jeffery Deaver. A positive response to the second option—a preference for character-centered novels—might lead us to books featuring a series character or Literary Fiction.

It is also important to try to discover characteristics of books that do not appeal to particular patrons. After all, the goal of readers' advisory is to give the patrons what they are comfortable reading. For example, we note preferences as to time period and setting. We all know patrons who would prefer not to read books that have frank language or explicit sex. A tactful way to elicit this information is to ask if there are books the patron may not have enjoyed. If we are not sure exactly what to suggest, we offer a range of books. If a reader says she enjoys Romances, for example, but is not more specific, we might show her a Contemporary Romance, one of the more romantic Gentle Reads, and a sensual Historical Romance. Patrons' responses to our suggestions give us clues to their preferences.

As readers tell us what they enjoy or what they dislike, we listen for the appeal elements and how patrons express them. Fans of Elmore Leonard's Crime Thrillers may enjoy another writer in the same genre, perhaps someone like George V. Higgins or Joe Gores, but they may also simply be looking for another fast-paced, cinematic, engrossing book. Or perhaps they would like one that features a similar type of character: the quirky, streetwise, small-time crook, caught in a scam that sometimes threatens his own life. For this reader, Carl Hiaasen's darkly humorous heroes may suit, as might Donald Westlake's lighter touch. From having considered the range of ways a book might appeal, we now fall back on that knowledge and listen for the clues patrons give us about the types of books they are looking for or do not enjoy. Having mastered the idea of appeal, we can respond appropriately to patrons' requests for similar titles.

If possible, suggest at least three titles, giving the patron an overview of each one and describing each generally in terms of appeal. Here is where we put into play all the book-describing skills we have been practicing. For example, we will talk about what is best in the book, special features that might appeal to readers, how the book fits into the genre, or what other readers have said about it. We may not want to refer to all these factors every time, but these are some of the elements we draw on in talking about books. It is important to recognize that we do not necessarily need to know the plot of every title we describe; we talk instead in terms of appeal, highlighting aspects patrons have said they enjoy. Describing several possible titles reinforces the concept that readers' advisors suggest rather than recommend, thus allowing the reader to make the final selection. We are not providing the one and only "perfect book" for the reader. Since readers typically have a wide range of tastes, there are usually many books they would find satisfying. We suggest several so they can make choices, in the library and at home, about what they are in the mood to read.

One important point to bear in mind as we talk to readers and suggest books is that we are going from the readers' tastes and mood to possible book suggestions, from the reader to the book, rather than simply suggesting popular titles or the book we have just finished and enjoyed. Readers' advisory would be far easier if we could simply keep a stack of our favorite titles at the desk and offer them to everyone who asks for help. We talk with readers and make suggestions of titles that might meet *their* interests. Occasionally, we will find a reader who shares our taste and is in the mood for something that we have enjoyed, but more frequently readers are interested in something very different. We certainly place our favorite titles on displays when appropriate, but when we work individually with readers, we must learn to focus on what they enjoy reading and offer suggestions that meet their criteria for a good book.

Readers' advisory inquiries, like many reference questions, do not necessarily require immediate responses. Some patrons are perfectly happy to have us take notes about the kind of book or author they are interested in and then call them later with suggestions. This gives us an opportunity to discuss queries with fellow staff members and to follow leads in reference materials at our leisure. We frequently leave notes about difficult-to-answer patron requests at our service desk and solicit suggestions from other staff members before we post the query on Fiction_L, the electronic readers' advisory mailing list. A patron who is looking for something specific usually does not mind the wait and, moreover, appreciates the interest and personal attention. In addition, we have validated the importance of the question.

Putting books in patrons' hands is not the end of the readers' advisory interview; it is equally important to close with an invitation for the reader to return. Since more than one person does readers' advisory in our library, it is especially important to establish that whoever is working at the readers' advisory desk can provide this service, not just the person the patron is talking with. Encourage patrons to check back and tell the readers' advisor at the desk what they enjoyed and, even more important, what they did not care for, as that also provides useful information. When readers' advisors assure readers that they are interested not only in what readers enjoyed but also in the books that were not quite right, they are reinforcing the idea that the readers' opinions are valued and that there are many more titles that might appeal to them. Advising patrons is a process in which readers' advisors work not only with what they know about popular reading but also with what the reader brings to the exchange.

Parallels between Readers' Advisory and Reference Interviews

Although I describe the readers' advisory interview as a conversation about books, it does have a structure that closely parallels one many of us have learned in order to conduct better reference interviews. In the early 1980s, unobtrusive testing in Maryland public libraries revealed that the correct answer to reference questions was provided only about 55 percent of the time. To improve this situation, a model for the reference interview was developed and used successfully in Maryland and across the country.

The interview process was broken down into four stages.[7] The first stage, "Setting the Tone," emphasizes approachability. Librarians smile, make eye contact, and greet patrons. In stage two, "Getting the Facts," the process stresses showing interest in the patron and the question, paraphrasing and clarifying the patron request, asking open-ended questions to solicit further information, and negotiating the inquiry by thoroughly consulting sources. "Giving Information" constitutes stage three. Here, all the earlier techniques come into play, as does citing sources. Finally, stage four requires a follow-up query: "Does this completely answer your question?" It takes little effort to apply these steps to the readers' advisory interview.

Stage one

Approachability—welcoming body language and acknowledging the patron— sets the stage for our encounters. Readers need to be made comfortable asking librarians for assistance, especially with questions about leisure-reading suggestions, which so many readers have been taught to see as less important than "real" questions.

Stage two

As in a reference interview, we need to get the facts, although leisure readers often have more nebulous questions than do patrons seeking specific information. When readers describe the kinds of books they enjoy, we follow up by paraphrasing their response. "It sounds as if what you enjoy about Tom Clancy's Thrillers is all the technical detail and action, as well as the community of men, and the fact that the hero solves the problem through ingenuity." The next question follows automatically: "Are you in the mood for something like that, or would you rather have something different today?" Whether our searches lead us to the fiction or nonfiction shelves, to catalogs of our collection, to print or electronic resources, to displays, or to book lists, we involve the readers in the search to validate the importance of their questions.

Stage three

As we provide information, we highlight the appeal of the books, emphasizing those elements in which the reader has already expressed an interest. If readers do not provide specific information, we ask probing questions: "Do you like a lot of action in your books, or do you prefer to know the characters very well?" As stated earlier, we offer a range of titles and encourage readers to take several. As we offer these books, we watch for and listen to their reactions to make certain we are providing the kinds of suggestions they want.

We can also use appeal to introduce readers to authors or genres they may not be familiar with. If a reader enjoys the action of Dan Brown's Thrillers but talks also about a preference for strong, interesting characters, we might also suggest an author such as Daniel Silva. We might point out that Silva has a series character, Gabriel Allon, who is an art restorer, and that although the books feature similarly elaborate frames combining art history with espionage and often religion, they also display more cerebral twists and turns of plot as well as more emphasis on characterization. We provide readers with information about authors and titles and allow them to make their own choices. We have not said this book is just like what they read or guaranteed that they will enjoy it. We offer a range of books and give the readers the kind of information they need to make a decision.

Stage four

Finally, just as in the reference-interview model, we ask a follow-up question at the end of the interview. In this case, it is not whether we have completely answered the question, because in readers' advisory work there is almost never one right answer. Rather, we might ask if the suggested books seem interesting. Or whether the readers have enough to choose from. (This is also a good technique to use when we begin to fear that readers do not know how to tell us they have enough, as is often the case with young adults.) We also follow up by encouraging readers to come back and tell whoever is on the desk whether they liked the books or not. We invite them to return for further suggestions, stressing that there are so many books that, whether they like these titles or not, there are always others they might find satisfying, and we would welcome the opportunity to help them find more.

Even though we emphasize the process of suggesting and describing individual books to readers, the goal is not primarily to get readers to take home the particular books we suggest. Certainly nothing is so satisfying as to have patrons seek us out and tell us how much they enjoyed the books we previously suggested to them. As rewarding as that can be, however, readers' advisory would be very frustrating and limiting if that response were all we expected from the exchange. Patrons do not always take the books we think they will like, and they foolishly dislike titles we just know are "perfect" for them. The true measure of the success of the service is not the number of books taken out but the frequency and quality of readers' advisory exchanges.

In summary, there are two important points to remember about the readers' advisory interview. First, we are suggesting, not recommending, a range of books in which a reader might be interested. We do not look for one perfect book; rather, we offer possibilities. Second, readers usually are not seeking books on a particular subject; they are looking for books with a certain feel, and we do better when we share books in these terms. Thus, although it is helpful to be able to identify books by subject, we, as readers, all know there can be real differences between them. In Historical Mysteries, for example, a comparison between Elizabeth Peters's humorous Mysteries, which feature Egyptologists Radcliffe and Amelia Peabody Emerson in the swashbuckling adventure style of H. Rider Haggard, and Anne Perry's much bleaker Victorian Mystery series, which features William Monk, demonstrates that not all Historical Mysteries are the same.

Acknowledging this, we need to rethink how we describe books to readers. Mini booktalks are not necessarily the answer. The responsibility of giving a mini booktalk for every book we suggest puts us under a lot of pressure. For one thing, it implies we know and can describe the plot of every book. It even suggests that we have read all the books we talk about with readers and remember them well enough to describe them and, thus, that to do our best readers' advisory, we should limit ourselves to books we know and remember. Such thinking puts us all in a real bind. However, if we focus on appeal elements when describing books to readers, we do better. Not only can we remember more about books we have read or read about if we think about them in terms of appeal but we can also talk invitingly about books that we have not read and know much less about. Following this approach, we might simply say to the reader who enjoyed Kate Wilhelm's *The Deepest Water*, "You might like Laurie R. King's *Folly*.[8] It also has a strong female character, elegant writing, building suspense, and a plot that turns on family secrets."

This approach takes practice and means we must change our focus as we read and read about books, but it is really more natural than giving mini booktalks. We start simply by considering what an author does best. All our practice thinking and talking about books helps to prepare us for this approach, which capitalizes on appeal—the way we naturally think about books—and enables us to present the kind of information to readers that allows them to choose for themselves what to read.

Special Situations

The following examples, which portray situations readers' advisors are sure to encounter, will clarify the nature of the readers' advisory interview. The examples are based on questions I have been asked, and the responses reflect what has worked for me; however, they are not necessarily the only, or even the best, ways to handle each case. Other readers' advisors will undoubtedly work out their own strategies.

How do you talk about a book, subject, or genre in which you have not read?

When talking with a patron about a book we have not read, we pick out the elements that indicate the book's appeal to readers. The skills we have mastered in analyzing the books we have read transfer to the more limited information provided by reviews, book jackets, conversations with readers, and even "speed-reading" books, as discussed in chapter 5. We draw on all these sources to talk about what each book is like and how it fits within a genre. Nothing replaces actually reading a book from cover to cover, assuming we remember in detail everything we have read, but trained readers' advisors can talk comfortably about books they have not read because they can extract and compile useful information from various sources.

There is no shame in admitting we have not read a book; we cannot read everything. In fact, even when they ask if we have read a book, patrons do not necessarily expect us to have read that particular title. They are really asking if it is acceptable for them to take the book. Has anyone read it? Our job is to reassure them. We relay any information we have heard about the book from other readers—staff and patrons—or reviews as well as anything we know about the author or genre. We can also go to the book itself. As discussed in chapter 3, "Articulating a Book's Appeal," flipping through a book often tells us whether there is a lot of dialogue or whether each page is filled with text, and we can comment on pacing or characterization based on what we discover. We also remind patrons they do not have to read the book if they do not like it. They can come back later or tomorrow, and we will help them find something else. Whether we are familiar with the book or subject or not, we work to find an answer for the reader. We use all available resources to answer this kind of question, just as we would an informational question on an unfamiliar topic. We do not refuse to find information about diabetes because we have not had the disease and thus know nothing about it; nor do we refuse to answer questions about plumbing just because we are not plumbers.[9] Treat these questions like all others, researching them to find answers for readers.

Best sellers constitute a special class of book because patrons often ask about them. They want to know what the book is about, so we need to know some particulars of the plot. That information is fairly easy to come by, using resources such as the *New York Times* best-sellers list, with its one-sentence annotations, as well as reviews and comments from patrons and colleagues about the book. Since most best-selling authors are repeaters, however, it is also helpful to have, at some point, read at least one typical book by that author. Combining what we know about the current best-seller's plot or subject with our general knowledge of the author, the kind of books he or she writes, and how readers and critics perceive the author, we can readily say enough to satisfy an interested patron.

Suggesting in a genre or on a topic we are not familiar with is harder. We really need resources: reference books on the genre, useful web resources, lists of popular fiction and nonfiction, and annotated book lists. If we are uncomfortable with Science Fiction, for example, but we get many requests for suggestions from readers, we talk with fans of the genre about their favorites and then have ideas to share with other readers. It behooves us to become familiar with fiction and nonfiction genres popular with our patrons. Just as the only way to answer difficult reference questions is to explore the material and gather aids, so it is in becoming familiar with a genre. There is no quick and easy way to get the job done, but it can be interesting and exciting. I talk more about this activity in chapter 5, "Background for Readers' Advisors."

What do you do when you draw a blank?

We have all experienced that familiar sinking feeling when someone asks for something to read—something ostensibly simple, such as a good Romance with a little bit of mystery or just a good book—and nothing comes to mind. At times like these, the best solution is to go and stand by the books. Walking from the desk to the stacks or a book display seems to get our minds moving, and I am convinced that the books themselves give off an aura. They seem to know we need help and come to our aid. I am amazed at how frequently I will think of a title or an author to fit the situation once I am near the books and handling them. I may be standing at one point in the stacks, when something I see reminds me of a book in another part of the alphabet.

Many of the reference resources discussed in chapter 2 can also be useful at this point. They serve as memory joggers that help us get our minds working. They also reinforce patrons' perceptions that we are taking their questions seriously. Consulting these resources often helps us start a conversation about books, and that is usually the impetus we need. Once we have overcome this mental block by searching in a reference source, we are usually able to go on to other suggestions. If not, these reference tools are designed to provide further assistance. We should remember, too, that readers often find these resources fascinating and, once familiar with them, browse for interesting information and reading suggestions. We should take every opportunity to introduce readers to our resources.

This is also the perfect time to pull out a genre list, such as a Popular Fiction List or Popular Nonfiction List (see appendixes 1 and 2), if we have one. Patrons may recognize an author they have enjoyed, and readers' advisors will have a list of other popular authors who write in that same genre or about the same kinds of topics, although perhaps not in the same style. Annotated book lists can also be a useful resource to give readers. Book lists often will bring to mind a book that can be suggested, and patrons can have a list of all the authors and titles that interest them.

How do you talk about books, subjects, and authors you personally do not enjoy?

Posted at our readers' advisory desk is "Rosenberg's First Law of Reading: Never apologize for your reading tastes." We believe that it is important for patrons to feel comfortable talking with a readers' advisor about any type of book, from so-called trash to classics. Even if we accept this philosophy, however, it does not mean that we will like everything patrons ask about— and we do not. When a patron asks about an author or a title we personally do not like, we rely on the techniques discussed earlier and talk about what the author does best. What is the strength of the book? What kind of book is it—Intrigue, Fantasy, Mainstream Fiction, True Crime? What have other readers praised? If we have heard fans of a particular author talk about the book, we share that information with readers. For example, we might say that fans of Bill Bryson's travel adventures have really liked this book. We may describe the book specifically, if we are familiar with it, or talk generally about the kind of books the author writes. This approach allows us to speak in nonjudgmental terms, without betraying our personal feelings. We may also talk about an author's popularity and appeal to other readers, again without interjecting our own assessment. It is important to develop some nonjudgmental phrases to employ in situations like this. For example, the author may be "quite a storyteller," or the book may be "a real page-turner," a "Cozy English Village Mystery," or have "quite a following among readers who enjoy this type of nonfiction." A readers' advisor should develop conversational lines that simultaneously respect a patron's taste and leave the advisor's senses of honor and humor intact.

We should make a conscientious effort not to make negative comments about a book or author. Even if we are certain the reader we are speaking with will understand our intent, another reader who overhears the remarks may not and may be offended. If a new book by a popular author has been poorly reviewed, we might suggest interested readers try it anyway and judge for themselves. If readers have told us they enjoyed a poorly reviewed book, we share that fact with other readers. On the other hand, we might suggest an alternative—an earlier book by the author or a similar title that other readers have praised.

What do you do when a patron refuses your offer of reading suggestions?

There are times when we cannot give book suggestions away, when patrons would not take our suggestions even if we paid them to do so. It happens. Unsatisfactory and discouraging as this situation is to us as readers' advisors, we need to recognize patrons' right to privacy as well as their right to be made aware of library services. The question is, of course, how can we offer readers' advisory service without seeming to badger readers who enjoy the pleasure of browsing on their own? This takes skill and experience, and staff should work through just what to say. Patrons have a right to decline our help, and both they and we should feel comfortable when they do so. Do not be discouraged by a refusal or even by a string of rejections. When patrons turn down our offer of book suggestions, we remind them that the service exists and that they should feel comfortable asking for suggestions whenever they are interested. We say, "The staff at this desk are all readers, and we would be glad to offer reading suggestions. Stop by if you ever want some ideas."

How do you handle the question,
"Can you 'recommend' a good book?"

Does any other question strike such fear in a librarian's heart as this? In most cases, we fall back on the interviewing techniques described earlier in this chapter. However, sometimes a patron does not have anything specific in mind or is asking for books for someone else. In both cases, the patron may just want a "good read." This is when we call on standby titles or "Sure Bets"—books that appeal to a wide range of readers (Sure Bets are discussed in depth in chapter 5; see also appendix 3). These are usually titles we and other readers have read and enjoyed, and we can often "sell" them to readers simply by sharing our enthusiasm for the book. When we fall back on Sure Bets, we use them as much to elicit a response from the reader as anything else. Hearing books described, the readers react, either by taking the book or by telling us something else they might enjoy.

The best Sure Bets are older titles that we can expect to find on the shelves. Advisors should cultivate Sure Bets in genres both familiar and personally unexplored. A list of Sure Bets kept at the advisory desk and updated regularly by staff eliminates the librarian's fear of being unable to remember them. We should be prepared, however, for all the readers who will want to take the list away. The only drawback to this strategy is that extra copies of these favorites will have to be ordered, because they will rarely be found on the shelf. It is also a good idea to have Sure Bets available in multiple formats. Then, if the regular print version is checked out, we might have the large print or paperback version on hand. This also enables us to expand our coverage of Sure Bets and meet the needs of a broader range of patrons.

How do you suggest books to patrons
who have reading restrictions?

We all know the stereotypical little old lady who is supposed to enjoy only gentle English Pastorals but is, in fact, just as likely to read and enjoy a really bloody serial killer Suspense novel. It is awkward when readers' advisors make the wrong assumption about a person, and this can be embarrassing both to us and to patrons. More important, it is not fair either to patrons or to readers' advisors to try to outguess readers or for readers' advisors to try to put restrictions on what we suggest when we have no good reason to believe that restrictions are desired by the reader.

On the other hand, some readers do have restrictions, and they will often voice them during the readers' advisory interview. The restrictions our readers most often mention are sex and violence; as a result, we get requests for "clean" books or for authors who simply tell a "nice story." This limitation may not be the most common one among your readers, but undoubtedly some limitation will come up. You will want to keep a list of titles that meet your readers' needs and update it whenever you come across titles that fit the criteria.

Explicit sex and violence are not the only restrictions readers' advisors encounter. We have readers who prefer only books written by men, and others, only those written by women. One reader likes Spy Thrillers but only if they take place in the United States. Another wants sea stories but not those set during World War II. By offering a range of books to readers and by being sensitive to their reactions, we can often help readers identify their own less obvious restrictions and more readily suggest books that appeal to them.

We also deal with patrons who have physical restrictions when it comes to reading. They may need more white space on the page or might have difficulty holding books that are too heavy or don't lie flat on a table. These physical characteristics of books can also be noted and kept on similar lists. We do serve a growing population of disabled and of older patrons—people who enjoyed reading in the past and want to continue to do so.

In dealing with patrons' content and style restrictions, it is also important that we, as readers' advisors and librarians, remain nonjudgmental; it is better not to take sides if a patron is talking on and on about "the terrible state of fiction today," even if we agree. We try to restate patrons' objections in positive terms, reinforcing our position of accepting the entire gamut of reading tastes. For example, we might say, "It sounds as if you're looking for what we call a Gentle Read. Let me give you some authors." The tone we adopt is important; our goal is to meet the needs of all readers, not just those who enjoy what we enjoy and who share our prejudices. We need to be aware of differences in attitudes and of how the written word may strike a variety of readers so that our comments inform rather than offend. We should also remember the public nature of our readers' advisory interviews. Our comments are easily overheard, and a disparaging remark about an author or type of book made to one patron may offend someone else in the area.

What do you say if a reader asks if a book is "safe"?

Related to readers' restrictions is the issue of whether a book is "safe" to read, either for the person asking or for someone else, usually a child, for whom the person is collecting titles. Never guarantee that a book is safe. What offends us may not offend another reader, but we certainly can never predict what someone might find unsavory in any title. If this is a parent asking for suggestions for a child, we encourage the parent to read the book first, before sharing it, if he or she has any concerns. (This is another instance when we are far better served by suggesting, rather than recommending, appropriate titles, since recommending may seem to imply a guarantee.) When readers are concerned for themselves, we tell them to try the book, but if they find anything that disturbs them, they should simply close the book and bring it back.

What do you do when readers ask for authors similar to an author you are unfamiliar with?

First, do not hesitate to admit to the patron that you are not familiar with a particular author. It is better to admit that you have not read everyone than to "fake it" and be found out by the patron. We use lines such as "I'm not familiar with any of the titles. Can you tell me something about them?" Asking patrons for information often uncovers what they like most about an author and allows us to make decisions about that author's appeal and suggest other, possibly similar, authors.

Second, check for information about the author in reference resources. Read the entries in the genre reference sources as well as those in general reference books, looking for clues to traits that will remind us of similar authors or for overt statements of similarities. Check electronic sources for reviews that might lead to suggestions of similar authors. This is certainly the type of question to post on Fiction_L, along with a description of what the reader particularly likes about that author. It is not enough simply to write, "I have a reader who likes Susan Elizabeth Phillips and wants more books like hers." We need to state that the reader likes her books because of the witty repartee between hero and heroine, the extended family whose members appear in many of her books, the satisfying romantic relationships, or whatever the reader tells us. Then our fellow readers' advisors have specific appeal elements to match.

How do you start a reader on a series?

If the series builds one book on the other, so that readers are lost unless they see the progression, then the only reasonable way to start is with the first book. Sometimes, however, the first book in a series is not the best choice. For instance, since authors refine their fictional detectives over time, the first book may not be the most representative of the whole series. Once Mystery fans are hooked on a detective series, they will read all the books in the series, but the first one they read has to be right. This same phenomenon is true for series in other genres as well. We always alert the potential reader that we are suggesting a book from a series and that we are not suggesting the first one, especially since some readers prefer to read a series in order, no matter what. The rule of thumb we follow is that unless reading the books in the order of their publication is absolutely necessary, we start a reader with the best title we know, no matter where it falls in the series. Some sources list "best" works by an author, and these can help identify titles for advisors who are unfamiliar with the series.

In some genres, especially Science Fiction and Fantasy, it is not unusual to have a series for which the internal chronology is not the publishing chronology. Anne McCaffrey, Lois McMaster Bujold, Marion Zimmer Bradley (and her collaborators), and Catherine Asaro all have long-running, multivolume series of this type. Even fans disagree about whether these should be read in publication or time-line order. Here, it is best to introduce the reader to the series through an award-winning or acclaimed title.

How do you comfortably suggest a fiction book for nonfiction readers and vice versa?

If a reader's favorite novelist has also written nonfiction, these books often make good crossover suggestions. Many fans of Amy Tan's heartwarming novels of the Chinese American experience also relish her essays, *The Opposite of Fate: A Book of Musings*, which offer personal insights into her novels.[10] Barbara Kingsolver's nature essays fulfill the same function for readers of her fiction. Fans of Calvin Trillin's food and travel essays may also enjoy his humorous novels, and we have seen many of Dave Barry's fans read his fiction and nonfiction with equal relish.

Readers' advisors who move readily between fiction and nonfiction often find it possible to suggest across this border, offering the reader titles that match the appeal elements they enjoy. Certainly, fans of Survival stories find much to interest them in both collections, but readers who appreciate the investigative forensic details in the Mysteries of Patricia Cornwell and Kathy Reichs might also enjoy William M. Bass's *Death's Acre: Inside the Legendary Forensic Lab—the Body Farm—Where the Dead Do Tell Tales*, with its description of the creation of the original body farm, where many of the forensic standards these authors apply were established.[11] Readers are generally pleased when we can suggest background materials on the type of novels they enjoy—history as well as books on customs, dress, and manners to match their Historical novels or books that explore an issue raised by a novel—or a novel or nonfiction book that expands on topics of interest. For example, readers of Patrick O'Brian's nineteenth-century naval adventures might be fascinated by nonfiction guides to the ships and battles as well as Robert Harvey's biography of the man on whom O'Brian's hero is based—Thomas Cochrane, in *Cochrane: The Life and Exploits of a Fighting Captain*.[12]

Sometimes it is easier to offer this crossover service through displays. A collection of fast-paced Adventure or Survival titles might include fiction and nonfiction; a display might feature Crime novels (including Mysteries, Suspense, serial killer tales) and True Crime; or "Intriguing Lives" might include novels about famous people and biographies. Creating these displays helps us gain a familiarity with both collections that we might otherwise not have.

How do you suggest books for readers who are not present?

We often receive requests from patrons who come for their own book selections and then also need to find something for another family member—husband, mother, grandmother, son. These interviews are always difficult, because the person making the request often has no idea of the other person's taste. If the request is for another adult, it is safest to fall back on your Sure Bets list, offering a range of titles and appeals. Sending copies of annotated book lists on potentially interesting topics, based, of course, on the requester's knowledge of that person's reading interests, allows us to suggest that the person mark titles that might be of interest. We have also e-mailed or telephoned an absent reader for further details. With requests for children, there is always the issue of appropriate titles, and we fall back on recommending that the parent read the title if there are any questions. Sometimes asking what television shows or movies the youngster watches helps us narrow our suggestions.

In summary, the readers' advisory interview—basically a conversation between the librarian and the patron about books and reading—is the crux of readers' advisory service. Thus, it is not surprising that extensive preparation and practice are necessary to master the skills involved. Readers' advisors should always keep in mind, however, that the goal of the readers' advisory interview is not to get readers to take the books they suggest but to establish a connection between readers and librarians so that patrons see readers' advisory as a library service in the same way that answering reference questions is a library service.

Finally, although the structure of this chapter, and indeed of this entire book, could be seen to imply a step-by-step process through which readers' advisors progress, this is not actually the case. None of us has the time or the opportunity to master all the reference sources and become familiar with the library's leisure-reading collections before we actually encounter patrons and start suggesting books. In fact, learning the many aspects of readers' advisory takes place simultaneously as we work with readers and resources. Having become familiar with the techniques described to this point, readers' advisors are now ready to tackle the more involved aspects of readers' advisory discussed in chapter 5.

Notes

1. Duncan Smith to Joyce Saricks, e-mail, February 13, 1996; and Kazuo Ishiguro, *The Remains of the Day* (New York: Knopf, 1989).
2. Helen Fielding, *Bridget Jones's Diary* (New York: Viking, 1998); and Jane Austen, *Pride and Prejudice* (London, 1813).
3. Margaret A. Edwards, *The Fair Garden and the Swarm of Beasts: The Library and the Young Adult* (Chicago: American Library Assn., 2002), 17–18.
4. Christopher Morley, *Parnassus on Wheels* (Philadelphia: Lippincott, 1917); and Helene Hanff, *84, Charing Cross Road* (Old Tappan, N.J.: Grossman, 1970).
5. Sharon L. Baker, "A Decade's Worth of Research on Browsing Fiction Collections," in *Guiding the Reader to the Next Book*, ed. Kenneth Shearer (New York: Neal-Schuman, 1996), 130.
6. Ross King, *Michelangelo and the Pope's Ceiling* (New York: Walker, 2003).
7. Ralph Gers and Lillie J. Seward, "Improving Reference Performance: Results of a Statewide Study," *Library Journal* 113 (November 1985): 32–35.
8. Kate Wilhelm, *The Deepest Water* (New York: St. Martin's Minotaur, 2000); and Laurie R. King, *Folly* (New York: Bantam, 2001).
9. Duncan Smith, "Reinventing Readers' Advisory," in *The Readers' Advisor's Companion*, ed. Kenneth D. Shearer and Robert Burgin (Englewood, Colo.: Libraries Unlimited, 2001), 59–76.
10. Amy Tan, *The Opposite of Fate: A Book of Musings* (New York: Putnam, 2003).
11. William M. Bass, *Death's Acre: Inside the Legendary Forensic Lab—the Body Farm—Where the Dead Do Tell Tales* (New York: Putnam, 2003).
12. Robert Harvey, *Cochrane: The Life and Exploits of a Fighting Captain* (New York: Carroll & Graf, 2000).

5 Background for Readers' Advisors

Whether they are a staff of one or part of a team, readers' advisors quickly come to recognize that just reading and talking about the books they know with patrons does not ensure the success of their service. Readers' advisors fare well when they work with readers who share their own reading interests and tastes, but when they happen upon a reader who is interested in an author or a type of book they are less familiar with, they realize how much more comfortable they are with a broad knowledge of popular fiction and nonfiction, even though reference resources may be right at hand.

In this chapter, I discuss in detail the ways in which readers' advisors acquire this knowledge of popular fiction and nonfiction and learn to relate more confidently to a wide range of readers and books. Since familiarity with popular leisure reading is vital, readers' advisors need to set up a personal reading plan in order to acquaint themselves with genres and authors who are popular with their patrons. In chapter 2, I explained how to use lists such as our Popular Fiction List and Popular Nonfiction List as reference tools; in this chapter, I show how, when the lists are structured carefully, they can also become reading guides. Next, since readers' advisors need a way to remember information about the books they and other staff members have read, I suggest both formal and informal ways to collect impressions of these books. A section on creating readalike lists follows, with guidelines to help staff answer one of the most difficult readers' advisory queries: who writes just like a reader's favorite authors? Readers' advisors also need to study genres, their characteristics and appeal, in depth. I describe this process and examine the rewards such studies bring to readers' advisors. Finally, I address strategies that help readers' advisors keep from feeling overwhelmed as they gain this necessary background.

Designing a Reading Plan

To be conversant with the types of popular titles patrons request, readers' advisors need a broad background. We designed our library's Popular Fiction List to serve both as a reference tool and as a reading outline that would help acquaint us with authors in the genres our patrons frequently request. Appendix 1 shows the Popular Fiction List used in our library in summer 2004. A prototype Popular Nonfiction List is in appendix 2. (The Adult Reading Round Table of Illinois has created a similar, self-diagnostic, and more extensive fiction list, *The ARRT Genre Fiction List: A Self-Evaluative Bibliography for Fiction Librarians*.[1] It is available through the organization [http://www.arrtreads.org] or can be downloaded from NoveList.)

You may not need lists as formally structured as this to develop a reading plan, but some sort of basic list of popular authors is a necessity. Using information gained by identifying the reading public's tastes and creating lists of popular genres and authors, we readers' advisors can structure our reading in a way that helps familiarize us with the authors readers consistently request, particularly those with whom we are less familiar. Such lists provide advisors with the foundation on which to build a reading plan—a place to begin as we work to familiarize ourselves with the leisure reading that is popular with our patrons. These lists must be comprehensive enough to provide a broad overview of each genre—fiction and nonfiction—popular in the library yet narrow enough to allow the readers' advisor to begin to understand the appeal of both the genre and representative authors without undertaking an unrealistic reading program.

Detailed suggestions for compiling these lists were presented in chapter 2. Once the lists have been developed, they can be used in assessing personal and staff reading strengths and in the consequent development of suitable reading plans. After writing their initials by the names of authors they have read, staff can identify the genres in which they have read the least and concentrate on unfamiliar areas, beginning with those most popular with patrons. A good way to start is for each readers' advisor to set a goal of reading a certain number of authors in an unfamiliar genre, one typical title per author, within a set time period. It is useful to set a formal time for discussing the reading and the conclusions drawn about the author's appeal with a supervisor or another reader. In very small or remote libraries, this might involve an online partnership or a mentoring project. Establishing a time to talk may not always be possible, but it is important that all readers' advisory staff keep reading and discussing what they read in order to expand their knowledge of authors, titles, and genres popular with patrons. Since titles are not included on our Popular Fiction List and Popular Nonfiction List, readers' advisors must rely on reference sources, as well as discussion with patrons and other staff, to identify which authors from the lists to read first and then to discover a representative title by each author.

Discussion of the titles read is an important part of learning about popular fiction and nonfiction. Figure 5.1 offers examples of the kinds of questions important to consider in both reading and talking about these books. The questions draw heavily on the nature of appeal, as discussed in chapter 3,

Figure 5.1 ▦ **Suggested Discussion Questions**

1. What does the author do best?
2. Does the book/author emphasize characters or story more?
3. Do you fall into the book immediately or learn the story and characters at a more leisurely pace?
4. Is there an especially detailed background, full of those fascinating extra details we find in some books? (For example, there are details of archaeology, nineteenth-century Egypt, and the status of women in Elizabeth Peters's Amelia Peabody mystery series. The chocolate lore and manufacturing details in *The Emperors of Chocolate*, by Joel Glenn Brenner, offer a nonfiction parallel.)
5. What other authors/titles does the book remind you of (not subject but feel and appeal)?
6. Who else might enjoy reading the book and why? (For example, someone who likes Adventure novels or True Adventure? Puzzles? Novels with strong characters or Biographies? An interesting setting? Action? Or a Gentle Read?)
7. If it is a genre book, how does it fit in that genre?
8. What makes the book popular?
9. Why do readers like the book? Have you overheard or picked up comments about the title or author?

but they also focus advisors on techniques that can help them share the appeal information they discover with patrons. As readers' advisors become comfortable with questions such as these and the thought patterns they reflect, we can use variations of them to question readers and to extract information about the kinds of books that might appeal to them. These questions also help us think about books and appeal in ways that make discovering similar authors easier. For example, reading Jacquelyn Mitchard's *The Deep End of the Ocean*, one of Oprah's Book Club books, reminded more than one advisor of the thought-provoking, elegantly written novels of Rosellen Brown (*Before and After*) and Jane Hamilton's *A Map of the World*, another Oprah pick.[2] Although not linked by subject, these books reflect similarities in writing quality, and all feature strong characterizations in their stories of how families cope with tragic events. These are the kinds of connections that readers appreciate and that a thoughtful, directed reading plan teaches readers' advisors to make.

Using these techniques a readers' advisor can also more easily make connections between fiction and nonfiction titles. Simon Winchester's *Krakatoa: The Day the World Exploded, August 27, 1883* might appeal to a fan of Robert Harris's *Pompeii*, not only because both offer fascinating details on vulcanology but also because both feature Adventure tales, grounded in fact, that might please the same readers.[3]

In addition to formal discussions with our library peers, there should be other formal and informal channels of discussion so that all readers may share some of their discoveries about the titles they have been reading. One quite effective way to communicate this information is through written summaries of the books read, a technique discussed in the next section. These summaries should be shared with staff members in addition to being made available for the public. A time set aside to discuss books at staff meetings or regional gatherings can provide another opportunity, as can the informal discussions among staff that we stressed in chapter 4. Sharing information about authors and titles helps all staff doing readers' advisory: this practice allows us to gain valuable insights from the reading experience of others, and this knowledge helps us make useful connections between authors more readily. There is also a particular pleasure in sharing newfound titles and authors that is contagious and seems to flow seamlessly from staff to patrons.

In some cases, only one or two staff members may be providing readers' advisory service in a library, and they may not be part of a department that has readers' advisory as a defined responsibility; in fact, they may be the entire library staff. If you are in this situation, do not be deterred; developing and working through a reading list is a useful activity no matter how few people are involved. Anyone who provides readers' advisory service should attack the Popular Fiction List and Popular Nonfiction List in the same way that a team of advisors does, that is, by starting with the genres that are most popular with their patrons.

As we discuss the value of reading and establishing a reading plan, it is important to address a question that is often raised: how much reading is required to be a successful readers' advisor? Since looking for appeal is primarily an intellectual exercise, it is important to acknowledge that there is more than one way to go about this activity successfully. Some of us feel that we must read several books before we are comfortably certain of the appeal of an author or genre; others feel they can read fewer titles and work with reviews, book jackets, reference materials, and readers' comments to ascertain the appeal. Both approaches are sound. My feeling is that when readers' advisors have reached a certain level of expertise, we develop a sense of how much primary material we personally need to read, and we can balance our reading and research patterns accordingly. Whether readers' advisors read numerous books or just representative titles, we will certainly need to rely on other sources; in fact, we learn to pull information from every source available to discern an author's appeal to the reader more clearly.

Thoughtfully constructed and current lists of popular fiction and nonfiction provide invaluable resources for readers' advisors. They lay the foundation for individual or group-directed reading plans and can be the basis for advanced genre study, discussed later in this chapter.

Writing about Books

Although developing a reading plan and starting a conscientious reading program are logical starting places for gaining expertise in leisure-reading genres, these are only the first steps. Reading and talking about books are not enough unless some written record is also kept, for without a written record it is difficult to retain the impressions and insights that were gained when the books were fresh in our minds.

When we began doing readers' advisory, we developed the format, shown in figure 5.2, to create book annotations. These were first part of a card file, perused by both staff and patrons, and then a database. We developed the form out of pure desperation. In 1983, there were neither books

Figure 5.2 ▩ Book Annotation Format

AUTHOR:

TITLE:

PUBLICATION DATE:

NUMBER OF PAGES:

GEOGRAPHICAL SETTING:

TIME PERIOD:

SERIES:

PLOT SUMMARY:

SUBJECT HEADINGS:

APPEAL:

SIMILAR AUTHORS:

NAME:

---

nor databases that offered reviews or plot summaries that would genuinely help readers' advisors remember important information about books in order to assist other readers. Since that time, the readers' advisory market has been inundated with tools, both print and electronic, that provide summaries useful for readers' advisory work. (Many of these were discussed in detail in chapter 2.)

As summaries of books became more readily available, we developed other ways to keep track of and share our thoughts on books we had read.

However, as more and more readers' advisors make their personal annotations available in a searchable form, on their library's intranet for fellow staff members and on library web pages for their patrons, we all begin to see the value of a standard form that focuses readers' advisors on appeal. This format serves that purpose and ensures consistency among all staff who write annotations.

The "Book Notes Format" in figure 5.3 complements the more formal annotation form above. I use this form as a bookmark in order to keep track of appeal information about a book as I am reading it. Printed on 8 ½ x 11 inch sheets, this form encourages me to record my impressions while they are fresh in my mind. I simply jot down, under each of the appeal characteristics, thoughts as they strike me while reading. Thus, this form provides an extraordinarily useful way to keep track of personal reactions that can be turned into more formal annotations, even years after reading the book.

Figure 5.3   ▓   Book Notes Format

AUTHOR:	DATE READ:
TITLE:	PUB. DATE:
GENRE:	PAGES:
APPEAL CHARACTERISTICS:	PLOT SUMMARY:
PACING:	
CHARACTERIZATIONS:	
STORY LINE:	Geographical setting:
	Time period:
FRAME:	Series:
SIMILAR AUTHORS:	Subject headings:

Recording our thoughts as we read also helps us remember more about the book, and the form ensures that we focus on the appeal factors covered in chapter 3. We might use some of the appeal vocabulary to note quickly that the book seems fast paced or densely written. We can indicate series information, elements of the frame that add to the appeal, and a range of general impressions that might help us later in composing a more formal description of the book or when offering it to readers.

Making notes like these as we read helps us capture valuable details and impressions we might otherwise forget. When we finish a book, we may also consult the appeal questions covered in chapter 3 (figures 3.1 through 3.4) since they help us focus on specific appeal elements as they relate to that book. When we consider the book in light of these elements, we can organize our impressions better. Whether we actually write a formal plot summary or annotation for each book or not, we keep these book sheets for reference. They often prove invaluable when we are trying to remember more about a book we read, are putting together a list of books on a particular subject or with a specific appeal, or are participating in a genre study and want to refresh our memories of books we have read in that genre.

Although it is not required, we encourage staff to compose more formal annotations in the space for "Plot Summary." We all know that it is easier to write annotations immediately after we read a book, and the more frequently we write annotations, the easier they are to compose. Writing more structured descriptions of books we have read is an excellent way to keep track of what we have read and, more important, what we have learned about the appeal of those books. Once the information is in written form, it can more easily be made available to others, whether they are staff working with readers or the readers themselves.

The plot summary should reveal enough of the story to entice a reader without giving away any details the author did not intend the reader to know ahead of time, and, like the reviews discussed in chapter 3, it should highlight the appeal. Our descriptions are not intended to be critical reviews. Instead, they indicate why a certain book appeals to readers and give the readers' advisor enough information to share the book. These differ from the briefer, more directed annotations used on annotated book lists and discussed in chapter 6. We put no stipulation on length, but all staff understand the importance of avoiding lengthy and involved summaries. Most important, these are written for readers, to provide them with enough information to help them decide if they might want to read a book. *Sequels: An Annotated Guide to Novels in Series*, by Janet Husband and Jonathan F. Husband, is a good place to study summaries written for readers.[4] The Husbands' characterizations of authors set a standard to emulate. Also helpful is Margaret A. Edwards's *The Fair Garden and the Swarm of Beasts: The Library and the Young Adult*, which has a section on annotation writing.[5]

There is also a subject headings section on the form, and if you plan to use these forms to create a searchable database, it is important for all annotators to use a controlled vocabulary, such as that in *Fiction Catalog* or EBSCO's NoveList. For nonfiction titles, Library of Congress headings could be used, duplicated or expanded from the catalog. However, the sometimes obscure phrasing makes them problematical in describing nonfiction, and these seldom provide the range that novels require. Subject headings are assigned only if they are an important access point to the book. Assigning subject headings forces annotators to look at the book in terms of what might interest a potential reader. However, since headings also provide an access point when we are searching for a book a patron—or someone on the staff—remembers reading, but for which we have no bibliographic information, we try to assign a range of headings that might be useful retrieval points.

Two features that make these "Book Notes" unique are the inclusion of places to list appeal elements as well as similar authors and, sometimes, specific similar titles. We add appeal terms, drawing inspiration from the limited thesaurus of terms listed in chapter 3. In contrast to the subject headings, which are more objective and straightforward, appeal terms are frequently individual and more personal; they reflect the more subjective nature of the readers' experience of a book and respond to readers' requests and moods in a way that transcends the limitations of subject headings. Adding these appeal terms, just as we apply subject headings, provides access points that address the "feel" of the book, not merely its content.

Determining similar authors requires readers' advisors to place the books in the reader's context and to think of other authors and titles with the same appeal, as discussed in chapter 3. By looking in the section listing similar authors, a patron or readers' advisor who wants other books "just like" an annotated author can find suggestions. This is one of the real advantages of devising a system that is accessible by patrons. If these "Book Notes" become the basis of online annotations, readers may search for their favorite authors and then follow up on the suggestions given in the "Similar Authors" section.

Instead of simply listing the names of authors we think are similar, we include notes that make these similarities clear. I believe it is extremely important to indicate why one author is similar to another rather than relying on a vague feeling that the authors might "go together." This more precise information is far more helpful than a simple listing of authors or authors and titles. When we later include this information in a formal annotation or on a bookmark of readalike authors, other staff and readers can see what similarities we are comparing. Seeing that the linked author shares a particular element with the author of the book being summarized allows readers to decide if the particular appeal element is what they appreciated and want to pursue in a similar title. Or the comments may simply intrigue them and prompt them to try the suggested author.

Every readers' advisory staff should develop a formalized system for keeping track of what staff are reading. You may not need or want to list everything we include in ours, or you may feel that you require information I have not mentioned. Whatever the case, every library that is serious about doing readers' advisory work should develop a standard method of recording what the staff is reading in a way that allows retrieval of the information when it is needed. This works best when all readers' advisors are required to write a set number of annotations each month. We require at least two written pieces a month from all of our staff, although most staff members read and write well beyond that number. Written pieces include annotations for any annotated book list the staff member is currently working on as well as a monthly annotation for our "What We're Reading" column on the library's web page. Putting information about what we read into writing forces us to concentrate on using precisely the right words. Annotators also focus on the book's appeal, and this leads them to take a good look at the title as it compares to others in the collection and to readers' tastes.

Although writing and making these annotations available may seem like a lot of work, the effort is worthwhile for both readers' advisors who write them and the staff and patrons who use them for reference and reading suggestions. Writing the summaries makes a readers' advisor focus on the aspects of the books that appeal to readers, and these are the same elements readers' advisors need when talking with readers. In time, this ability to summarize is naturally carried over to books that one reads but does not annotate, as experienced readers' advisors unconsciously annotate books they are reading. Nothing equals actually writing about books, however, and even the most experienced readers' advisors need to continue writing formally about books they read, if for no other reason than to ensure that others have access to readers' advisory information about as many books as possible.

Creating Readalike Lists

Readalikes are those "Similar Authors" from the "Book Notes" form above, authors who write books "just like" the author a reader has read and loved. They are what readers expect us to pull from our hats by the dozens whenever they come to the desk and tell us they need more books just like their favorite author writes. This quest for readalikes, or similar authors, constitutes one of the most popular requests we receive at the public service desk, yet it can still strike fear in the heart of the most experienced readers' advisor. Often readers ask about authors we have not read; sometimes we do not even recognize the name of the author a reader is asking about. Even if we are familiar with the author, we still do not know what it is about this author that the reader enjoys and seeks in the titles of readalike authors.

Providing lists of readalikes, or similar authors, becomes far easier for readers' advisors who understand the appeal of books and authors. Just as we do in a regular readers' advisory interview, we ask readers what it is about a particular author that they enjoy. Then we seek other authors who share this appeal. We follow this strategy frequently in individual interactions with readers, but what sets this activity apart is the possibility of creating lists that identify appeal and that might help many readers, not just the one currently standing in front of us.

Creating readalike lists reinforces some of the most basic readers' advisory skills. Thinking about who else writes like a particular author helps us be open to a wider range of possibilities. If a reader talks about Janet Evanovich's wacky bounty-hunter Stephanie Plum and her romance with both Morelli and Ranger with a twinkle in her eye, we will offer different suggestions than we would to a reader who talks about the quirky characters in the series or about heroine Stephanie as a lady with an attitude. Even if we are familiar with the authors requested, we listen to what readers say they enjoyed about the books, and, whether this is what we noticed when reading or not, we look for authors who share similarities to what the readers enjoyed.

Thinking through and creating readalike lists reinforces our readers' advisory interview skills. Readers tell us what they love about an author, and we make certain we understand what they are looking for. Then, when we offer suggestions, we follow the same pattern, responding along these lines: "If you like James Patterson for his fast-paced stories of Suspense, you might want to try these other writers who offer similar page-turning, suspenseful stories." In this way, we go readily and naturally from what the reader enjoys to book suggestions, and readers become familiar and comfortable with this approach.

This process also allows us to cut across genres, to match what readers enjoy, without concern for whether authors fit within particular categories. Although we understand that it is important to know genre classifications and authors associated with those genres, we know that not every book fits within a genre and that authors change what and how they write; their writing and popularity with readers forces us to modify our definitions of genres. We also realize that even if a reader enjoys a particular type of Mystery, he might also enjoy books not classified in the genre if they share the elements that he seeks. For example, if readers like to participate in police investigations, they may also enjoy such authors as Robert K. Tanenbaum and Ridley Pearson, whose suspenseful series are often not classified as Mysteries. Creating readalike lists helps us see the bigger picture of how books and authors appeal within and across genres, fiction and nonfiction, and this process makes us better readers' advisors.

Working on readalike lists also reminds us we do not work in a vacuum. No one has read everything or thought of all the ways a reader might read a book and a book might appeal. Working with other readers and readers' advisors to brainstorm and generate these lists forces us to think more broadly and certainly provides more possibilities than each of us could if we were limited only to the books we personally know.

Because readalikes are frequently requested by readers, lists abound on the Web, especially on library home pages. Although some of these lists make valuable and interesting connections, others seem subject matches at best, with little consideration for what it is about the author that readers enjoy. Unfortunately, many of these lists simply offer a dozen diverse Horror writers, claiming they write "just like" Stephen King. It is one thing to create a list of popular Legal Thrillers that includes titles by both John Grisham and Scott Turow, but it is another matter entirely to suggest that either is a readalike for the other without including clear reasons for linking these authors. Readers are more discriminating than that; they deserve thoughtful, appeal-based lists, not subject- or genre-based lists that claim to offer readalikes.

Before going further, however, I should say that, in fact, the actual answer to the question "Who writes just like . . . ?" is "Nobody." There is not another author who provides exactly the same satisfactions as the one the reader loves. Just as there is not a perfect book for each reader, there is not a perfect match, a perfect readalike, for every popular author. What we are looking for, or rather what our readers want, is another author to tide them over until their favorites publish more books or until they discover another favorite. They are looking for authors who share some of the same appeal as their favorite and ones whose books will provide some of the same satisfactions. From this vantage point, we see that we are again basing our responses on what that reader enjoys about the author. This is just the kind of information we are accustomed to look for as we read for appeal and what we have learned to ask about in the readers' advisory interview.

When we first started thinking about readalikes at our library, we realized that an understanding of appeal was at the heart of readalike matches. When we brainstorm readalikes, we naturally and almost unconsciously fall back on appeal. What is it about the story Grisham told in his early novels—beyond the fact that they dealt with the legal profession—that readers enjoyed? If it is the David and Goliath theme, with an independent lawyer battling against corrupt corporations, might they also like Robin Cook's stories of good doctors fighting big medicine? The key is not the subject of the story but the way the author tells the story. The following discussion helps elucidate how we apply appeal to the problem of finding readalikes.

Beginning our examination of appeal with pacing, we consider whether the action starts on the first page and continues at a relentless pace, with twists and turns throughout, or whether the story unfolds at a more leisurely pace, drawing the reader into a deeper understanding of characters along the way. Might a fan of either type appreciate diverse books that feature that particular pacing, no matter the subject or genre?

If a reader particularly likes a certain type of series character, perhaps the loner, hard-boiled detective, might he enjoy Sue Grafton's Kinsey Millhone as well as James Lee Burke's Dave Robicheaux? Or if she enjoys Robert B. Parker's one-liners in the Spenser series, what other authors display a similar flair with dialogue?

When examining story line, we should be careful not to rely solely on subject similarities. We might find two mysteries that feature journalists as detectives, but one author probes the underlying and provocative issues, exposing layers of meaning and detail, while the other skims over issues but offers quirky series characters and a lighthearted tone. Both have their audiences, but readers do not read them for the same reasons.

Sometimes the frame is the main appeal. Readers appreciate the detail the author builds into the story. Fans of the late Ellis Peters's Brother Cadfael books loved the feel of twelfth-century Shrewsbury, of the monastic life, of the community of characters she created. She gave us far more detail than she needed for the mysteries, and this is what many readers cherished. Who else provides that level of detail? Must it be another Historical novel? Or another Mystery—or might either type work? Or something else entirely?

Readalikes are suggestions of possibilities. We tell our readers that we are not claiming that these authors write just like the ones they love but that they share particular characteristics. Then readers can decide for themselves whether we have identified what they like and, if they take the book, whether it works for them. These suggestions and possibilities become part of the ongoing dialogue between readers and readers' advisors.

Providing individual readalikes for the reader we are currently helping is one approach; creating lists that might satisfy many readers is another. With individual readers, this is a straightforward readers' advisory interview, and we gauge our suggestions by the reader's reaction. When preparing a list for distribution it is important to identify what aspects of that author's appeal we are matching. (Figure 5.5, discussed more fully below, shows a readalikes bookmark, for example.)

There are many ways to collect information on readalikes. Ours works well, in part, because our approach is straightforward. When we begin receiving requests for readalikes for a popular author, we start a page in our readalike notebook at the desk. At the top of the page we put the author's name and then list appeal characteristics, using some of the vocabulary from chapter 3. Working with reference sources to generate more characteristics and readalike authors usually comes later. At first we consider what we know about this author from our own reading of books, from reviews, and from our knowledge of what fans say when they talk about this author.

At the bottom of the page, we list authors who might be possible readalike suggestions and how they are similar to the author for whom we are developing the readalike. It is not enough for each of us to "know" why we think one particular author works for fans of another. Our colleagues may not make that same leap, and readers who glance through our working lists certainly will not. It is important to identify the appeal elements that we are matching and make certain that this information is clear.

All staff share in these brainstorming activities (figure 5.4 shows the kind of notes we collect as we compile readalike information). Then one staff member takes charge of filling in useful information from reference resources, print and electronic, and checking the Web for other readalike suggestions. We check genre resources when appropriate, but we also consult standard sources, such as *Contemporary Authors*, for information about strengths and keys to appeal. An easy way to check for other readalike lists

Figure 5.4 ▨ **Readalike Notes**

Susan Elizabeth Phillips

humorous

upbeat

multiple points of view

series characters

strong secondary characters

conversational style

verbal sparring—always amusing dialogue

fast paced

racy

domestic

family centered

romantic

appealing characters

sensual, heartwarming stories

romantic romps

contemporary

"good ole boys" and strong, seductive heroines, women
who aren't afraid to speak their minds

"sophisticated flair"

"well-developed sense of the ridiculous"

linked characters throughout several books and series of books

stories may be familiar, but characters and dialogue add twists

classy, vulnerable heroines

humorous situations and sparkling dialogue make her books comic delights

Sophisticated yet comfortable, sexy and humorous, and filled
with an engaging cast of memorable characters, these
are satisfying, contemporary tales of romance and women's lives.

Even though a happy ending is inevitable, she doesn't let us have it too soon.

delightful, emotion-filled trip

characters sometimes hide deep emotions beneath humor

Readalike suggestions

Jayne Ann Krentz—humor, sometimes mystery, sexy stories, strong heroes and
heroines (*Truth or Dare*)

Millie Criswell—humor, contemporary stories, small-town feel, strong heroines (*The Trouble with Mary, Trials of Angela, What to Do about Annie*)

Jennifer Crusie—humor, contemporary, pushes borders of genre with themes and language (*Bet Me, Faking It*)

Meg Cabot—smart heroines, witty dialogue, contemporary stories, heartwarming (*The Boy Next Door, Boy Meets Girl*)

Rachel Gibson—sassy heroines, humor, contemporary, verbal sparring, quirky characters (*True Confessions*)

Susan Andersen—humor, contemporary, smart dialogue (*Be My Baby, Head over Heels*)

Georgette Heyer—even though historical, books provide many of same satisfactions of character, situation, humor, dialogue (*Talisman Ring*—more of a romp with adventure)

Barbara Metzger—also historical but madcap, romantic romps, with quirky characters, humorous dialogue, but no sex, family, domestic (*Wedded Bliss*)

---

is to use Google and search, "If you like [author's name], try." This search yields a variety of lists, some of which include interesting, viable suggestions that we can then pursue further.

Despite the fact that we understand how readalike lists must be constructed and that we can spend hours considering these links, our notes do not provide perfect matches; they simply offer possibilities to readers. We do feel confident that they reflect the range of an author's appeal. We know from experience that authors appeal to different readers for a variety of reasons, that every reader reads a different version of a particular book and relates to different elements of that book. For example, some readers like Larry McMurtry for his western settings and landscape details, and they enjoy a range of books with similar settings. Others read him for his elegant writing style and depth of characterization. No list of readalikes is perfect for every reader; no reader will like all the suggestions on a readalike list.

When completed, our lists—available for readers in our library and on our web page—take the form of bookmarks that proclaim, "While You Are Waiting, " followed by a popular author's name and genre and an indication of the appeal of the author we are matching, as shown in figure 5.5. We used to do "If You Like" bookmarks for popular authors, but we have found this focus more satisfying, in part, because it allows us to address demand for popular writers and offer alternatives. From our list of notes, we might be able to compile more than one bookmark, each featuring an aspect of an author's appeal.

Figure 5.5 ■ Completed Readalike Bookmark

While You Are Waiting

For Susan Elizabeth Phillips' next humorous contemporary romance...

Try one of these novels featuring quirky characters and sparkling dialogue.

FICTION/ANDERSEN
Andersen, Susan
Be My Baby

FICTION/CABOT
Cabot, Meg
The Boy Next Door

FICTION/CRISWELL
Criswell, Millie
The Trouble with Mary

FICTION/CRUSIE
Crusie, Jennifer
Faking It

FICTION/GIBSON
Gibson, Rachel
True Confessions

FICTION/KRENTZ
Krentz, Jayne Ann
Truth or Dare

Literature and Audio Services
April 2004

Downers Grove Public Library

1050 Curtiss Street   Downers Grove, IL 60515
(630) 960-1200   TDD (630) 960-1345
www.downersgrovelibrary.org

By following this procedure, we have greatly increased our knowledge of the appeal of these blockbuster authors. In addition, we have created thoughtful, appeal-based lists, not available elsewhere, of similar novelists and titles for popular authors. An example of the type of readalike article available on EBSCO's NoveList is included in appendix 4.

Studying a Genre

Over time, we realized that in-depth studies of specific genres were absolutely essential. At first we looked primarily at individual titles for their appeal elements. Then we began to set up readalikes, groupings of authors and titles that we discovered had similar appeal for our readers, and we started to create lists in the pattern of "If You Like" and "While You Are Waiting," discussed in detail above. Although we have been pleased with the useful lists we have created and the way in which we have refined our knowledge of an author's appeal for the reader, we have, unfortunately, had to start pretty much from scratch each time. Therefore, rather than just reacting to the current popular authors one at a time, we realized that we also needed to take a broader view. We thought that if we expanded this process to a whole genre, we would be well on our way to an understanding of popular fiction—and nonfiction as well—based on the attraction it has for the reader. We decided to work our way through, one genre at a time, the fiction genres on our Popular Fiction List. Based on our experience in working with a single author, we expected the following results from genre study: a basic understanding of the characteristics and pattern of the genre, a clearer picture of the appeal of the genre, a greater familiarity with the range of authors in that genre, a sense of which authors appeal to the same readers, the ability to communicate better with readers of the genre, and increased staff comfort levels when dealing with unfamiliar genres. Such a study would direct our energies.

Our comments and experience relate to the study of fiction genres, yet we believe that the same techniques could be applied to nonfiction "genres" as well. In studying each genre, we first tried to identify the standardized pattern—that is, the rules for constructing plot and characters—that structures each genre. We theorized that if we could understand the pattern, we would have a better sense of the appeal of the genre. We asked some of the same questions regarding pacing, characterization, story line, and frame that we used when looking for the appeal elements in individual books. We began by brainstorming these characteristics.

First, we asked about what common characteristics books in a particular genre share. We could establish fairly quickly, for example, the fact that Romances all seem to revolve around a romantic relationship and end happily; Mysteries have a body and a detective/crime solver; Suspense novels have characters placed in jeopardy; and so forth. We would consider the same appeal issues discussed in chapter 3 and apply them more generally to the genre as a whole rather than merely to individual titles. As might be expected, we found this to be an intellectually challenging and very satisfying activity. An example of this process and the results of such a study, figure 5.6 shows the list of genre characteristics from our study of Suspense. (These were further updated in *Readers' Advisory Guide to Genre Fiction*, where there are similar schema for fourteen other genres.)[6] The connection between these characteristics and the appeal elements described in chapter 3 is readily apparent in this schema, with each characteristic relating to a specific appeal element: pacing, characterization, story line, and frame.

When we first embarked on a genre study in the mid-1980s, we selected Thrillers, a genre that was in great demand and at that time was synonymous with Espionage. Fortunately, it was also one many staff members already read and enjoyed. Our familiarity with these books allowed us to focus on developing the genre study skill itself, not just the content. As we looked at genre reference material, we tried to identify the elements and the pattern of the genre that made it so popular. We found that, with a little extrapolation, both the "Themes and Types" section of Betty Rosenberg's first edition of *Genreflecting* and books about writing genre fiction, such as

Figure 5.6   ■   Characteristics of the Suspense Genre

General Characteristics

1. The reader empathizes with the protagonist and feels the same sense of peril. However, the reader often follows the antagonist's thoughts and actions, too, and thus knows more than the protagonist.

2. The action usually takes place within a narrow time frame, often in only a few days, and the reader is made aware of the danger to the protagonist early on, generally in the first chapter or even in a prologue.

3. Stories follow a similar pattern, with unexpected danger from an unknown source intruding into the protagonist's normal life. The resolution is brought about through a confrontation between the hero/heroine and villain, and the protagonist survives.

4. A dark, menacing atmosphere is essential and underscores the danger to the protagonist. As the story unfolds, tension grows, and the reader, recognizing the danger, feels a sense of uneasiness, uncertainty—even before the protagonist senses anything is wrong.

5. Books take place in the present day; that is, they are set in the time period in which they are written.

Softer-Edged Suspense

1. The bodies of the victims are usually offstage, and they are not described in grisly, clinical detail.

2. Although the protagonist is stalked by the villain, there is more threatened danger, more atmosphere, more building of emotion and tension than actual physical peril. The suspense is generated more by atmosphere than action.

3. The protagonist is often a woman who is resourceful and who saves herself in the end. The police may be present, but they often play a less important role in the final confrontation and resolution.

4. Details are more likely to relate to descriptions of characters than to the crimes or crime scenes.

5. Roller-coaster pacing is typical. It builds and then eases up, only to build again.

Benchmark author: Mary Higgins Clark (*We'll Meet Again*)

Hard-Edged Suspense

1. The protagonist is often a detective who may or may not be in immediate danger himself but may be working against time to protect someone else. Details of the crimes and of the police procedures play an important role because of the protagonist's occupation.

2. Descriptions are more graphic, and these books often include sexual situations, physical violence, and strong language.

3. The suspense is generated more through action than atmosphere.

4. The pacing feels relentless. The novel seems to stay in high gear throughout, as tension builds the suspense.

_____

Benchmark author: John Sandford (*Rules of Prey*)

Source: Adapted from Joyce G. Saricks, *Readers' Advisory Guide to Genre Fiction* (Chicago: American Library Assn., 200I).

Dean R. Koontz's *Writing Popular Fiction*, were particularly helpful in understanding the traditional genres.[7] Writer's manuals often provided useful clues to the pattern of the genre. We also often picked up some useful information from the introductory material contained in genre reference books. We read, talked, and brainstormed as we tried to identify the elements that made the genre as a whole so appealing and to determine a preliminary list of characteristics.

We found that as we identified the pattern and appeal of a particular genre, we could use this information right away in our readers' advisory interviews. For example, if a reader told us he liked books in which a tourist or other innocent character was unexpectedly caught up in a situation involving spies and international intrigue, we knew he would be unlikely to enjoy Ian Fleming's novels of superhero James Bond but might very well be satisfied with novels by someone like Helen MacInnes. When we finished Thrillers and embarked on Mysteries, we recognized early on that most Mysteries are dominated by the character of the detective or problem solver and that much of their appeal revolves around that character's personality. Using this observation, we began to ask readers seeking Mysteries to describe the main character of the Mystery series they enjoyed. A reader who described little old ladies who stumbled upon cases wanted quite different books from one who described hard-boiled detectives. Then we compared this information to our own mental list of types of detectives and could suggest authors whose detectives seemed similar.

Extending the pattern we used when working with individual authors, we picked one of the most popular authors in the Thriller genre and read some typical titles by that author. We compared the novels we read with what we felt was the pattern and appeal of the whole genre. We identified the most prominent appeal elements—attitude of the main character, pacing, frame, and so forth. When we were studying Thrillers in the mid-1980s, Robert Ludlum was the premier Thriller writer and was enormously popular in our library. Thus, we read his Thrillers, looking for their appeal, and we were able to identify several elements that were evident in the majority of his books: strong male characters with extraordinary training and stamina who operate under a personal moral code, fast-paced plots with many sudden twists and turns, frequent and graphic violence, and international settings.

Every Thriller may have some of these characteristics, but novels with Ludlum's appeal usually contain this specific combination of features. After identifying the Ludlum appeal elements, we continued looking at other well-known and frequently read authors in the genre and compared them with Ludlum: Did they have the same elements or something different? Which Thriller authors also appealed to Ludlum fans? Did they share the same elements? Naturally, we also found Thriller writers who did not appeal to Ludlum fans. For instance, John le Carré's central male characters certainly possess personal moral codes and superior intellectual powers, but many of our Ludlum fans did not like le Carré. By reading le Carré's novels, as well as about him, and talking with his fans, we decided that John le Carré has a dark quality and slower, more measured pacing that is not typical of the action-packed Ludlum-type novel. The difference does not mean that we would never suggest a le Carré novel to Ludlum readers, but it is unlikely that we would suggest him to readers who tell us they read Ludlum for his energetic pacing. The next step, then, was to follow the same pattern to compile a list of Thrillers with le Carré's pacing and style for his many fans.

And so the process was repeated for the most-asked-for (benchmark) authors. Most popular Thriller writers could be placed in one of the five groupings we had tentatively identified, each one with its own unique appeal elements. These were as follows:

Action—Robert Ludlum, benchmark

Superhero—Ian Fleming and John Gardner's James Bond, benchmarks

Cynical Realism—John le Carré, benchmark

Amateur/Adventure—Helen MacInnes, benchmark

Technology—Tom Clancy, benchmark

Defining the characteristics of these subgroupings or subgenres in exact yet nonexclusive terms is often very difficult; we are still grappling with this issue. Defining subgenres is useful in helping us classify the rapidly growing body of information we are learning about the genre. We may sense that a set of novels has the same appeal, but putting that appeal into words is often very challenging. When we did succeed in creating and defining a grouping, we could use the terms decided upon, not only in our own discussions with colleagues but with readers as well, and this proved very satisfying. Patrons also began to reflect and repeat the new terminology, and they quickly showed us where we did not have quite the right idea. For example, when talking with Tom Clancy fans, we might ask if the technical detail is the feature they most appreciate. Since we know Clancy and the Techno-Thriller subgenre, we know this is one of the elements that distinguishes this subgenre from others. If the patrons respond that they do read Clancy for the technical detail, other authors, such as Dale Brown and Craig Thomas, who also include many technical military details, may be good suggestions. Sometimes readers respond that they read these books for another feature, perhaps strong characterizations, an integral element of the Cynical Realism subgenre. Understanding the subgenres and asking readers questions based on our knowledge can lead to more satisfying readers' advisory interactions, for us as well as for patrons.

We have learned through experience that none of these subgroupings is mutually exclusive. From working with readers and their varied interests, we know there is crossover among subgenres, just as there is among genres, based on what readers say they enjoy and are in the mood to read. For example, figure 5.6 identifies two major subgenres in the Suspense genre and lists characteristics and benchmark authors for each. These are opposite ends of the spectrum, because, in reality, writers of Suspense range from softer- to hard-edged. While the Sandford readers may not read Mary Higgins Clark and vice versa, they may both read someone like Thomas Perry, whose series heroine Jane Whitefield creates new identities for people on the run. Books in this series offer characters and situations similar to Clark's but also contain more violent episodes. Identifying subgenres and thinking of authors in terms of narrower groups with set characteristics makes gaining an understanding of the genre and where authors generally fit much easier. This understanding helps us see the appeal characteristics that allow us to take readers across genres or subgenres. We need to know the subgenres but not be limited by them.

Figure 5.7 outlines how to conduct a genre study. In addition, we have some observations and guidelines to share, drawn from our experience leading and participating in genre studies over the past twenty years.

First, effective genre studies take time. We allow about two years to study a genre in order to have time to read extensively, to discuss the genre and representative authors among ourselves and with patrons, and to reflect

Figure 5.7 ▨ Tips for Studying a Genre

---

1. Select a high-demand genre—one that staff read and enjoy.
2. Gather resources to gain an overview of the genre (reference books and online sources as well as staff knowledge).
3. Make a preliminary list of the genre's appeal characteristics and pattern; note possible subgenres.
4. Identify the benchmark (most popular) author, in general and for each subgenre. What characterizes that author's books?
5. Read other authors in the genre. Do they fit with the benchmark, or are they different? How?
6. Formulate a list of appeal characteristics of the whole genre. Define subgenres with their own unique list of characteristics and representative authors.

---

on our discoveries and draw conclusions. In his book *An Aesthetics of Junk Fiction*, Thomas J. Roberts discusses a comment from James Gunn, professor, editor, and writer of Science Fiction, who says, basically, that to know a genre, one needs to read about a hundred books.[8] It takes that much reading not only "to acquire the internal map of the genre" needed to read pleasurably but also to understand whether a story fits the basic pattern of the genre or does something new and to be able to recognize the difference between reworkings of genre conventions and innovation. Daunting though this number may seem, it is probably accurate if we are exploring a genre on our own.

Second, genre study should not be a solitary activity. We really need at least one other person reading and reacting to reap benefits. Our department is always engaged in a genre study, and we know of other librarians, often those in smaller libraries, who participate in genre studies with staff from other area libraries. We know of some who even do this by e-mail. By participating with others in a genre study, we receive the benefit of having read the hundred books without actually having to read more than one or two a month over a two-year period. Although some reading is absolutely essential to discover the appeal of authors and the genre as a whole, readers' advisors, as we have said earlier, are trained to glean information from a variety of sources, and genre studies provide an opportunity to practice those skills.

Third, although we read and discuss books as we explore a genre, we do not discuss them in the same way we might in a book discussion. We are reading to discover the book, author, and genre's appeal to fans. We are not reading for plot but to discover why the author and genre are so popular. Our discussion reflects this emphasis. We focus on the following: How do these authors and titles fit with others in this genre? Which of these authors are similar and fit together in subgenres? What do the books we read suggest about the appeal of the genre as a whole? What do readers tell us about these authors and others they enjoy? These discussions help us focus our thoughts and discoveries, and the results direct our future reading. For example, the group might consider questions such as those listed in figure 5.8 for a discussion of Sue Grafton and other female Private Investigators. It is easy to see how such questions focus the discussion and lead to conclusions about a particular author as well as genre and subgenre.

Fourth, in an organized genre study, one person should be designated as the leader to direct the reading and focus the discussion. Preferably, this should be a person who knows something about the genre, but fans need to be careful not to skew the reading list and discussion only toward aspects

Figure 5.8 ■ Questions to Consider in Discussing Sue Grafton
and Authors of Female Private Investigator Mysteries

1. What characteristics/appeal elements do these books illustrate?
2. Why are these Mysteries so popular?

    Immediacy of first-person narration?

    Likable protagonist?

    Series character?

    Lower level of violence?

    Social and moral issues inherent in her cases?

    Step-by-step investigation (as opposed to the "snooping" in many Cozies)?

    Sense of place?

    Self-reliance of the protagonist?

3. What is the difference between Grafton's books and Private Investigator Mysteries and Police Procedural Mysteries that feature women characters, such as those by Stephen Booth, Elizabeth George, and Jill McGown? Would fans of Grafton also like these or other Police Procedurals?
4. Who is Grafton's audience? Women or men? Does the sex of the author (and the P.I.) make a difference?

they enjoy. This leader reads widely, gathers resources about the genre, determines reading assignments, and helps the group draw conclusions.

Fifth, in determining which genre to study first, select a genre popular both with readers and with the librarians studying it. This allows you to become comfortable with the process of the genre study while expanding your book knowledge. This is not to say that it is not important to study genres the staff do not personally enjoy, but do not begin the process of studying genres by choosing one that is unfamiliar or unpopular. We speak from experience in saying that it can be very difficult to keep up enthusiasm for an unpopular genre and to understand why readers enjoy it. If we start with a genre participants read and enjoy, they will be more comfortable reading widely and sharing their knowledge of books already read, and they will have a wider array of familiar authors to draw upon. Later, when participants are familiar with the techniques and benefits of a genre study, move on to more difficult, less familiar genres.

Finally, we have some more specific suggestions related to the organization of a genre study group.

1. In making reading assignments, have everyone read at least one specific benchmark title together rather than many different titles. Then everyone has the same frame of reference to draw on in discussing that author and title. If three books are being read during a two-month period, we might assign two specific titles and allow one free choice by a similar author. (For example, in reading female Private Investigators, we might assign titles by Sue Grafton and Marcia Muller, plus one other similar female investigator of the reader's choice.) We encourage participants to read widely in the genre, beyond those authors and titles assigned, but by assigning specific titles and encouraging participants to draw on reader opinions for suggestions of other authors to read, we both focus on known works and force ourselves to talk with readers about other authors they enjoy.

2. Talk about the genre with staff and patrons. As noted earlier, genre study is another example of readers' advisory as a collaborative activity. Talking with staff—all staff, not just those who work with fiction—and readers forces us to put our thoughts and discoveries into words, and readers either affirm or redirect our conclusions. In addition, all genre study makes us more conscious of pattern and appeal in all genres, not just in the genre we are studying. Genre study focuses us on appeal and the concept of similar authors; it reinforces

the nature of the readers' advisory interview. We do better readers' advisory when we draw on our expanded understanding of genre fiction and share our enthusiasm with other readers.

3. Organize monthly or bimonthly meetings. A genre study is a commitment of time to read and reflect and of time to meet and discuss. Regular meetings allow participants to share their discoveries of current reading as well as to fit them together with authors read previously.

4. Read widely and follow up on suggestions from staff and patrons. The leader, especially, needs both to read ahead of the group and to remain flexible enough to change direction if the discussion warrants this.

One question we are frequently asked is what kind of product a staff can expect at the conclusion of a genre study. Obviously, from an administrative point of view, a commitment of two years to extensive reading and discussion should produce something that reflects all the hard work. In addition to the greatly increased understanding of the genre and the ability to work with readers and fans of genre fiction in general, other products can be created. One possibility is a schema of the genre. Figure 5.6 shows such a schema for the Suspense genre, with general characteristics of that genre followed by those of the two subgenres identified in the study, along with benchmark authors in each.

Another product might be a bookmark or book list. When we studied Suspense, we were able to update two very popular bookmarks, "If you read Mary Higgins Clark's novels of Suspense, try one of these" and "If you read Thomas Harris's novels of Suspense, try one of these," with appropriate lists of authors and titles we had discovered in our reading. Our study of Historical Fiction led to a popular annotated book list, with each of us contributing three or four annotations of books we had read during the study. Tangible products can be a relatively straightforward result of a genre study, but they should not be our focus. We study genres to expand our knowledge and skills. The time and effort we invest are far more than that needed to develop bookmarks and book lists, and the results of genre studies are more far-reaching.

The plan for a genre study we present and pursue requires time and energy. We realize it may seem intimidating; it may sound like so much work that it is not worth even trying. But all directed reading helps readers' advisors work better with patrons. Smaller steps, such as those described above in "Designing a Reading Plan," send us in the right direction and may inspire us to participate in more ambitious reading plans, such as those for genre studies. Whatever genre reading we do, we will gain a greater awareness of the authors and their appeal to readers. We begin to see the pattern that a genre follows; we see links between similar authors. We learn quickly when we embark on any reading program that, with our heightened and directed perceptions, we more readily uncover links and useful information in books we have read about or heard about as well as in those we read or skim.

Whenever readers' advisors undertake a genre study, the benefits are immediate. We quickly improve our ability to identify the appeal of that genre and to recognize where new authors fit within them. We gain confidence in our ability to work with a wide range of readers, as many of our patrons are genre readers. Genre studies are particularly helpful in making staff more comfortable with genres less familiar to them. Studying a genre allows readers' advisors to gain a kind of control over our expanding knowledge of popular fiction and nonfiction, to refine our ability to define a genre and the groupings within it, and to apply what we learn about one genre to others. We see genre study as an ongoing pursuit, one that is perhaps never ending but is certainly rewarding and stimulating.

Strategies to Prevent Overload

As readers' advisors expand their skills and awareness, reading and exploring popular fiction and nonfiction, we reach a point at which we begin to feel overwhelmed. There are so many books, so many patrons with diverse interests, so much to learn to be effective readers' advisors. It is important to take stock of what we do know, but it is also important to recognize that we will never have read or learned enough to help every reader every time. Sometimes it helps to remind ourselves that one of the intellectual satisfactions of doing readers' advisory is that we know there is always more to learn. There are also strategies that help us conquer this helpless feeling. One is a technique for "speed-reading" books; another involves collecting Sure Bets, books that satisfy many readers.

Speed-Reading

Over the years many guides to speed-reading or reading a book in five minutes have circulated among librarians. One of the best was developed by readers' advisor Georgine N. Olson, and it differs from its predecessors in both her recommendations for how one evaluates books, samples sections, and draws conclusions and in her insistence that one also needs to record one's impressions of these books and discuss them. Figure 5.9 is the handout Olson developed to explain this method.

Figure 5.9 ■ Speed-Reading Books; or, How to Read a Novel in Ten Minutes

Basics of Speed-Reading

Select a book to "read."

On a card, sheet of paper, or form: Record the Author, Title, Genre, Series Info, Call Number. As you "read," jot down notes about items listed below that seem pertinent.

Hold the book and look at its basic features. Is it heavy? When you open it, do the pages lie flat?

Look at the typeface, the space between lines, the general layout. How easy to read is it? Is there much white space? Is it densely printed?

Look at the cover. What does it tell you about the book (or what the publisher wants you to think about the book)?

Read the blurb. Does it give you an idea of the story line? Does it tell "everything" (or maybe it doesn't tell you anything)? Is it inviting, teasing, ominous?

Read the first chapter. Does it pull you right into the story, or is there a slow buildup? If it's a series title, how smoothly does it deliver background info?

Skim and read bits and pieces here and there throughout the book. Does it seem to flow? What's your general impression of the book?

Read the end (sorry, but this is important!). If it has an epilogue, read a couple of sections before the epilogue. Is there a conclusion or is it open-ended? Does the ending read like a checklist, wrapping up all loose ends?

What can you tell about the following?

Style:	humorous; serious; length of sentences, sections, or chapters; dialogue
Pacing:	leisurely or action oriented
Format:	straight-line narrative, flashback, single or multiple points of view (How smooth are transitions?)
Characters:	Many or few? Are they a recognizable "type"? Does it seem character or action oriented?
Setting:	time; place; integral or wallpaper
Story line:	character or plot driven
Genre:	Does it follow genre conventions? Subgenre?

(cont.)

Figure 5.9 (*cont.*)

From the Readers' Advisor's Viewpoint

Does this bring to mind any other authors or titles as possible readalikes?

Which readers could enjoy this? Why would they?

Think about how you would phrase a recommendation based on speed-reading versus cover-to-cover reading versus what you might have learned from reviews or other readers.

Becoming Proficient at Speed-Reading (and Learning Its Value and Limitations)

Practice. Set a goal (five books an hour; thirty books a week, etc.).

Speed-read five books you read and enjoyed a long time ago (at least several years). How much comes back to you? How much of what you are "speed-reading" reminds you of what you so enjoyed the last time you read the book? Are you getting a "feel" for the book? Does it seem like the same book you read before, or does it seem different?

Speed-read five books that you haven't read but would be at the top of your "I want to read" list. Then read the books from cover to cover as you normally would. How different are your impressions of the book speed-reading versus "regular" reading?

Find people (preferably with some knowledge of readers' advisory) who read in a genre you do not read. Ask them to select five newish books in the genre that they have read and enjoyed. Speed-read the five books and discuss each with the person recommending the title. How well have you "read" these?

Get together with several others and speed-read the same book. Have a mini book discussion to compare your impressions and notes. What is similar and different in the various readings of the book? How does this compare with the usual book discussion experience?

Source: Georgine N. Olson, Fairbanks, Alaska, 2003. Reprinted with permission.

Following these suggestions can make a real difference in a readers' advisor's ability to gain familiarity with the ever-growing list of "must reads." It is not a substitute for reading a book from cover to cover, yet it is a sensible plan for delving into books and drawing conclusions, discussing them, and recording impressions that makes it easier to share books with other readers, particularly when you have some familiarity with the genre and are simply searching for additional authors and titles.

Sure Bets

Sure Bets were mentioned in chapter 4 as useful titles to fall back on when readers are not forthcoming in the readers' advisory interview about the types of books they enjoy or dislike. In fact, a thoughtfully constructed list of Sure Bets can become the ultimate readers' advisory fail-safe, a list to consult when our minds go blank, when readers are simply looking for something "good" to read, when our selections for displays seem never to find their way into readers' hands and book bags. A list of Sure Bets should be compiled by every library doing readers' advisory, not only for the experience of thinking about what makes a book a Sure Bet in your community but also, and perhaps more importantly, for the lifeline such a list provides to staff.

Sure Bets have a good hook; we can talk about their appeal easily, and our patrons can then decide if they might want to try them. Readers do not always take Sure Bets, but talking about the books usually elicits a reaction from readers, and that often leads us in the right direction—and we all know that is more than half the battle when we are desperate. Sure Bets are especially important for staff new to readers' advisory who are not yet comfortable with a wide range of books and genres. New staff can use this list to fill the Good Books You May Have Missed book truck (discussed in detail in chapter 6), to peruse and become familiar with popular titles, to consult when they run out of ideas, and to jump-start their genre knowledge.

We started a notebook of these Sure Bets years ago, when we suddenly had several new staff members. We labeled each page with a genre—Mystery, Science Fiction, Romance, and so forth—and staff wrote down the authors and titles of books they had given successfully to a wide range of patrons. Lists tend to be library specific. What readers appreciate at our library may not be what readers elsewhere enjoy, since most libraries have specific regional authors or topics. A list for one library may not be successful at another, although there will certainly be some carryover. Sure Bets do not have to be new books; frequently, they are favorites that might be lost in the stacks with the older books. As we describe them to readers, they will react—they may have heard of them or even read them. This can set the stage for their accepting our suggestions of other titles.

Among our Sure Bets are books such as Dorothy Gilman's *Caravan*.[9] Unlike the somewhat wacky Mrs. Pollifax tales, this is an elegant, evocative tale of an older woman looking back on her life, which involved her kidnapping and subsequent tale of adventure in the Sahara in the early twentieth century. Both the fascinating character and her intriguing life please readers, as do the exotic setting and the stylish prose.

Before he became famous for his massive Historical novel of the Central Intelligence Agency, *The Company*, Robert Littell wrote a wonderful and much smaller novel, *The Amateur*.[10] When his girlfriend is killed by terrorists and the government refuses to investigate, a CIA cryptographer, who is trying to discover who really wrote Shakespeare's plays in his spare time, decides to search for her killers himself in this intelligent, fast-paced adventure.

First Ladies, by Margaret Truman, has proven a successful suggestion, especially for many fans of Biography and History.[11] She offers an intimate look at American history and the lives of the women behind the presidents, from Martha Washington to Hillary Rodham Clinton. Her role as a former First Daughter gives her insider insights into the subject that few others possess, and she offers fascinating details of their lives and the times in which these interesting women lived.

Truman Capote's *In Cold Blood: A True Account of a Multiple Murder and Its Consequences* retains its power to shock readers, even almost forty years after it was written.[12] This classic True Crime tale, a nonfiction novel that explores the murders of a rural Kansas family in 1959 and the subsequent investigation, delves into the crime and the lives of the killers. Younger readers may never have heard of this book, but older readers will remember this chilling tale—and may want to reread it.

These are just a few examples of our Sure Bets; more are included in appendix 3. Working with staff to create a list for one's library is worth the time and effort. This is the kind of ongoing list that continues to serve staff and readers well. Our actual list is not annotated because of the time involved, but any notes about the books' appeal add to the value of the Sure Bets list.

In conclusion, the thinking processes described in this chapter evolve as readers' advisors work more and more closely with readers and become more and more familiar with books. As readers' advisors become more skilled, we initiate activities that help us provide better service and continue to challenge us intellectually. We also begin to realize that in print and electronic reference sources we cannot find all the information we need to help readers, and we therefore begin to create our own tools. As I pointed out, our Popular Fiction List came about in just this way and remains a source of authors to read to broaden readers' advisors' backgrounds in genre fiction and, in its revising, serves as an exercise in analyzing the current genre interests of readers who use our library. Formal and informal methods of recording our impressions of the books we read are another example of the kinds of tools readers' advisors develop. Analyses of the appeal of certain books and of individual genres provide readers' advisors with intellectual tools of a sort and with a framework that allows readers' advisors to work both in greater depth and with more ease in helping readers find books that interest them. Finally, as we become more deeply immersed in trying to learn about leisure-reading titles in fiction and nonfiction, we find we need these strategies to keep us from being overwhelmed. All this prepares us for the next step, marketing our leisure-reading collections.

Notes

1. Adult Reading Round Table, *The ARRT Genre Fiction List: A Self-Evaluative Bibliography for Fiction Librarians*, 2nd ed. (Woodridge, Ill.: Adult Reading Round Table, 2003).
2. Jacquelyn Mitchard, *The Deep End of the Ocean* (New York: Viking, 1996); Rosellen Brown, *Before and After* (New York: Farrar, Strauss & Giroux 1992); and Jane Hamilton, *A Map of the World* (New York: Doubleday, 1994).
3. Simon Winchester, *Krakatoa: The Day the World Exploded, August 27, 1883* (New York: HarperCollins, 2003); and Robert Harris, *Pompeii: A Novel* (New York: Random, 2003).
4. Janet Husband and Jonathan F. Husband, *Sequels: An Annotated Guide to Novels in Series* (Chicago: American Library Assn., 1997).
5. Margaret A. Edwards, *The Fair Garden and the Swarm of Beasts: The Library and the Young Adult* (Chicago: American Library Assn., 2002).
6. Joyce G. Saricks, *Readers' Advisory Guide to Genre Fiction* (Chicago: American Library Assn., 2001).
7. Betty Rosenberg, "Themes and Types," in *Genreflecting* (appears at the end of each chapter) (Littleton, Colo.: Libraries Unlimited, 1982); and Dean R. Koontz, *Writing Popular Fiction* (Cincinnati: Writer's Digest, 1972).
8. Thomas J. Roberts, *An Aesthetics of Junk Fiction* (Athens, Ga.: Univ. of Georgia Pr., 1990), 213–14.
9. Dorothy Gilman, *Caravan* (New York: Doubleday, 1992).
10. Robert Littell, *The Amateur* (New York: Simon & Schuster, 1981).
11. Margaret Truman, *First Ladies* (New York: Random, 1995).
12. Truman Capote, *In Cold Blood: A True Account of a Multiple Murder and Its Consequences* (New York: Random, 1965).

6

Promoting and Marketing Readers' Advisory Collections and Services

This chapter covers some activities that promote readers' advisory service. Although many of these activities can be used for other, equally valid purposes, they will be considered exclusively from the viewpoint of the readers' advisor. Signs, book displays, bookmarks, booktalks, and the layout of the readers' advisory area—all will be touched on briefly. Basic how-to information on these topics can be found in the current library literature and won't be duplicated here, although this book's bibliography offers two lists of interesting resources, historical and contemporary (as well as websites for book discussion leaders). Also, you'll find a more detailed section on how to produce annotated book lists. When we started creating book lists at Downers Grove Public Library, we found little information available about the basics involved in their creation, and even less that applied to the type of book lists we recommend for readers' advisory work, so we developed our own techniques. Because marketing and promotion activities are often closely linked to the measurement of the readers' advisory service and statistics, some thoughts on that aspect of promoting the department to administration are also included.

First Impressions

Often, unfortunately, an individual librarian can do little about the physical arrangement of the library or department. Decisions such as where the librarian's service desk is located, how the books are arranged, and what signs are being used are often made by others or cannot be altered. To the extent possible, however, readers' advisors should make sure that the library's layout and design call attention to their activities and encourage both patron contact and easy book selection. As was mentioned earlier, readers' advisors cannot expect that patrons will necessarily seek them out; thus, the location of the service desk should be thoughtfully chosen to draw the notice of readers. Ideally, readers' advisors should situate themselves as close to the book collection, especially to the new books, as is convenient, because these are often a reader's first stop. Readers' advisors not only need to be visible; they also need space at their service area for reference materials, book lists, and bookmarks as well as computer access. While it is certainly advantageous to have separate desks for readers' advisory and reference, this is not always possible. If a desk and staff serve the dual function of providing assistance with both leisure reading and information, an effort should be made to advertise and fulfill both roles.

Consider and pursue any options that make the library as comfortable as possible for readers as they look at books and talk with readers' advisors. For example, shelving that displays book covers forward, seating that allows better vision of low shelving, and good lighting are details that encourage browsing and facilitate conversations about books. Comfortable seating in the fiction and nonfiction areas also helps create an atmosphere that underlines the importance of reading and is conducive to leisurely book selection. At least once a month, make a point of entering the library through the same entrance as your patrons and try to see it as they do. Often, simple yet effective adjustments will come to mind if we take a good look at the library from the reader's point of view. Since studies have shown that a high proportion of fiction readers are browsers, everything we can do to make browsing easier will benefit our collection and its users.[1]

Clear and readable signs should advertise and promote the readers' advisory service. Signs such as Ask Here for a Good Book, Not Sure What to Read? Ask Here, Reading Suggestions, or even the simple Readers' Advisory Service all alert readers with their mention of books and reading. As mentioned earlier, we post "Rosenberg's First Law of Reading: Never apologize for your reading tastes" behind our service desk because it reinforces our philosophy about suggesting books and encourages patrons to approach us to discuss books. Patrons have often commented on the sign, and it has provided the impetus for many very satisfying readers' advisory interviews.

Providing good, clear signage and an inviting and efficient physical arrangement are the first steps in creating an atmosphere conducive to readers' advisory activities. Time spent looking at possible options will be repaid in increased visibility and a more accessible readers' advisory service.

Segregated Genre Collections

In chapter 1, I mentioned that the arrangement of both the fiction collection—alphabetically by author—and the nonfiction collection—arbitrarily by Dewey or Library of Congress cataloging systems— creates problems for browsing readers and argues in favor of providing readers' advisory to assist readers in finding books they will enjoy. Grouping the fiction collection by genre or placing genre identification on book spines is often suggested as the solution to providing readers with better access to the fiction collection. Unfortunately, nonfiction may be more difficult, but certainly grouping Biographies and indicating popular collections—such as Sports, Cooking, Classical Music, or History—on the ends of appropriate stacks may help. We readers' advisors know how frequently readers request materials by genre, and research supports the effectiveness of genre fiction categorization.[2] In addition, a recent study indicates the popularity of genre categories in libraries serving larger populations, with "Science Fiction and/or Fantasy," "Westerns," and "Detective and/or Mystery and/or Suspense" used in more than 90 percent of the libraries surveyed.[3] More than 80 percent of those libraries also shelve these collections separately.[4]

Although I have advocated some genre fiction classification and collection segregation, I do not believe that classification alone is the answer. One problem is that genre labeling and classification are not straightforward tasks. As anyone who has tried to classify fiction realizes, it is difficult to label novels or authors by genre with any integrity or consistency. For example, who decides whether a book goes in the Mystery or Fiction collection? The librarian who selected it? The cataloger? Since it is impossible to read every addition to the collection in order to ascertain its genre, there must be written guidelines that are relatively straightforward to follow.

There is also the danger that classification will segregate readers, allowing them to believe that if they like Mysteries, for example, they will find books they will enjoy only in that area. Furthermore, for some readers, classification and separation by genre may reinforce the misconception that leisure-reading selection should be done without bothering the library staff.

In addition, classification systems alone do not help readers find the particular types of authors or titles they are looking for within a genre or a classification number. As anyone who has worked with readers knows, locating books within a genre is only the first step for genre fans in selecting reading material. Classification systems create similar problems for readers' advisors and leisure readers in the nonfiction collection. That a reader enjoyed *Seabiscuit: An American Legend*, by Laura Hillenbrand, does not mean that he or she will also like everything else in 798.4 (Horse Racing and Flat Racing).[5] Readers' advisors provide assistance in locating the type of book a particular reader might enjoy, suggesting from among numerous genres, subgenres, and appeals.

Although standard reference aides—subject classification, subject headings, and pathfinders—can be helpful to nonfiction users, these reference tools are not expected to do the whole job in answering reference questions. The full potential of information and reference material is realized only when patrons have expert reference librarians available to assist them. The same standards and philosophy that underline our reference service should be applied to the service provided to users looking for leisure reading.

Although both can help, neither a classification system nor increased subject and genre access can truly serve the readers' advisory function. Facilitating optimum use of the library's collections and serving individual readers well require trained staff. Certainly, some level of genre classification and segregation can help readers and readers' advisors alike, but we need to be careful in choosing which genres we segregate, selecting those in which fairly clear distinctions, easily understood by all users of the collection, can be made. As distinctions between genres increasingly blur and writers publish in more than one genre, the practice of segregating genres becomes more and more difficult and the need for trained readers' advisory staff for fiction and nonfiction collections more vital.

Book Displays

A book display consisting of a small group of books and a descriptive sign is one of the most effective ways to promote and market parts of our collections. It is important to situate the readers' advisory service desk as close to the book collections as possible, but if we cannot be physically close to these stationary collections, we bring the books to our desk and immediate service area through displays. In this section, we discuss a more or less permanent display we have found particularly useful as well as short-term displays.

An ongoing Good Books You May Have Missed display has, in fact, been one of the most successful book promotion ideas we have ever had. On a metal book truck near the readers' advisory desk, which is at the entrance to the fiction section, we keep a small, selected group of books. Instead of trying to find a "good read" from the rather daunting numbers of books available in the book stacks, here patrons have a small group of suggested titles from which to choose.

The Good Books You May Have Missed cart has up to twenty-one books spread out on the three shelves of a one-sided library book truck. A large sign above the cart now proclaims Good Fiction You May Have Missed. (With an expansion of the library, we now share the second floor with the reference department. They, too, have discovered the advantages of such a display. Their parallel display is labeled Good Nonfiction You May Have Missed. To avoid confusion, I will continue to refer to it as the Good Books truck.) Books are displayed with covers out, alternating with books displayed with spines out.

The Good Books truck is monitored by readers' advisory staff during their scheduled time at the desk, and one of their responsibilities is to see that this display is kept well stocked. If some of the titles have been removed by patrons, the books remaining on the book truck are first rearranged so that titles that were spine out are now cover out and vice versa. The books are also moved upward, leaving all empty spots on the bottom shelves. To maintain the twenty-one-book maximum, staff add new books to the bottom shelves. One day a week, a staff member notes what is on the top shelf. Any books that remain on the book truck after a week are removed and new titles added, again always moving the remaining books upward and adding new titles at the bottom. This simple system gives every book an equal chance at exposure and ensures that the collection is always fresh. We keep track of the number of books we add to the truck and cumulate the figures monthly, comparing figures over time.

Books to be placed in the Good Books display are those with our longest checkout period, that is, our older books. We include primarily hardcover books with book jackets because they are the most attractive and eye-catching. We choose mass-market paperbacks less frequently, as we find that the smaller size does not display as well. Larger, trade paperbacks work better and are often included. The titles we put on the book truck are some of the best examples of the different genres. We also strive to have a variety of genres on display, making sure that the most popular genres in our library are represented.

Patron response to this ongoing display has been gratifying, to say the least. On rare occasions, we have had to discontinue the display for a short time, and at those times there has always been a great deal of consternation among the patrons who visit the display regularly. Patrons often tell us that it is their first or last stop when they come to the library.

There are a number of advantages to the Good Books display. It is easy to maintain, and it places the better, older fiction before the public. Because the Good Books truck is filled by whoever is at the readers' advisory desk, we all have an opportunity to refresh our memories of titles we might suggest to readers. This system also guarantees a wider variety of titles than if only one person always makes the selections. Since we make an effort to select good books and try to maintain a variety of genres, the act of deciding which books to add to the display heightens our awareness of the quality and the genre classification of various titles. In addition, watching which types of books are circulating and which are not gives us an informal assessment of what is popular at any given time. The display is also a form of readers' advisory lifeline. Here is a preselected group of books we draw upon when our minds have gone blank or when we want to ascertain a reader's tastes by describing several genres or types of books, for we are likely to find a representative selection on the book truck.

Our Good Books You May Have Missed book truck is an ongoing display, but thematic book displays of shorter duration are another way we showcase our collections. We find that for readers' advisory work, the most effective displays are ones from which readers can select books and immediately check them out, not the locked-cabinet type. If the displays are movable (for example, books on a single-sided book truck), they become even more flexible.

Displays of twenty to thirty books are about the right size, and we have found them to be most successful. A display showing only three or four books looks uninviting, and too many books can be overwhelming. The key is to make sure, before we put up the book display, that enough good titles are available beyond the first twenty so that the display can be properly stocked for the expected time it will run. A display for which we have only twenty or so possible titles will have a short life and will rapidly look fairly bedraggled since patrons will check out most of the titles, and we will not be able to restock the display. Occasionally we will do weeklong, rather than monthlong, displays of books on a subject for which there may be a great deal of interest but not enough titles to support a longer display.

In our experience, good displays capitalize on the elements of books that appeal to readers. For example, we have put fast-paced Espionage Thrillers under the sign If You Like Robert Ludlum's Thrillers, Try One of These. We also use displays that take advantage of readers' moods. For instance, in the dead of winter, we used a collection of Family Sagas and Storyteller novels under the sign Books for a Long Winter Night. Subject displays are still another type—sea stories or books with foreign settings, for example. A query on Fiction_L, the readers' advisory mailing list described in chapter 2, asking for suggestions for appropriate titles for a display will elicit an astounding number in a very short time. Since the archives are also searchable, one can check to see if others have mounted similar displays and find endless suggestions without even posting the question.

We also display staff-produced bookmarks and book lists along with appropriate titles. We choose themes that reflect what we feel our readers would enjoy reading. Like the books in the Good Books display, the selected titles for all our displays are ones that have been read by someone in the department or that are suggested by a reliable source. We do not display just any book that happens to fall within the theme; we try to be more discriminating. Readers grow to trust the quality of the books we put on display, so we make a point of selecting them carefully.

In contrast, an example of a display that may be fun but that does not promote readers' advisory service is the Books That Have Never Been Checked Out type. Unless the book selection for this kind of display is very carefully done—focusing on good material that will truly appeal to readers and *should* be checked out—the display will be of limited value to both readers and readers' advisors. Perhaps there is a good reason why the titles have not circulated.

In dividing up the total time set aside for creating book displays, we spend the majority of time choosing a theme that will appeal to readers and selecting titles to include. The smaller percentage of time is spent creating the display itself. Because of the time and care taken with book selection, these displays become a reliable source of titles for readers and readers' advisors alike. Signs advertising the display need not be elaborate; the simpler the better is the rule we try to follow. Since the purpose of the display is to put books in readers' hands, we try to make it attractive and inviting without it appearing to be part of a do-not-touch display. We find that a clear, basic setup and good titles are what bring readers back. Librarians fortunate enough to have talented artists with time to devote to creating more elaborate displays can build on this basic display format. On the other hand, it should be reassuring to librarians who lack the budget, staff, or skills to devise more decorative displays that basic displays can be just as successful and popular among readers. We all know that readers gravitate to small universes of books, even clamoring for the musty books we are trying to weed from the collection! Since we have experienced their propensity to take titles from displays or any book trucks available, we understand that it is better to select carefully, so they come to know that they can rely on our displays.

We have tried to capitalize on every display area we can find. When remodeling moved us to the second floor, we realized early on that we did not have the foot traffic or the circulation we had when we were near the front door and checkout desk. We have alleviated that problem by creating two display areas, which feature both fiction and nonfiction, on the first floor. As a result, we have seen higher circulation and greater patron satisfaction. We also employ slatwall shelving on the ends of the aisles for easy, attractive displays that feature books from particular sections, or the themes of the book lists and bookmarks can be highlighted there. I would encourage all readers' advisors to examine their service space carefully, with an eye to adding displays for readers. Even a small grouping of selected books at the service or checkout desk with an inviting sign—perhaps, Try One of These—will serve a readers' advisory function and remind readers of our role in offering book suggestions. It is important to use high traffic areas and the points of purchase—service and checkout desks—as prime candidates for displays of materials that patrons can check out.

An additional, related promotional idea that we have found to be very effective is an ongoing, and regularly changing, display of the bookmarks and annotated book lists our department has produced over the years. We all know that many patrons like to browse for their leisure reading on their own, and they are pleased to find a selection of book lists on a wide range of topics; they can choose one or more and simply take them into the stacks with them as a guide to reading suggestions. This is another low-maintenance display. We have a file cabinet of bookmarks and book lists, and a clerk changes half of the display every week. Our library has a display unit that holds a mix of approximately sixteen bookmarks and annotated book lists, but even a spot to put out copies of lists at the service desk, at the checkout desk, or in a unit that attaches to the end of a book stack would inexpensively serve the same purpose.

Library web pages offer a relatively easy means of spotlighting collections and highlighting displays, bookmarks, and book lists. Many libraries have sections of their web pages devoted to readers' advisory, and through these they provide links to other library web pages and to sites of interest to readers as well as information on their own collections. Current technology suggests that these will become more and more important vehicles for promotion and information.

I believe it is important to designate physical and virtual locations for both ongoing and short-term book displays, as this affects patrons' perceptions of the library's attitude toward leisure activities. One of the benefits of an established display area is that patrons know where to go to find a changing and interesting selection of materials, which might include audiobooks and video titles. Marketing our collections has become such an important element of library service that readers' advisors need to be proactive in discovering and utilizing promotional locations and techniques. A library literature search will reveal a wealth of articles on the topic, but we should also explore such authors as Paco Underhill, a marketing researcher who can take us beyond the library sphere for inspiration and sound marketing tips (see the bibliography for an Underhill book).

Bookmarks

Bookmarks are another method we use to highlight parts of the collection. A bookmark, as you might expect, is more complicated and time-consuming to produce than a display. The advantage of a bookmark, however, is that the reader can walk away not only with a book to read but also with a list of authors and titles to pursue on a later visit. Each of our bookmarks consists of a list of authors and titles. They are printed on sturdy card stock so that they will stand up in a display unit. They usually are not annotated. Of course, even a one-line comment about each title makes a bookmark more valuable to the user, but producing such a description increases the workload for the bookmark's creator.

We have found that the more useful bookmarks focus on limited subject areas for which full annotations are not necessary. The subjects of bookmarks need to be straightforward and self-explanatory, and not every topic lends itself to this format. Whenever the reader will need more information to choose among the titles, it is better to undertake an annotated book list. Examples of bookmarks with a narrow-enough focus are Locked-Room Mysteries and If You Like [Author's Name], Try These. When produced, the bookmark is made available for patrons, along with a display of the listed books. *And just a reminder:* Any and all printed materials need extensive proofreading. We will discuss proofreading in more detail in the next section, "Annotated Book Lists."

Bookmarks have several advantages. They require much less work than an annotated book list but at the same time give readers a selected list of authors and titles that are available in the library. Bookmarks can be compiled to aid readers' advisory staff in meeting the need for books on popular topics, such as novels featuring lawyers or Romantic Suspense. Creating a bookmark also exposes a novice bibliographer to the process of choosing a theme and selecting books related to patrons' interests and to the rigors of proofreading, which can be substantial, as is made obvious in the next section.

As well as having their own place in the promotion of reading, bookmarks are a good first step for someone who wants to create annotated book lists. There is, in fact, a progression with respect to the skills and time required from designing displays, to compiling bookmarks, to creating book lists. Another more specific and difficult bookmark links similar authors under a title like "If you enjoy the Suspense novels of Mary Higgins Clark, try one of these," or the "While You Are Waiting" readalike bookmarks described in detail in chapter 5.

Annotated Book Lists

Because locally produced annotated book lists provide readers with a printed list of suggested books available in the library, they are an important tool for readers' advisory work. Despite this fact, not much has been written about them from a readers' advisory point of view. For this reason, we believe that it is important to consider book lists—their construction and their value—in some detail.

It is worth noting at the outset that producing good, original annotated book lists takes time. The staff member must choose a topic, select appropriate books, read the books, write annotations, prepare copy for printing, and set up the display of books with the finished book list. Although we have worked to streamline these activities, we have found that each requires considerable time and effort. We believe, however, that the advantages of locally produced annotated book lists make the effort an extremely valuable exercise and worthwhile to the creator, the staff, and the patrons. We strive to create eight new annotated book lists a year, one from each of the staff members who work the readers' advisory desk.

Producing an annotated book list on a topic extends the creator's knowledge of the topic and of the range of books that fall within it. Staff narrow or expand a topic to suit the scope they define, and they both read and read about books within that topic. Then they crystallize their impressions of the chosen books into inviting annotations. Again, this is no small task, but it is not one without rewards.

For patrons, annotated book lists furnish booklets that include not just book titles but descriptions as well. Readers go away with a list—something tangible—in addition to any books they select. In fact, there is nothing more satisfying than coming upon a patron in the stacks, clutching a dog-eared book list and choosing from among the books included on it. Annotated book lists provide some of the benefits of readers' advisory to patrons who feel uncomfortable talking with staff about their reading interests.

Before discussing the process of creating book lists, let me elaborate on two points: book lists for fiction and nonfiction need to be annotated, and they should reflect the local library's collection. Although the time required may be the same, our time is far better spent producing one annotated book list than four nonannotated ones. One reason for annotating book lists is obvious: it is often impossible to tell anything about a work of fiction solely from its title, and nonfiction titles are often just as obscure. Annotations are necessary to describe the book. Second, although it is possible to reap some benefits from commercially produced book lists, I believe that the real advantage to readers' advisors and patrons alike comes from locally produced book lists that include books from the library's collection on topics based on the staff's perceptions of reader interests.

The procedure we follow in creating our book lists is explained below. It concentrates primarily on how readers' advisors think through both the theme and content of a book list, and it offers some guidelines for proofreading and display. The process falls into five stages: choosing a topic and defining the scope, selecting the books, writing the annotations, preparing the book list for printing, and displaying the completed book list.

Choosing the Topic and Defining the Scope

Choosing a topic that reflects reader interests is the first step in producing an annotated book list. Sometimes an appropriate topic comes easily to mind. This can be as straightforward as responding to a number of requests for books with western themes. Or it can be a more complex topic, such as a need for a book list of "page-turners," a topic for which authors cannot easily be found in either book or electronic reference sources. When we are having difficulty choosing a topic, we check our log of patron comments and questions. A number of requests for a genre such as Horror or for a specific writer such as Clive Barker may mean that Horror would be a good candidate for an annotated book list. We might consult the Fiction_L archives for book list topics or browse library web pages for ideas, as these activities often remind us of a topic that would interest our patrons and make a good book list. Brainstorming ideas among readers' advisory staff has also proved useful when we are at a loss for a topic. In fact, at least once a year we have a session to generate ideas for future book lists, based on our perception of reader interests.

Although we need to choose a topic that reflects the needs and interests of our patrons, we also have to be certain the staff member is comfortable with and enthusiastic about the chosen topic. After all, since the staff member will likely be reading and annotating almost two-dozen books, the topic must reflect the readers' advisor's interest as well. When we have needed a book list on a topic about which no one was enthusiastic, we decided to do a department book list, with everyone contributing just a few annotations, rather than assigning it to someone or even taking it on personally. Not only were the discussion and title negotiations interesting and useful and the process relatively painless but the finished book list was often superior to anything we could have created individually.

Once a topic has been chosen, the next step is to collect a large number and variety of books for the book list. As the readers' advisor begins making decisions about which to include, questions arise; in answering these questions and in considering the purpose of the book list, the advisor defines its scope. This task requires the staff member to decide what to focus on within the topic and to determine the audience for the list. For example, with a book list highlighting new books on a subject, the readers' advisor quickly sees that in order to select books, an appropriate cutoff date is needed, and only books published after that date should be included. When a book list of foreign fiction was compiled in our library, for instance, the advisor was forced to consider whether to include only native authors whose works had been translated into English or simply books with foreign settings. In the case of the proposed book list of Family Sagas, terms had to be defined. For example, what constitutes a Family Saga? Is it about two generations of a family? Three? What makes a book a Family Saga and not a family story, a Historical novel, or simply part of a series?

In defining the scope of the topic, readers' advisors should also ask who the intended audience is. Is a genre book list compiled for fans who have read within the genre or for nonfans in order to provide an overview or an introduction? Is the book list directed at a particular age group, such as young adults? Or is the subject something like Small-Town Life, with a mix of books ranging from Romance and Gentle Read to Mystery, Horror, and nonfiction designed to appeal to a wide variety of readers? Considering the audience for whom the book list is designed and evaluating titles from that point of view help readers' advisors define the book list's scope and make decisions about which titles should ultimately be included.

It is always useful to put the topic and scope into words as early as possible in the process, defining what ties the books together. We will occasionally discover that the proposed scope is too narrow, that there are not enough acceptable and appropriate titles available, and we must rethink and expand the scope. In fact, this statement explaining the scope is often included at the beginning of a printed book list because it sets the stage for the books and annotations that follow. As an example, the following is the scope statement for an annotated book list entitled "Novels with a Touch of Science":

> To read a book that explores science in a painless manner, try one of these books that teaches an aspect of the natural sciences or the scientific method using a fictional setting. The books range in topic from physics to paleontology to geology and beyond.[6]

Selecting the Books

Once we have a clear definition of the book list's scope and an idea of the list's intended audience, we make final decisions about which books to include. The titles chosen for a book list must fit the scope, but they must also meet certain standards. Books included in a book list must be *known* to be books of an acceptable quality, either because we have read them ourselves or because they are listed in a trustworthy source to which we can refer if questions of suitability ever arise. On the other hand, we do not necessarily *love* every book included. If they meet our quality standard and are thought to appeal to the intended audience, they become part of the book list. Annotated book lists allow us, as readers' advisors, to put our book suggestions into print for patrons. Thus, we want to be careful in our selection of titles.

How many books should be included? We generally annotate eighteen to twenty-four titles, primarily because that number fits comfortably on a folded legal-sized sheet of paper, the size we most frequently use. We feel that fewer titles provide too small a sample for the user and make the process hardly worth the effort for the readers' advisor. More titles make the book lists cumbersome to produce, as additional pages are required and more time is needed to write annotations. We do, however, make certain that we own more than just eighteen to twenty-four listed titles on this theme, since we always display the book list with books, both those we have annotated for that list and other appropriate titles.

Our selection guidelines include two additional caveats. First, we include no more than one book by an author. If readers like the title by that author, they will read others. The rare exception is if an author writes different types of books and more than one type fits the scope of the book list. Second, we try to include as wide a variety of titles as fit within the defined scope. For example, a book list of fiction set during World War II covered not only stories of battles but also life away from the front in England and America, Espionage novels, and Suspense stories, appealing to a larger audience than had it concentrated only on battle stories.

Writing Annotations

After the topic has been selected, the scope defined, and appropriate books read and chosen, the advisor is ready to begin writing the annotations.

> To shun the hackneyed phrase, the threadbare adjective, to find the word that conveys the nature of the book's style or distills the essence of its theme, to integrate its substance, quality, and value clearly, logically, and with graphic brevity, is to practice the fine art of annotation.[7]

Thus wrote Helen E. Haines in 1950, defining the art of annotation writing—another art to which readers' advisors aspire, and one closely related to the technique of describing books orally. Just as some readers' advisors have the facility to talk easily about books with readers, others can do the same in writing: they can capture the essence of a book in a sentence or two and make us want to pull the book off the shelf and read it immediately.

Good annotations should be both informative and inviting; they should describe a book in a way that makes readers want to read it and yet give enough appeal information to allow readers to judge if this is the book for them. Annotations should focus on the story line and on the book's appeal to the reader. The text of the annotation should leave no doubt about the kind of book being described. The annotation should show how the book fits within the scope of the book list, and it should focus on the book's best features, just as readers' advisors do in their conversations with readers. The key is to write an inviting annotation without overpraising the book—and without giving the ending away.

Regarding style, the best annotations are written in the active rather than the passive voice. We found that, although annotations need not be grammatically complete sentences, they must flow. It is not necessary to use a subject if the subject would be the book's title or the words *this book*; in fact, there is no point to repeating the title or information implied by the title in the annotation itself. Reading the annotation aloud is a technique that sometimes helps determine if it will be readily understood. Finally, annotations should be concise, preferably just one or two sentences long and fewer than one hundred words. We have learned that each staff member has a different style of writing annotations; the above guidelines are not intended to stifle creativity, but we have found them helpful in structuring the annotation.

We have all experienced those difficult times when we simply cannot seem to write *anything*, not to mention something as difficult as good annotations. We have found that the best way to get around this block is to think about each of the books with respect to the scope of the book list: What is it about the book that makes it fit? Why would the person who picks up the book list want to read that particular book? Thinking in these terms often gets us writing again.

Another difficulty we have discovered in attempting to write inviting annotations is that there are very few good models to follow. Among ourselves, we librarians often discuss books in critical terms. Book reviews are designed to do the same—to be critical of the book, to point out faults as well as strengths in order to help a librarian decide whether to purchase a particular title. Thus, the reviews we spend so much time reading are poor models for annotation writing. Annotations for book lists focus on the parts of the book that appeal to readers. Annotators select and promote good books; they do not need to evaluate them critically as well. For more tips on writing annotations, consult Mary K. Chelton's "Read Any Good Books Lately? Helping Patrons Find What They Want," where she discusses "How to Write a Reader's Annotation," and Sharon L. Baker's "Book Lists: What We Know, What We Need to Know."[8] Although we agree on some points, our styles and opinions often differ, thus giving prospective annotation writers varying points of view to draw from in developing their own styles.

Although there are some similarities between annotations for book lists and plot summaries for "Book Notes" (see chapter 5), they differ in focus and purpose. The "Book Notes" have a uniform format that requires the same information about all titles (setting, subject headings, etc.) and a more extensive plot summary based on the range of the book's appeal to the reader. Book list annotations, on the other hand, briefly highlight one or more aspects of appeal and focus on how the book fits the scope of the book list. For example, if a readers' advisor were to use Jane Langton's *Dead as a Dodo* for that annotated book list of "Novels with a Touch of Science," mentioned above, the annotator might highlight the discussion of Darwin and his evolutionary theory, which permeates the text, and the fact that Langton uses appropriately chosen passages from Darwin's writing to head many chapters.[9] A book list on Mysteries in a college or university setting would certainly place greater emphasis on the book's Oxford setting—especially the Museum of Oxford—the cadence of university life and interactions between professors and students; perhaps the additional quotations from Lewis Carroll, which balance the more serious lines from Darwin; and Langton's multiple drawings, which evoke the Oxford scene. The "Book Notes" summary would mention all these aspects of appeal and subject interests. Clearly, book list annotations are shorter and more focused than other plot summaries and reflect the more limited scope of the book lists.

We are still grappling with another issue involved in writing annotations for book lists: what is and is not copyrighted? As with many issues related to copyright law, no absolutely clear guidelines are provided. Haines wrote in 1950,

> In the preparation of such lists, annotations in current and standard bibliographical guidelines as well as terse comments from reviews or graphic summations from publishers' announcements are drawn upon for information, for adaptation or paraphrase.[10]

The issue is, of course, when is it paraphrase and not quotation?

For example, what about the book description on book jackets? Are they copyrighted or "fair game"? When asked, legal experts replied that the material on a book jacket is exempt from copyright law if the information being quoted is factual information about the book or an outline of factual information. This information is considered advertising for the book. If the information to be quoted is a fairly elaborate synopsis of the plot, it is protected by law. Again, the issue is not straightforward, but it seems likely that anything beyond the basics, any character or plot description, would be protected by copyright.

Although I do not have any clear-cut answers on the copyright issue, I believe that readers' advisors need to be conscious of and sensitive to this issue. Certainly, one cannot copy annotations from another source and not credit the source. However, there is obviously a very fine line between copying and Haines's concept of "adaptation or paraphrase." I advise reading the book or about the book and writing annotations from our impressions of everything we have read. If we take something word for word from another source, we put the material in quotations and credit our source. The rights of the original authors to their own words must be respected, and we feel that it behooves all librarians to be aware of the dangers of simply copying someone else's words. In the same way, if libraries use bookmarks or book lists from another library, they should ask permission and credit the original source.

This discussion brings up another issue that arises whenever book lists are considered: do we need to read every book we include? I do not believe that it is necessary to read every book; however, I do believe that we must be doubly certain that the books we have not read are of the desired quality and that they fit within the scope of the topic we have chosen. As we all know, book reviews and book jackets do not always give a complete and accurate picture of a book, so we are careful not to rely on them exclusively. When considering a book we have not read, we talk to people who have read the book, check several reviews and other descriptions of the book, and practice the speed-reading techniques described in chapter 5. Staff develop strategies that allow them to gain the information necessary to decide whether a book should go on their list and to write the annotation.

All these issues—from style to content—should be considered in writing annotations for book lists. In the end, I believe that the secret to writing inviting annotations is enthusiasm for the book, just as it is the key to talking about books with readers. Some readers' advisors can write inviting annotations but have difficulty talking with readers about those same books. Others can "sell" almost any book verbally but have trouble doing the same in print. The art of annotation writing is the ability to capture a reader's enthusiasm for a book, to think about the best elements of the book, and to convey each of these aspects in writing to other readers.

Preparing to Print

Choosing a topic and defining its scope, selecting books to include, and reading the books and writing annotations make up the first three stages in compiling an annotated book list. At the fourth stage, the book list is prepared for printing, which involves setting up the final format, editing, and proofreading.

First, a few words about format. In our annotations, we include the following bibliographic information: author, title, publication date, and number of pages as well as the call number or location in our collection. Our policy is to put the name of the bibliographer, the date the book list was produced, a request not to copy without permission, and the library logo with library name, street and web addresses, and telephone number at the end of our book lists. What a library can do regarding the physical format of its book lists often depends on the resources available and the amount of money it chooses to put into the production of such materials. We have found that colored, legal-sized paper folded in half to make four nearly square pages is a convenient and workable size. We devote the top three to four inches of the first page to the title and to any graphics, and then we simply run the annotations—usually in alphabetical order by author. This format requires a minimum of time, effort, and money, and it produces a simple but attractive book list.

Editing is the next aspect in this process. We designate one person as editor for each book list. It need not be the same person every time, but it is important to have someone fill this role from the book list's beginning. In the early stages, the editor is a sounding board for ideas—someone to provide assistance in defining the scope, selecting books, and writing annotations. The editor asks several questions at this stage: Is there a good mix of book types? Is there as much variety as possible within the scope of the topic? Are there too many examples of one kind of book? The editor works with the creator in striving for a balance among all the possible types of books that could be included.

The editor reads for style and content as well as for grammatical errors: Is the style of the annotations consistent without being monotonous? Are the annotations approximately the same length? There is certainly some room for variation in the length of the annotations, but if some are quite long and others quite short, this may be a problem that needs to be addressed. Is there a legitimate reason for the variation? Do the shorter annotations say enough? Are the longer ones simply wordy? Do the annotations adequately describe the story line and address the book's appeal? Simply saying that the book is "a good read" is not sufficient; the bibliographer needs to provide evidence to convince readers of this fact. Are the annotations inviting? Do they describe the story in a way that will intrigue the reader? Are there jarring remarks or language in the annotations? In our experience, the last sentence of the annotation is often crucial and should be constructed with care to be especially interesting and hook the reader. The editor should read carefully and check that the annotations are nonprejudicial and noncritical. If there are any reservations about a book, that book should not be included on the list.

Proofreading is the final step in creating a book list. We place a lot of emphasis on this step because we have *never* had a book list in which the proofreader has not found errors, no matter how careful the creator and editor were. Proofreading should be done after all editorial changes have been made and the book list is essentially ready for printing. The first rule of proofreading is that this task must be done by someone who has never seen the book list before; therefore, both the creator and the editor are excluded from this process. You may need to enlist colleagues or others outside the library to help. The easiest method we have found is to collect all the books included in the book list and have the proofreader sit down with the books and the book list and verify the information using the proofreading checklist (see figure 6.1).

We do not mention checking for spelling errors as being among either the editor's or the proofreader's responsibilities; however, both individuals must look for misspelled words. For the most part, finding spelling errors hinges on whether a word looks questionable to the reader. Both the editor and the proofreader must take responsibility for checking for spelling errors and look up any questionable words. We have learned not to rely on the computer spell-checker exclusively because it will not catch mistakes such as homonyms if the inappropriate word has been correctly spelled.

Now for some final cautions. In general, we advise our staff never to include any detail in a book list annotation that they are not willing or able to check. Again, no matter how accurate you are, *you cannot proofread your*

Figure 6.1 ■ Downers Grove Public Library Proofreading Checklist

Check each annotation for the following:

    Alphabetization or organization of entries

    Author's full name—exactly as it appears on the title page

    All title words and punctuation in the title—exactly as they appear on the title page

    Publication or copyright date

    Number of pages

    Call number or location information

    Any personal and place-names used in the annotation

own work. Doing this is possible theoretically—if you are willing and able to read the book lists backward, word by word—but it is hardly advisable if it can be avoided. It is better to find good proofreaders among your colleagues and friends and to employ their skills. Our experience is that good proofreaders generally enjoy the task and are willing to help. Furthermore, if you make changes in the original, the altered entries need to be checked again after the corrections have been made. Proofreading takes time—always more than expected. However, the assurance it gives that you are providing accurate material for publication makes proofreading necessary and worthwhile.

Displaying the Book List

Displaying the book list is the final stage of the production process. We display all newly produced book lists alongside the listed books and other appropriate titles. It is important to display the book lists with the books, even if we simply put both on a book truck at the end of a book stack. The completed list can then be included in the display of our older book lists in a freestanding display unit. As mentioned earlier, patrons often browse through these lists when they are looking for book suggestions; readers' advisors, in talking with readers, can also refer to book lists on the display and easily give them to patrons as part of the readers' advisory interview.

It is important for a library that wants to provide annotated book lists to produce its own lists, featuring books from its collection and focusing on subjects of particular interest to its readers. However, this activity should not be limited strictly to professional librarians. Book lists of the type we describe can be created by anyone who is willing to make the commitment in time and effort. The key is enthusiasm for books and for the subject.

Booktalks

Library staff are frequently asked to provide book programs for community groups, and we have some tips to make this less threatening and to capitalize on this opportunity to promote the readers' advisory service.

Booktalking is an art, and when done well, it can be entertaining as well as informative for the audience. If booktalking is an activity you are unfamiliar with, a survey of the literature, especially in the young adult and children's areas, should provide you with several informative sources; some are also listed in this book's bibliography. My purpose in adding a section on booktalks, as in several other sections in this chapter, is not to discuss the basic techniques but to suggest an approach that I feel complements the philosophy and general goals of readers' advisory service.

We had been looking for a way to use booktalks to reflect the work we were already doing as readers' advisors. When we came upon the answer, it at first seemed so simple that it took us awhile to appreciate its advantages: we began to apply the same guidelines to booktalking that we use in our readers' advisory interviews and in other promotional activities. Readers' advisors quickly learn the art of booktalking in the stacks, offering information about multiple titles, focused on the reader's interests, many times throughout the day. For more formal booktalks, we simply expand on that process.

When gathering the titles for a booktalk, we do not limit our choices only to books we personally have read. We think instead about the types of books that might appeal to the audience; thus, the more we know about the group we are to address, the better we can focus our selections. We plan to spend about five minutes presenting each book, although we are fairly flexible from book to book. When describing each title, we use the techniques outlined in the section of chapter 4 called "Talking about Books." We emphasize the elements that make the book appeal to a reader; we describe the best features of the book, perhaps even reading a passage to help make the point; and then we make comparisons to well-known authors and titles, or even to other books by that same author, including remarks such as, "If you are the kind of reader who enjoys [popular author's name], you may enjoy this book, too." We also take copies of our annotated book lists and bookmarks and describe the service to members of the group, making it clear to the audience that one of our jobs as readers' advisors is to suggest books and to evaluate titles in terms of how they appeal to readers; they should come ask us whenever they want reading suggestions.

Again, some staff are naturals at talking before a group—they make books sound irresistible. Still, by using the skills of describing and selecting titles already practiced in conducting readers' advisory interviews, *all* readers' advisors can learn how to do this type of booktalk. The booktalks we are recommending directly support the readers' advisory service because they introduce the audience to the way readers' advisors regularly suggest books. Developing booktalks can also expand the skills of readers' advisors in describing titles, again encouraging readers' advisors to focus on a book's appeal and on readers' tastes.

Book Discussion Groups

With the continuing popularity of Oprah's Book Club, no public library can afford not to offer an opportunity for patrons to gather to discuss books, both fiction and nonfiction. With the increase of interest in book groups, materials abound—in both books and electronic resources; sometimes discussion questions are even provided by publishers in the books themselves. Whether or not libraries offer book discussions led by staff, they should certainly offer assistance to leaders in finding information on organizing and running a group and locating materials, including suggested titles that make good discussions, biographical information about the author, reviews and other printed material about the book, and published questions if available. Some libraries even circulate complete book discussion kits, with the above material as well as copies of the books. Useful titles and websites are listed in this book's bibliography.

Measuring the Success of a Readers' Advisory Service

Since measurement has become crucial in proving the success of a service or tool and ensuring its continued funding, it is important to think about statistics related to readers' advisory service. Unfortunately, many of the measures of a successful readers' advisory service, such as patron satisfaction and improved service orientation, are nebulous, and increased circulation is hard to attribute solely to readers' advisory. If your library surveys patron satisfaction, increased satisfaction with the development of a readers' advisory service should be evident, but libraries do not undertake expensive surveys annually, and not all surveys demonstrate this kind of satisfaction. Patron comments, too, can bolster the reputation of the service, but our patrons may be more likely to identify poor service rather than to applaud good service.

Two measures that speak directly to readers' advisory techniques—the number of interactions and the number of titles added to displays—provide evidence of the success of a service. Many libraries are required by their states to count the number of reference interactions in order to obtain state money. Whether this is the case for your library or not, we encourage you to count reference and readers' advisory interactions. We simply added an extra column to our daily statistics sheet, and we make a hash mark every time we talk with a reader and suggest books. If a reader needs books for himself, his wife, and his mother, we make three hash marks, as we have provided suggestions for three separate readers. When our director reports the reference statistics to the state, he simply adds together the reference and readers' advisory numbers, properly counting both as reference. If your library makes a distinction between ready reference—quickly answered questions—and research, you will want to count readers' advisory queries with research, not ready reference. Consider the amount of time an advisor is "connected" with the reader. Even the shortest conversation when offering a book to a reader takes more time than ready reference.

Duncan Smith reports on a technique he used when working in a branch library in Atlanta, Georgia. Two jars of pennies were kept in the staff room, and whenever a staff member placed a book in a reader's hand, a book that reader would not have checked out had the staff member not been there to suggest it, the staff member moved a penny from one jar to the other. Seeing the jars also reminded staff to offer books to readers. At the end of the month, Smith could calculate exactly the benefit of having readers' advisory staff, because, in the pennies, he had a physical count of how many books circulated because advisors put them in readers' hands. He could report that a service that cost no money, because staff were at the service desk anyway, increased circulation by 3 percent.[11]

We also keep track of the number of titles we add to various displays each month. Since we choose these titles based on our skill and knowledge—we do not add just any books to our displays but ones we know to be good—we believe it is important to acknowledge that we selected these titles for readers, even if we did not specifically talk with every reader who took books from the display. It is important to recognize the thought and care involved in choosing books for displays; keeping track of these numbers and reporting them monthly provides that satisfaction and acknowledgment. We have a fairly elaborate system of keeping track of the number of titles we add to each display every day, but that is not necessary for every library. It is enough to make hash marks indicating the number of books added. At the end of the month, count the number of items remaining on the displays and subtract that from the total added for the number of books that circulated each month from displays. If you have not done this in the past, you will likely be astonished at the number of titles readers take from displays.

Certainly, circulation figures over time will reflect reader satisfaction with the readers' advisory service. The marketing techniques discussed above help us highlight and promote our collections. We provide free access to a wealth of materials to meet our readers' leisure-reading needs, and the more inviting and available we make these books, the more likely they will circulate. Adding popular new titles, weeding and refreshing copies of popular older titles, adding them to lists in print and on our websites, putting them in displays (which means it behooves us to keep our displays filled), and placing books in readers' hands ensure that our circulation figures will continue to rise.

Just as we market our collection and service to readers, we need to learn to market our service and skills to administration as well. Monthly reports provide an easy opportunity for highlighting upcoming displays and book lists and reporting on the popularity of current displays. We should share anecdotal evidence—and encourage our patrons to share their comments with administration as well. Even administrators who support and use the service welcome hard data as justification for continued support for this program, as they do with all aspects of library service. We need to consider what kind of data we can provide and make that readily available. Marketing inside and outside the library helps ensure the success of a readers' advisory program.

In summary, all of the activities discussed in this chapter have a place in readers' advisory service. The value of these promotional suggestions as readers' advisory tools is that they rely on and support basic readers' advisory techniques and acknowledge the reader's perspective with respect to the layout of the department, displays, printed bookmarks, book lists, booktalks, and book discussion groups. However, it is important to remember that we are marketing and promoting a service as well as materials. Everything we do that promotes our collections also underscores our ability and willingness to work with readers in the library. Our displays and web pages remind readers that we have interesting materials to help them find books for their leisure reading. Readers' advisory is an integral part of the public service libraries provide, and as we promote our collections, we market our image as a library interested in meeting our patrons' informational and leisure interests. The next chapter, "Training," looks at a readers' advisory training program, a way to support the initial and continuing education of a readers' advisory staff.

Notes

1. Sharon L. Baker, "A Decade Worth of Research on Browsing Fiction Collections," in *Guiding the Reader to the Next Book*, ed. Kenneth Shearer (New York: Neal-Schuman, 1996), 127–47.

2. Ibid., 141–47.
3. Gail Harrel, "Use of Fiction Categories in Major American Public Libraries," in *Guiding the Reader to the Next Book*, ed. Kenneth Shearer (New York: Neal-Schuman, 1996), 150.
4. Ibid., 151.
5. Laura Hillenbrand, *Seabiscuit: An American Legend* (New York: Random, 2001).
6. Sue O'Brien, "Novels with a Touch of Science" (annotated book list, Downers Grove Public Library, Ill., April 1992).
7. Helen E. Haines, *Living with Books: The Art of Book Selection* (New York: Columbia Univ. Pr., 1950), 145.
8. Mary K. Chelton, "Read Any Good Books Lately? Helping Patrons Find What They Want," *Library Journal* 118 (May 1993) 33–37; and Sharon L. Baker, "Book Lists: What We Know, What We Need to Know," *RQ* 33 (winter 1993), 177–80.
9. Jane Langton, *Dead as a Dodo* (New York: Viking, 1996).
10. Haines, *Living with Books*, 140.
11. Duncan Smith, in discussion with the author, July 2004.

7 Training

Training staff in the art of readers' advisory is, in many ways, the most difficult task we undertake. Training requires energy, inspiration, and enthusiasm as well as the ability to work at the top of our form as we model correct behavior. Providing ongoing training that is designed to keep staff enthusiastic, up-to-date, and growing as readers' advisors is as challenging and time-consuming as instilling philosophy and skills in new staff.

The focus of this chapter will be on *what*, not *how*, to train, and it will draw on information presented in more detail in the previous chapters. All of us have our own styles and timetables. How we implement readers' advisory service and train staff to provide this service is not the essential issue; what we train and that this training provides a sound basis for skill development are critical.

Very few librarians required to provide readers' advisory service have had formal library school training in public service techniques useful in dealing with patrons or any background in popular fiction and nonfiction. In probably no other aspect of library work is on-the-job (and even less-formal) training more often the rule rather than the exception. Only in recent years are library schools beginning to offer such training, acknowledging that preparing graduates in this area is absolutely crucial in enabling them to work successfully with adults in public libraries. Many individual public libraries and library systems, on the other hand, have instigated extensive and elaborate continuing education programs that focus on readers' advisory training. Some libraries provide genre overviews or offer formal instruction to increase staff knowledge of popular genres, in addition to teaching basic readers' advisory techniques. Other libraries have implemented directed-reading programs and assign readers' advisory reference questions as training exercises. Whatever we do, we need to help staff gain familiarity with readers' advisory techniques and popular leisure reading through reading, practice, and discussion.

This chapter highlights those areas in which training is vital, providing both an intellectual and a philosophical justification for such training, and presents specific activities that help staff build skills. First, however, it is important to consider the goals of such training. What do we want to achieve with a readers' advisory training program? Training of readers' advisors should accomplish the goals listed in figure 7.1. Because these goals form the basis of training activities, it is important to consider them individually in more detail.

Figure 7.1 ■ Goals of Readers' Advisory Training

1. Help staff (and the administration) recognize the importance of and the need to provide readers' advisory service in the library.
2. Teach readers' advisors to be comfortable, skilled, and nonjudgmental in their interactions with readers.
3. Provide strategies so readers' advisors can be successful in going from readers' interests, moods, and needs to books as they suggest a range of possible titles patrons might wish to read.
4. Help readers' advisors understand the concept of appeal and its essential role in readers' advisory work.

The Goals of Readers' Advisory Training

Teaching staff to understand and acknowledge the importance of readers' advisory service in the public library constitutes the first training goal. Not all of us are fortunate enough to have staff and administration committed to the idea that assistance with leisure-reading interests in both fiction and nonfiction is as important as any other service the library provides. Staff and administration must understand that when we do not help leisure readers looking for suggestions, we essentially deny service to a large part of our clientele. Readers' advisory questions are fundamentally no different from any other reference question. We need to acknowledge this fact and help staff to understand it as well. As library professionals, we pride ourselves on the level of service we provide to answer information questions, but popular leisure-reading collections, especially fiction, too often remain self-service. We should actively train staff to help patrons with their leisure-reading inquiries, and we should support our collections with reference sources and guides that allow both staff and readers to use them more effectively. Staff must learn to acknowledge that the patron asking for a book that is "just like" those that Stephen King or Bill Bryson writes deserves the same level of service as the person who wants information on building a deck.

This is not always an easy concept to accept. Over the years, we have all encountered many justifications for this denial of service to leisure readers. We may argue we are too busy with "legitimate" reference questions to handle readers' advisory requests, which, because they often involve the fiction collection, are somehow "illegitimate" and not worthy of consideration. Or we may complain that there are too often no straightforward, easy-to-find answers to readers' advisory queries. A reference book will not give an accurate list of books exactly like those by John Grisham or Calvin Trillin. To help the reader who asks for more books "just like" Grisham or Trillin writes, we need to discover what it is about the author that the reader enjoys before we can identify similar titles, and even then, reference sources are often deficient. It takes time to become familiar enough with popular fiction and nonfiction to be able to help readers. That there is often no training and that there are few reference sources make these questions seem even more difficult. A third argument can be summarized in the frequently heard justification, "We don't get questions like that at our reference desk, so why bother learning about the collections?" Since libraries in general have worked hard to teach patrons over the years that asking for a "good book" is an inappropriate question, we should not wonder at the lack of queries. On the other hand, it would be interesting to discover in how many of these libraries this request is made in the stacks and at the circulation desk, since readers have been made uncomfortable asking at the reference desk.

The biggest deterrent, in our experience, is that many of us really are too busy to answer all questions in the detail they deserve. That readers' advisory questions are not straightforward makes them seem even more difficult and time-consuming. However, no other questions are actively excluded from reference instruction and training in the way that these are. We do not single out any other questions or groups of users and say we will not handle their queries. Libraries are inundated with difficult health and business questions, but we have never heard of a library that has designated those as areas in which questions simply will not be answered. Until we are also willing to say we will not answer business or health or any other group of questions because we are too busy or the questions are too complicated, we need to reconsider the appropriateness of doing just that with questions dealing with leisure-reading interests. Thus, the first goal of readers' advisory training is to provide tools—physical and intellectual—that ensure that we treat these questions with the same professionalism and tenacity that we bring to info-oriented questions. Staff must learn to see readers' advisory as an *integral part of their job responsibilities* in order to provide good reference service as well as good public service.

Once we accept the inherent necessity of providing readers' advisory service, we need to ensure that the staff are comfortable, skilled, and non-judgmental in their interactions. This is the second training goal. Betty Rosenberg's motto, "Never apologize for your reading tastes," should set the tone for all readers' advisory activities and interactions. We all know that if readers ask for titles and authors we dislike or find frivolous, and if we let our attitude show, those readers will never ask again. Nor will any patron who overhears the interaction. We do not have to like everything, but we must find phrases to use in talking about materials we do not enjoy so that we can preserve our own integrity yet acknowledge what it is about a type of book, an author, or a title that gives a reader pleasure. We must remember that there are books for the moment and others for the ages.[1] As readers, sometimes we appreciate one type and sometimes the other, but requests for both are legitimate and should be treated equally.

The third training goal is that readers' advisors must learn to discover what an individual reader is looking for: to move from readers to books, not from books we have personally enjoyed to every reader who asks. Readers' advisory work would be so much easier if there were an infinite list of perfect books that would satisfy every reader or even if we could simply keep a stack of copies of the last book we really enjoyed and pass one out to everyone who asks for suggestions. Our job might be easier, but readers are unlikely to leave satisfied, as was reported by Anne K. May and others in chapter 2. Readers expect us to suggest titles that meet their own personal reading needs and interests. We need to learn to do this and to teach our staff how to do it as well.

Finally, years of experience working directly with leisure readers, and particularly fiction readers, indicate that readers read for more than just plot or subject. They also look for books with similar appeal elements, which were discussed in detail in chapter 3. Staff must learn to describe books by appeal, not just by plot, because, as we have discovered, appeal-based descriptions allow readers to make choices more easily about what they are in the mood to read. Describing books by appeal also relieves us of the task of remembering the plotline of every book we talk about. Relying on appeal not only capitalizes on strategies we naturally employ in sharing books but also makes recalling and describing books easier. We learn to identify the connections we see between books and authors. Then, as we suggest that a fan of one book might enjoy another, we are able to elucidate the link between the two, clarifying why we think the reader might like this book. If we have mastered the techniques described in chapters 3 and 4 and learned to be alert to appeal elements in all we read and hear about books, we greatly expand the range of books we can discuss with patrons.

Training and supervising staff place an enormous responsibility on those of us in charge of these activities. I feel strongly that trainers and supervisors should also work the desk and model appropriate behaviors and techniques, since this helps create and foster a climate in which providing this service comes to be accepted by administration, staff, and patrons. We must teach and reinforce public service skills in order to show, as well as to tell, staff how to be nonjudgmental, positive, enthusiastic, and professional in all our interactions. We also must help staff fit readers' advisory into their desk responsibilities and help them become comfortable sharing books so this activity becomes automatic, a part of their daily routine.

Basic Training for Readers' Advisors

In training new staff, it is important to recognize and acknowledge what seem to be their two greatest fears:

How can I ever read enough so that I can talk with readers?

How can I remember what I do read?

It is all too easy for new staff to become overwhelmed. They shadow us in the stacks and hear us talking—knowledgeably, they assume—with a range of readers, whose tastes run the gamut from Cyberpunk to Henry James to True Crime writers. No wonder they are concerned! It is important to reassure new staff, to make clear to them from the first that there are strategies to use in working with readers, that they will be taught these techniques, that providing readers' advisory is not as impossible as it may seem, and that we all felt overwhelmed at first. Then we need to embark on training activities that help staff become comfortable and allay their fears. Initial training of readers' advisors involves providing mental and physical tools. The former includes ways to think and talk about books; the latter covers reference sources, annotated book lists, and other written means of sharing books. We also provide reassurance and strategies for dealing with difficult problems, and we set up situations in which success is likely by providing a reading plan and opportunities to make talking about books part of their routine, even before new staff work with readers.

We have found that beginning readers' advisors need to master five basic skills, listed in figure 7.2, during the first year of training. Figure 7.3 illustrates "A Checklist for Readers' Advisory Training," which describes these skills and provides activities that can be used to teach them. This model can be readily adapted to meet an individual library's training and staff needs. Such a tool is useful for both trainer and new staff since it lays out the activities, in approximate order, that will constitute the training process. This example of a training program is specifically correlated to this book and thus requires reading, discussing, and completing the exercises described in the previous chapters. If your library lacks a training checklist, take this as an example and adapt it to meet your own needs. In my experience, it works best if one staff member oversees this training, acting as a mentor. In addition to regularly scheduled formal meetings, he or she touches base with the new staff member informally for five to ten minutes every week. Although one person is responsible for the training, all in the department benefit from this skills refresher course as everyone, at some point, works with the new staff member, either on the desk or informally in

Figure 7.2 ▧ **Basic Skills for Readers' Advisors**

1. How to build on and expand familiarity with fiction and nonfiction
2. How to think about books
3. How to talk about books
4. How to use reference sources
5. How to write about books

Figure 7.3 ■ A Checklist for Readers' Advisory Training

Assignment	Date	Discussed/Initials
Philosophy of service		
Read and discuss chapter 1	_____	_____
Assess reading background	_____	_____
Design reading plan and set discussion dates	_____	_____
Keep track of what is read	_____	_____
Appeal		
Read and discuss chapter 3	_____	_____
Description exercise	_____	_____
Book summaries	_____	_____
Readers' advisory interview		
Read and discuss chapter 4	_____	_____
Read and discuss Hanff and Morley	_____	_____
Reference sources and questions		
Read and discuss chapter 2	_____	_____
Peruse collection of department book lists and bookmarks	_____	_____
"Book Notes" form		
Read and discuss chapter 5	_____	_____
Unannotated bookmark		
Read and discuss chapter 6	_____	_____
Annotated book list	_____	_____
On-desk activities		
Keeping track of questions	_____	_____
Setting interview goals	_____	_____
Filling Good Books truck	_____	_____
Filling displays	_____	_____

the workroom, responding to questions and sharing favorite reference sources and authors. New staff learn early on that the best readers' advisory is not done in a vacuum; it is a team effort and involves sharing resources and techniques, not to mention books.

Since understanding and acknowledging the importance of providing readers' advisory are essential and form the basis of all later activities, start with a discussion of the philosophy of providing the service. Staff quickly see the value of the service they are being trained to provide, and their enthusiasm sustains them as they master the necessary techniques.

At the same time, we teach new staff how to build on and expand their knowledge of popular leisure reading. We start here to address and help counteract that fear of not having read enough. Our Popular Fiction List and Popular Nonfiction List (see appendixes 1 and 2) serve as the basis for an assessment of the new staff member's knowledge of popular reading and the formulation of a reading plan. Having new staff initial names of the authors they have read serves two purposes: first, they can easily see how much they really have read and know something about, and second, we trainers can see where to start in setting up a reading plan to expand that knowledge. See the detailed discussion, "Designing a Reading Plan," in chapter 5. There are many ways to set up such a plan, depending on our schedules, our expectations, and the other reading assignments in which the new employees will be expected to join. For example, we might assign a book a month and then discuss it, or we might assign two or three books with a longer reading time, again followed by a scheduled discussion. We start new readers' advisors in a genre popular with patrons so they will be able to use their knowledge immediately as they interact with readers. At first, the trainer should assume responsibility for selecting the titles to be read in order to guarantee they are typical of the author's writing. Later, when staff are comfortable using reference and staff resources to choose typical titles, they take on that responsibility themselves.

Whether reading may be done on library time is another important point to consider and discuss with new staff. When hired, readers' advisory staff at the Downers Grove Public Library are informed they will be required to read and write about two books monthly. Although much of our reading is done on our own time—we hire staff who enjoy reading—we have always said that staff may read on the desk, as long as they look up and greet patrons as they enter the area and are caught up on their other desk responsibilities. This plan has worked well. Staff have always read reviews or work-related articles while staffing the public service desk, and we know from experience that a reader can become as engrossed in those as in a book. The key is that staff must acknowledge patrons in the area and must look "interruptible." We have all seen staff members absorbed in a review journal or with eyes riveted to a computer screen, so preoccupied that patrons must speak to gain their attention. If staff are attentive to the arrival of patrons in the area, their reading can be a plus for a readers' advisory service. Not only are they becoming familiar with books they can share with other readers but by reading they also remind patrons that we are readers, too, and that sometimes helps start a readers' advisory conversation.

The scheduled discussion is the second part of this exercise. It is not enough simply to read popular authors and titles; readers' advisors need to learn first what to look for as they read, then how to think about books, and, finally, how to talk about books with readers. Thus, the reading plan with its concomitant discussion prepares the way for later training activities. When we meet to talk about books, we do not structure our conversation like a formal book discussion, and we do not talk about what is good or bad about a book or author. Instead, we focus on questions such as those listed in figure 5.1, which emphasize what an author does best; thus, we help staff see the appeal even in those books they do not personally enjoy. These might seem like a lot of questions for new staff to try to consider, but these questions reflect the thinking that makes us better readers' advisors. A list of questions to consider helps new staff focus more easily on what they need to be aware of and makes their reading assignment more manageable, not to mention comprehensible. Needless to say, staff become more skilled at responding to this directed reading as they progress through their training, but these questions provide an initial framework and direction that focus their energy.

At this point, we also encourage staff to keep track of what they read, simply by recording authors and titles in a notebook. This is discussed in detail in chapter 4. Later, we encourage more formal and detailed methods of keeping notes on books, described in chapter 5, but simply listing titles and authors in order is the initial step. Staff will soon realize the almost magical properties of this technique in their increased ability to remember what they have read. It is tempting to forgo such a simple step, but comments by readers and readers' advisors over the past almost twenty years have reinforced the importance of this activity as a valuable tool. Keeping a list and reviewing it sustain and reinforce the pleasure many of us find in reading and underscore the importance of offering a service that recognizes and promotes such pleasure.

As was mentioned earlier, the two greatest fears new staff face are not being able to read enough and not remembering what they have read. Setting up a reading plan, with scheduled time to discuss the titles read, addresses the first issue and sets the stage for confronting the second. Remembering what we have read does seem to become easier when it is our job to remember, but keeping track of what we read helps us remember more as well. The key to remembering more of what we read, however, is to think about books in terms of their appeal rather than their plots. As trainers, we need to demonstrate that books are more than plots or subjects and that patrons are usually seeking a book with a particular feel rather than one on a specific subject.

In chapter 3, I presented the idea of appeal in depth and discussed its role in preparing for the readers' advisory interview in chapter 4. Almost twenty years after this book was originally written, I feel even more strongly that appeal plays the most important role both in reading enjoyment and preference in future selections. Readers' advisors have seen that thinking about a book in terms of its appeal, rather than a plot summary, helps us remember more. Sharing a book in terms of appeal not only reflects the way we naturally talk about books, adding those appeal-based adjectives to our descriptions, but also allows readers to make choices more readily. Staff need to learn to read for appeal and to use appeal to share books more effectively. Figures 3.1 through 3.4 list questions to think about when considering a book's appeal. Practice makes these thought processes more automatic, and readers' satisfaction with these appeal-based suggestions reinforces their importance.

Mastering appeal also allows us to look at books we have not read and glean the same kinds of useful information we gain from reading. At this point in their training, staff also learn how to scan book jackets and reviews to find clues to appeal as well as how to abstract similar information from readers' comments about books they have read. None of us will ever be able to read enough to meet the diverse and changing interests of all the readers we help. Staff must learn to gather information from a range of print and reader comments and use that information to expand their own knowledge. Practice with the techniques explored in figure 5.9, "Speed-Reading Books; or, How to Read a Novel in Ten Minutes," is vital at this point.

An understanding of appeal forms the basis for the way readers' advisors think about books. It also provides a format to use in talking about books. There is an art to the way readers' advisors talk about books, and we are more successful when we learn to formulate our comments in terms of appeal rather than plot summaries. Learning to talk about books requires practice, first with staff and then with patrons. New staff meet formally with their trainer to discuss reading assignments on a scheduled basis. Talking about books informally should also be an integral aspect of the department's routine, a natural activity, a part of the regular interaction in the workroom and at the desk. All talking about books helps; it makes us conscious of appeal, of what makes the book popular beyond its subject or genre. Talking informally among staff allows us to practice structuring our comments in terms of appeal, to discover and share phrases that are effective, to become more comfortable sharing books so that we will be at ease working with patrons. Talking among the staff also reinforces that this is a legitimate activity for readers' advisors to engage in, and it emphasizes the importance of sharing information. Successful readers' advisory requires a team effort. The more a department works as a team, sharing books and techniques, asking each other for help and information, the better readers' advisory service we provide, and the better public service staff we become. Christopher Morley's and Helene Hanff's books, referred to in chapter 4, as well as more recent titles on the pleasures of reading noted in chapter 1, emphasize the satisfaction gained from sharing books.

Talking about books with patrons was discussed in depth in chapter 4. From a training perspective, we need to underscore the idea that the readers' advisory interview is a conversation about books between staff and patrons, with questions and suggestions handed back and forth. We suggest books based on what patrons say they enjoy reading, and we encourage them to come back for more and to let us know whether they enjoyed the books or not. As talking about books with staff becomes part of their routine, new staff become more comfortable talking with patrons as well. We train them to conduct successful readers' advisory interviews, covered in depth in chapter 4.

Many of the special situations, also discussed in chapter 4, relate to this training stage. Talking over these problems and suggested techniques for solving them increases the comfort level for new staff. They learn that all of us experience these situations, and they gain skill and confidence in dealing with them. They begin to develop their own sensible strategies to deal with potentially difficult situations. We help them devise and practice nonjudgmental phrases to use in talking about authors or genres they do not personally enjoy. Role-playing may be a useful exercise at this stage to help new staff feel more comfortable and prepare for interactions with patrons.

We offer four tips to help make the readers' advisory interview more manageable. First, there is no perfect book. Our job in working with readers is not to find the one and only perfect book that will suit them that day;

we suggest a range of titles that might appeal to this reader. Second, we reinforce the distinction between suggesting and recommending. In a library situation, we suggest several books that might appeal, based on what the patron has said about reading taste and mood. Third, we emphasize that the point of this readers' advisory conversation is to get the patron to talk, and we try to give new staff lines to use as suggestions of ways to elicit information. We remind staff not to ask, "What do you like to read?" A request such as "Tell me about a book you have enjoyed" encourages readers to talk. Finally, we reinforce that readers' advisory reference is not just print and electronic resources; it may be other staff, consulting on questions and calling readers back with answers or suggestions; and it may also be the annotated book lists or bookmarks staff have created.

We also begin setting goals for readers' advisory interactions every time new staff are scheduled at the desk. For example, we encourage a new readers' advisor to set a goal of two readers' advisory interactions during each four-hour on-desk shift. When they consistently meet their goals, it is time to increase the interactions by one or two. Just as we keep tally of reference questions for library statistics, we should keep track of readers' advisory interactions, as discussed in chapter 6. Keeping statistics is important, if only for the personal satisfaction of seeing the growing number of readers who seek and receive assistance. Statistics can also provide a tangible record of goals set and met. And when each goal is comfortably met, it should be increased. Setting goals reminds us to approach and talk with patrons about books, even when we are busy at the desk. Then, just as we encourage staff to keep track of what they read, we have them keep a log of their readers' advisory interactions. They discuss these—problems and successes—with their trainer.

An introduction to readers' advisory reference sources constitutes the next training step. These resources were discussed in detail in chapter 2. Beginning readers' advisors, especially, should be reminded that familiarity with these tools is important in providing good service. Reference sources provide added memory and take us beyond the limited number of books we have personally read. It is useful to have a list of the library's readers' advisory reference sources, print and electronic, so new staff can methodically review each source, examining indexes, coverage, tone of articles, and ease of use. We assign sample questions at this point. Figure 7.4 lists examples of assigned questions. These should be designed to highlight the range of material contained in the most useful sources as well as to direct staff to the more obscure tools. In most cases, there is not one correct source but rather

Figure 7.4 ■ Readers' Advisory Assignment

1. I just discovered Arthur Upfield's Mystery series. I'd like a complete list of the books in reading order.
2. I'm traveling to Italy, and I'd like some books set there so I can get a feel for the place. Where can I find those?
3. I need a short book to read for a high school book report due tomorrow. Can you find me one I'll like?
4. I think I have read all of Elizabeth Peters's books. I heard she wrote under another name. Can you find out what it was and the books written under that name?
5. I like Jean Auel's books. Who else writes fiction set in prehistoric times?
6. I would like to read some books about Australia in the 1700s.
7. I need questions so I can lead a book discussion group on Guterson's *Snow Falling on Cedars*. I've never led a book discussion before—where should I start?
8. Years ago there was a series of Mysteries in which the detective is a dwarf. Who wrote them, and what is the detective's name?
9. I like Thrillers, you know—spies, intrigue. Can you suggest any funny titles?
10. What is the order of the Dragonlance books?
11. I want to start reading Edith Wharton. Which novel would you suggest I start with?
12. I have to read a Mystery for school, but I really only like Science Fiction. Are there any books I might like?
13. It's been a while since I've seen a book by Rosamunde Pilcher. Is she still writing? Does anyone else write like her?

several resources in which the answer can be found. In talking over the questions and answers, we trainers can make suggestions about the best sources and share strategies we find useful. Although it is important for new staff to work primarily with a specific trainer, at this point they benefit greatly from discussing these questions and sources with all staff who work the desk. Just as we share information about books we read, we share tips for handling readers' advisory questions and hints about special features found in these sources. We all have favorite sources, just as we have favorite authors; new staff benefit from all our suggestions and experiences. Remember, among the library's best resources may be book lists and bookmarks developed by staff in response to reader interests and requests. New staff should be familiar with these as well, since they are a resource that patrons can take with them and refer to later.

At the Downers Grove Public Library, we start working with reference sources and questions when new staff begin to sit at the desk with us. At this time they are expected to shadow us on reference and readers' advisory questions. This is a time for absorbing techniques, discovering sources, and, especially, for talking about how we handle questions and patrons. New staff learn best by observing and by discussing what they see as we answer questions on the desk and what they discover as they begin working through the sample questions. When they finish these questions, we discuss them, pointing out additional and sometimes better places to discover the information they have sought. Once staff are assigned to the desk alone, they continue to keep track of questions asked and sources consulted so these can be discussed at weekly meetings with their trainer.

Writing about books is the last of the basic training skills. Writing gives precision to our comments about a book and its appeal. It helps clear up any muddiness we experience when talking about books, and it forces us to think specifically in terms of appeal and similar authors readers might enjoy. In addition to writing the monthly annotations, within their first year new staff prepare an unannotated bookmark and begin work on an annotated book list. Details of both these projects were discussed in chapter 6.

After all this, another crucial question arises: how do we keep new staff from feeling overwhelmed? When they see all there is to learn and recognize all they do not know, the first reaction of many beginning readers' advisors is panic and fear that they can never do this job. We all have days when we feel there is no hope, that we can never read enough, never remember what we have read, never figure out why an author appeals to readers, and never be able to talk comfortably with patrons. It helps to recognize that we cannot read everything—that reading everything is not even our goal. What we are doing is reading and learning about key authors and titles so we develop a frame of reference that allows us to interact successfully with readers. One way to counteract this feeling of inadequacy is to encourage staff to regularly take stock of what they have done. Check off authors on the Popular Fiction List and Popular Nonfiction List; look back over their reading record; realize that they can increase their goal for readers' advisory interviews; work on bookmarks and book lists; and review all they have learned from studying a genre. All this helps readers' advisors—beginning and experienced—to see how far they have come.

Ongoing Training for Readers' Advisors

While basic readers' advisory training provides tools and techniques to help staff become familiar with resources and comfortable working with patrons, ongoing training is designed to stimulate and motivate experienced staff, to keep them fresh and intellectually challenged in their work. Useful activities, summarized in figure 7.5, help meet this goal.

Just as a reading plan provides the basis for initial training, it can also stimulate more experienced readers' advisors. We use the same basic techniques discussed in chapter 5, selecting a popular genre with which the staff member is less familiar or may not enjoy, then reading and discussing specific titles to discover more about an author or genre's appeal. This is an activity that can be done with two or more staff, making it a mini genre study, or with a staff member and another reader. It is even possible to do this on one's own, but we feel we need the stimulation of discussing a book's appeal to gain the greatest benefit. We also encourage staff to sign up for a computer mailing list devoted to this genre, read the postings for at least two months, and share new insights into the genre with reading partners and other staff. In any case, talking about what we are reading or what we

Figure 7.5 ■ Ongoing Training Activities for Experienced Readers' Advisors

1. Design a personal reading plan.
2. Read in unfamiliar fiction genres and nonfiction topics.
3. Subscribe to a genre mailing list for two months, reading postings and sharing insights into the genre with other staff.
4. Read authors on the best-sellers lists.
5. Share discoveries with staff and patrons.
6. Practice talking about books—every day.
7. Collect and share Sure Bets.
8. Keep statistics of readers' advisory interviews, and set personal goals to increase interactions.
9. Create annotated book lists.
10. Brainstorm readalike bookmarks for popular authors.
11. Create readers' advisory tools such as popular fiction and nonfiction lists.
12. Undertake a genre study.

have learned about specific authors and titles from other sources must be part of the daily routine of all in an active and successful readers' advisory department.

Staff should also be encouraged to read authors on the best-sellers list. We used to require staff to read all titles on the best-sellers list. Now we simply require familiarity with the authors. Since most authors on these lists have appeared previously, it is necessary to read only new authors or books by best-selling authors if they pursue new directions. Still, staff need to be aware of best-selling authors, because many patrons come to the library looking for their books. We need to know something about them and, more important, other authors to suggest when the best sellers are checked out and unavailable. If they make a point of discovering these similar authors, knowledgeable staff, interested in helping readers find other titles to tide them over until their turn for a best seller, can set up readers' advisory relationships that encourage readers to return for more suggestions later.

Identifying Sure Bets, discussed in chapter 5 (see also appendix 3), is another valuable exercise for experienced staff. Such a list is especially useful for new staff in filling displays and talking with readers. Like the authors on the Popular Fiction List and Popular Nonfiction List, these are authors and titles that are popular with the readers in your library and appeal to a wide range of readers. New staff might use this list to fill displays. They might also read or "speed-read" unfamiliar titles and practice describing them to staff to make them more comfortable with readers, knowing they can talk about some very popular titles easily.

Experienced readers' advisors should also set personal goals to increase their number of readers' advisory interactions when they are on the desk. Although more readers approach the desk and request book suggestions in libraries with established readers' advisory services, we still need to encourage staff to check with readers in the book stacks and offer assistance. Setting goals reminds us to offer book suggestions and to talk with patrons in the stacks to ensure that all library users are finding the information they seek in both fiction and nonfiction collections.

Creating annotated book lists affords staff an opportunity to explore a topic in depth and produce a resource valuable to fellow staff members and patrons. We encourage staff to work on one every year, following the process outlined in chapter 6. Occasionally, we work as a team to produce book lists on topics or in genres no single staff member is interested in or willing to tackle on his or her own or to compile results of a genre study. Staff still benefit from the discussions to select titles, from their own reading and annotation writing, and from the finished book list, which becomes a valuable readers' advisory reference source. Staff can also cooperate to brainstorm readalike bookmarks for some of our most popular authors, who will never be able to write enough to satisfy their many fans. This process was discussed in detail in chapter 5.

Devising our own readers' advisory resources also offers useful training opportunities. If your library does not have popular fiction and nonfiction lists, you should consider taking ours apart and creating your own. (See appendixes 1 and 2.) This activity, described in chapter 2, provides an excellent training exercise for staff, as does updating and revising an already existing list. In constructing popular fiction and nonfiction lists, we must consider which authors truly are the most popular in our library and be able to justify our decisions. In fact, updating our fiction list has become an annual departmental training activity. In preparation, we review the current version of the list, considering which authors are still popular and which have become less so. We make a special effort to research authors who have become more popular in the past year and may now belong on the list. Reviewing best-sellers lists, tracking authors included in our Rental Books collection (always among the most popular), and checking reserve queues prepare us for the discussion—sometimes almost a battle—to see which authors are to remain on the list. Afterward, we have an up-to-date list that truly reflects the most popular authors our patrons read, and the process itself hones our skills in gathering information about our patrons' reading tastes.

Designing library-specific readers' advisory reference sources is a particularly valuable training exercise. Experienced readers' advisors can also find areas in which reference sources fall short and for which a specialized tool—a database or even a book list—can make the collection more accessible. For example, when we needed a reliable, up-to-date resource that identified Fantasy books in series, a staff member set up a database with this information, and our high school aides now update it. The listing—by title, series title, and author—is printed out regularly, and readers, especially a growing group of high school fans, consult it frequently.

Participation in a genre study constitutes the last, as well as the most advanced and time-consuming, of the ongoing training activities. As discussed in chapter 5, genre studies provide a way to learn about popular authors and the genres in which they write. To begin, we choose a high-demand genre, one both patrons and staff enjoy. We read in the genre and about the genre; then we discuss our discoveries at regularly scheduled meetings. We formulate a list of genre characteristics early on and refine it as we read. During the process, we identify benchmark authors and discover what it is that characterizes their work. Then we compare other authors to these benchmarks and create appeal-based subgenres with unique characteristics and a list of authors who seem to fit together within them.

All of this takes time—to read, react, discuss—and considerable effort. It requires commitment and dedication. Could the benefits possibly justify the work involved? One important reason to study genres is that many, if not most, of our library fiction readers are genre readers, and this in-depth study has immediate benefits both in our expanded knowledge of a particular genre and in our increased ability to recognize patterns and similar authors in all fiction we read. By identifying the appeal of the genre and discovering key authors within subgenres, we can also identify similar authors and become a valuable resource to readers.

Although a genre study requires an enormous amount of reading, reacting, and discussing, it also provides a large measure of intellectual satisfaction and enjoyment. Its collaborative and participatory nature involves sharing books and fosters the pleasure inherent in this activity. Studying a genre requires us to read and think about authors in terms of their appeal. No matter what genre we are studying, these benefits carry over into all our other reading and conversations with patrons. Information in reference books about an author or genre does not provide answers to questions about the nature of their appeal. We discover those answers when we take what we have read and combine it with what we have gained from our conversations with staff and other readers. We begin making important and useful connections; it is a very satisfying experience. When we are focusing on a genre, we begin to have more interesting conversations with readers as well. Our readers' advisory interview skills grow because we are asking readers questions that reflect what we want to discover about a genre. We become more aware of readers, books, and appeal elements. As we read a particular genre, we provide better readers' advisory suggestions for the fans of that genre, but we also do better readers' advisory in general because we are more aware of readers and the appeal elements they enjoy.

Genre study generates a certain excitement among the participants. In addition to the heightened awareness when we read and talk with patrons, there is the excitement of the chase, of following clues, and then of pulling all the information together. We find ourselves writing down bits from reviews or reference books—lines that characterize an author—and then tracking them down to see if they are correct and what they mean in terms of the pattern we have described for the genre.

Genre studies are also great confidence builders. As we read and explore a genre, we gain assurance from our growing knowledge and become more comfortable sharing what we have learned with patrons and soliciting their opinions. These conversations pique our curiosity so that we read further and discuss more comfortably. Genre studies are a jumping-off point for more experienced readers' advisors, a springboard from which more extensive work with readers and books is launched.

In addition, having studied one genre, we have a framework to use as we approach other, unfamiliar genres. Even though every genre study unfolds differently, we gain a sense of where to start and how to progress and comfortably apply our general knowledge of the process to this new situation with satisfying results.

Finally, genre study is an activity to be enjoyed. The pleasure in unraveling puzzles is one of the elements of reference and readers' advisory that has attracted many of us, and genre study is one of the best ways to experience this. Reading a genre to discover its pattern, reading books within genres to understand why they appeal to readers, and seeking other books and authors with the same appeal are stimulating exercises that provide both intellectual challenge and enjoyment. Although our experience with genre studies has been exclusively with fiction, we believe that these same techniques could be followed by readers interested in embarking on genre studies in nonfiction.

Devoting a chapter of this book to training goals and techniques confirms the necessity of a definite commitment from both library administration and staff to providing this service. Obviously, to provide even the most rudimentary service, readers' advisors must make a commitment of time and effort. We need preparation time to master the techniques of the readers' advisory interview, to learn to talk about books with readers, to gain familiarity with the broad range of fiction and nonfiction popular with leisure readers, and to discover and create tools to help readers' advisors assist patrons. A willingness to read—and to read widely—must be a prerequisite for all readers' advisory staff. However, even a staff composed of readers must make an additional commitment to expand the scope of their reading in order to gain the broadest background.

Administratively, it is important to acknowledge this commitment to a service that requires extensive preparation by providing library time, whenever possible, for reading and for creating tools to use with patrons and staff. Scheduled work time away from the service desk is a necessity. Readers' advisors need time to concentrate on developing the complex skills that are necessary to provide a comprehensive readers' advisory service.

In a library committed to providing readers' advisory, staff also need time and opportunity to offer the service to patrons. If the reference or circulation staff—or any public service staff who also provide other library services—provide readers' advisory, there is always the danger that readers' advisory, because it often lacks the immediacy of reference, circulation, or other transactions, will receive short shrift. Care must be taken to avoid this possibility and to acknowledge and promote the readers' advisory service. In a library that does commit itself to readers' advisory service, readers begin to see librarians as a reading resource, and readers' advisors become a very satisfying link in the chain connecting books and readers.

Since this chapter addresses the training of staff who work with leisure readers, I want to conclude by quoting not from a management text but from a work of fiction. In *No Witnesses*, by Ridley Pearson, his series detective, Lou Boldt, is teaching a police course in investigative techniques. At the end of the class, Boldt realizes,

> There comes a time when all the information must be set aside; there comes a time when passion and instinct take over. It's the stuff that can't be taught; but it can be learned.[2]

That encapsulates what I feel about training readers' advisors. We can provide reference tools and training exercises and more, but we cannot force staff to learn how to make connections between readers and books. With the right inspiration and a good grounding in basic techniques, however, the art of readers' advisory can be learned. We, as supervisors and trainers, are facilitators in this process; whatever we do and however we do it, we are forging links in the chains of readers who skillfully share their pleasure in reading.

Notes

1. Catherine Sheldrick Ross, "New Research in Fiction Reading" (lecture, Dominican University, River Forest, Ill., May 21, 2004).
2. Ridley Pearson, *No Witnesses* (New York: Hyperion, 1994), 1–2.

1

Popular Fiction List

Action/Adventure

Features a hero on a mission, overcoming danger and obstacles to reach goal

> Dale Brown
> Tom Clancy
> Clive Cussler
> W. E. B. Griffin
> Jack Higgins
> Wilbur Smith

Crime/Caper

Told from the point of view of the flawed, often amoral protagonists; complicated plots; runs the gamut from noir to more comedic

> Lawrence Block
> James Ellroy
> Carl Hiaasen
> Elmore Leonard
> Lawrence Shames
> Donald Westlake

Fantasy

Portrays magic in a world that could never exist

> Terry Brooks
> Jim Butcher

> Charles de Lint
> David Eddings
> Raymond E. Feist
> Neil Gaiman
> Terry Goodkind
> Robert Jordan
> Mercedes Lackey
> George R. R. Martin
> L. E. Modessitt Jr.
> Terry Pratchett

Gentle Reads

Feel-good books with no sex, violence, or strong language

> Jennifer Chiaverini
> Richard Paul Evans
> Philip Gulley
> Jan Karon
> Joan Medlicott
> Robin Pilcher
> Jeanne Ray
> Anne B. Ross
> Nicholas Sparks
> Adriana Trigiani
> Marcia Willett

Historical

Set in the past with a serious respect for historical accuracy and detail

Jean Auel

Tracy Chevalier

Donald Coldsmith

Bernard Cornwell

Diana Gabaldon

W. Michael Gear and Kathleen O'Neal

Margaret George

John Jakes

Sharon Kay Penman

Anne Perry

Edward Rutherfurd

Jeff Shaara

Horror

Produces fear in readers, contains a monster of some type, and super-natural elements figure prominently

Clive Barker

Poppy Z. Brite

Laurell K. Hamilton

Stephen King

Dean R. Koontz

Anne Rice

Literary Fiction

Critically acclaimed, often award-winning, character-centered, provoca-tive, elegantly written works

Margaret Atwood

Louise Erdrich

Alice Hoffman

John Irving

Barbara Kingsolver

Toni Morrison

Chuck Palahniuk

Arturo Pérez-Reverte

Richard Russo

Jane Smiley

Amy Tan

Anne Tyler

Mysteries

Puzzles, filled with clues, that readers and detectives (police, private, amateur) attempt to solve to discover whodunit

Nevada Barr

M. C. Beaton

Lilian Jackson Braun

Patricia D. Cornwell

Janet Evanovich

Sue Grafton

P. D. James

Jonathan Kellerman

Alexander McCall Smith

Sara Paretsky

Robert B. Parker

Elizabeth Peters

Romance

Focuses on the development and satisfactory resolution of the love relationship

Mary Balogh

Jo Beverley

Millie Criswell

Jennifer Crusie

Kathleen Eagle

Julie Garwood

Rachel Gibson

Jayne Ann Krentz/
Amanda Quick/Jayne Castle

Debbie Macomber

Susan Elizabeth Phillips

Mary Jo Putney

Nora Roberts/J. D. Robb

Romantic Suspense

Combines hard-edged Suspense with sensual Romance

Sandra Brown

Catherine Coulter

Tami Hoag

Linda Howard

Iris Johansen

Elizabeth Lowell

Science Fiction

Speculative fiction, often set in the future, that explores moral, social, intellectual, philosophical, and ethical questions, against a setting outside of everyday reality

Catherine Asaro

Greg Bear

Ben Bova

Lois McMaster Bujold

Orson Scott Card

Brian Herbert

Anne McCaffrey

Jack McDevitt

Elizabeth Moon

Michael D. Resnick

David Weber

Connie Willis

Suspense

Fast-paced stories in which tension builds, as protagonists are placed in perilous situations

Lee Child

Mary Higgins Clark

Harlan Coben

Michael Connelly

Jeffery Deaver

Greg Iles

James Patterson

Thomas Perry

John Sandford

Psychological Suspense

Thomas Cook

Ruth Rendell/Barbara Vine

Minette Walters

Thrillers

Gripping, plot-centered stories, set in the detailed framework of a particular profession that places heroes or heroines in dangerous situations from which they must extricate themselves

David Baldacci

Dan Brown

Robin Cook

Michael Crichton

Tess Gerritsen

James Grippando

John Grisham

Tim R. LaHaye and
Jerry B. Jenkins

Steve Martini

Douglas J. Preston and
Lincoln Child

Lisa Scottoline

Stuart Woods

Women's Lives and Relationships

Explores the reaches of women's lives, personally and professionally, and the distinctive way women deal with these concerns

Elizabeth Berg

Maeve Binchy

Meg Cabot

Barbara Delinsky

Katie Fforde

Kristin Hannah

Sophie Kinsella

Jodi Picoult

Anita Shreve

Danielle Steel

Joanna Trollope

Jennifer Weiner

Appendix

2

Popular Nonfiction List

Adventure/Survival/ Exploration/Disaster

True tales of human beings prevailing against the elements, the unknown, or both

Chris Bonnington
Barry Clifford
Tony Horwitz
Sebastian Junger
Jon Krakauer
Edward E. Leslie
Piers Paul Read
David Roberts
Tim Severin
Spike Walker

Animals/Nature/Natural History

Stories of the animal kingdom/natural world and its interactions with human beings

Diane Ackerman
David Attenborough
Gretel Ehrlich
Jane Goodall
Sue Hubbell
Jeffrey Moussaieff Masson

Peter Matthiessen
Farley Mowat
Michael Pollan
David Quammen

Contemporary Issues

Politics, social questions, and "hot topics" in civic life

Noam Chomsky
Barbara Ehrenreich
Thomas L. Friedman
Tracy Kidder
Michael Moore
Ishmael Reed
Eric Schlosser
Hunter S. Thompson
George F. Will
Bob Woodward

Crime and Criminals

True crime and tales of crimes and criminals, past and present

Jeff Benedict
Vincent Bugliosi
Alan Dershowitz
Robert Graysmith

Jay Robert Nash

Jack Olsen

Nicholas Pileggi

Ann Rule

Harold Schechter

Joseph Wambaugh

History and Microhistory

Examinations ranging from the history of the world to the intricacies of the smallest aspects of history and events

Thomas Cahill

Kenneth C. Davis

Antonia Fraser

Doris Kearns Goodwin

John Keegan

Mark Kurlansky

Erik Larson

David G. McCullough

Richard Rhodes

Simon Winchester

Humor

Includes the writings of contemporary humorists, from journalists to social and political commentators to comedians

Dave Barry

Roy Blount Jr.

George Carlin

Andrei Codrescu

Bill Cosby

Ian Frazier

Garrison Keillor

P. J. O'Rourke

David Sedaris

Gary Trudeau

Memoirs and Biography

Stories from the lives of the famous and not so famous, including intimate first-person accounts and sweeping studies

Maya Angelou

Rick Bragg

Jill Ker Conway

Annie Dillard

Joseph J. Ellis

Homer Hickam

Mary Karr

Kitty Kelley

Ross King

Garry Wills

Popular Culture/Sociology/ Lifestyles/Entertainment

Highlights the new and the popular; reflections on personalities as well as on the way we live

Art Bell

Roger Ebert

Anne Edwards

Marc Eliot

John Gray

Bob Greene

Michael Gross

Robert D. Putnam

Studs Terkel

Calvin Trillin

Popular Science

Scientific expertise, theories, and technology made accessible to the common reader

- James Burke
- Martin Gardner
- James Gleick
- Stephen Hawking
- John McPhee
- Richard Preston
- Oliver W. Sacks
- Dava Sobel
- James Trefil
- Carl Zimmer

Self-Help/Inspirational/Sociology

Wide-ranging advice on how to "live a good life"

- Richard Carlson
- Deepak Chopra
- Stephen R. Covey
- James Dobson
- Tenzin Gyatso, the Dalai Lama
- Harold Kushner
- Max Lucado
- Thomas Moore
- Kathleen Norris
- Robert Schuller

Sports

Captures the spirit of specific sports and those who participate in them

- Roger Angell
- Bob Costas
- Frank Deford
- John Feinstein
- David Halberstam
- Roger Kahn
- Rick Reilly
- Glenn Stout
- Rick Telander
- Richard Whittingham

Travelogues

Stories for armchair and intrepid travelers alike

- Bill Bryson
- Tim Cahill
- William Least Heat-Moon
- Peter Jenkins
- Frances Mayes
- Peter Mayle
- Jan Morris
- Eric Newby
- Jonathan Raban
- Paul Theroux

Appendix

3   Sure Bets

"Sure Bets are those titles that appeal consistently to a wide range of readers, from fans of the particular genre to others beyond."[1]

Fiction

A perennial favorite is *Vertical Run*, by Joseph Garber.[2] When a midlevel executive arrives at work one morning, he finds his boss in his office, waiting to kill him. And his day goes downhill from there. Neither the protagonist nor the reader understands until much later why trained assassins attack the hero at every step. Luckily he was a Green Beret in Vietnam, so his training helps him escape innumerable traps—and set some of his own. This action-filled and somewhat violent tale moves at a breakneck pace, and its mix of Adventure, Intrigue, and Mystery make it a good suggestion for a wide range of readers, men and women alike.

Thomas Perry's Jane Whitefield novels are a good example of a series that appeals equally to men and women. Jane runs her own witness protection service, producing new identities for people in trouble, but something always goes awry, putting Jane and her clients in deadly danger. These are suspenseful, atmospheric, and action filled, featuring a strong and very appealing protagonist. Her thoughtful approach in the midst of tense and often violent situations sets these complex Thrillers apart. *Vanishing Act* is the first.[3]

Harlan Coben wrote an interesting series of Mysteries featuring a sports agent, but when he turned to Suspense and *Tell No One*, he also hit the best-seller's list.[4] A mysterious Internet message leads Dr. David Beck to believe that his wife, killed eight years earlier, might still be alive, but his desperate efforts to verify this may lead to his own death. Edge-of-the-chair suspense and a story line filled with satisfying twists will keep almost any reader up burning the midnight oil.

Adriana Trigiani captured the down-home feel of the Blue Ridge Mountains with her Big Stone Gap trilogy, but *Lucia, Lucia* takes us to a strict Italian family and community in Greenwich Village, just after World War II.[5] Times are changing, and Lucia, who works in the custom department at B. Altman, wants more than marriage and family. Despite the cosmopolitan setting, readers will find the same heartfelt emotions in this touching, often humorous story.

Celaya, the only daughter with six older brothers, is the storyteller and the repository of family stories in the exuberant *Caramelo*, by Sandra Cisneros.[6]

Interweaving her own more flamboyant version of events with the actual, Celaya tells her family's story, a tale filled with humor and pathos, as intricately woven and beautiful as her grandmother's scarf, the caramelo of the title. This character-centered tale offers a heartfelt and often whimsical look at the history of a Mexican American family from the Mexican Revolution to the Vietnam War.

Jeanne Ray tells comfortable, charming stories, filled with humor and good will. Her unpretentious heroines are older woman, often caught between their grown children and their own parents, and the problems they face are generally domestic, relating to hearth and home rather than the greater world. Her first, *Julie and Romeo*, places Shakespeare's tale in contemporary Boston, with the lovers in their sixties, but the dissention between their rival florist families keeps them apart.[7]

Nonfiction

Because his writing ranges through a number of topics—travel, language, humor—Bill Bryson makes a good suggestion for many readers. *In a Sunburned Country* has something for almost everyone—humor, insight into Australia and its people, and a thoughtful yet unpretentious approach to his subject, not to mention an accounting of the incredible number of poisonous species supported there.[8]

Fans of both History and True Crime will find much to appreciate in Erik Larson's *The Devil in the White City*, the story of the building of the Columbian Exposition in Chicago in the 1890s and the serial murderer who stalked the city and the fair.[9] The vivid descriptions—despite the lack of pictures—of the physical preparations for the fair, as well as the personalities and politics involved, are as intriguing as the glimpse into the life and murderous acts of H. H. Holmes, the man who preyed on young women attracted by the fair, and both tales are supported by extensive historical research.

Often, older titles, forgotten in the stacks, remind readers of the books they have always meant to read. Maya Angelou's evocative, heartfelt autobiography, beginning with *I Know Why the Caged Bird Sings*, appeals to her fans as well as to others who appreciate fine writing and tales of triumph over adversity.[10] This gritty and bittersweet memoir of her early years speaks of lessons learned through hardship and struggle, and Angelou's elegant language creates a touching and dramatic portrait of a young woman.

Master of the Microhistory Mark Kurlansky has created gripping tales on limited topics in *Salt* and *Cod* and, most recently, *1968*, an entertaining and enlightening examination of a pivotal year in U.S. and world history.[11] For those who lived through it and those who have only heard of what happened, Kurlansky provides a provocative, detailed account of the people and events and their impact during that crucial year and beyond.

Positively Fifth Street, by poet and novelist James McManus, makes an unexpected reading treat.[12] Sent to Las Vegas to write about the annual world series of poker, he becomes a participant rather than an observer, and his engrossing and colorful narrative provides fascinating details of game and players alike, not to mention both the fantasy world and seamy underside of Las Vegas and casino life.

Humor may be the hardest nonfiction genre to categorize, as it appears in so many guises and appeals in different ways to readers. Bailey White's collections of her National Public Radio essays make a good suggestion for readers, displays, and booktalks. With its vivid and outrageous descriptions of rural southern life, *Mama Makes Up Her Mind: And Other Dangers of Southern Living* works well for readers of fiction and nonfiction.[13] The piece on roadkill is a guaranteed laugh.

Notes

1. Joyce G. Saricks, *Readers' Advisory Guide to Genre Fiction* (Chicago: American Library Assn., 2001), 8.
2. Joseph Garber, *Vertical Run* (New York: Bantam, 1995).
3. Thomas Perry, *Vanishing Act* (New York: Random, 1995).
4. Harlan Coben, *Tell No One* (New York: Delacorte, 2001).
5. Adriana Trigiani, *Lucia, Lucia* (New York: Random, 2003).
6. Sandra Cisneros, *Caramelo; or, Puro Cuento* (New York: Knopf, 2002).
7. Jeanne Ray, *Julie and Romeo* (New York: Harmony, 2000).
8. Bill Bryson, *In a Sunburned Country* (New York: Broadway, 2000).
9. Erik Larson, *The Devil in the White City: Murder, Magic, and Madness at the Fair That Changed America* (New York: Crown, 2003).
10. Maya Angelou, *I Know Why the Caged Bird Sings* (New York: Random, 1970).
11. Mark Kurlansky, *Salt: A World History* (New York: Walker, 2002); *Cod: A Biography of the Fish That Changed the World* (New York: Walker, 1997); and *1968: The Year That Rocked the World* (New York: Ballantine, 2004).
12. James McManus, *Positively Fifth Street* (New York: Farrar, Strauss & Giroux, 2003).
13. Bailey White, *Mama Makes Up Her Mind: And Other Dangers of Southern Living* (Reading, Mass.: Addison-Wesley, 1993).

4

A NoveList Author Readalike

DONALD GOINES
by David Wright
Genre: Noir Fiction; Thriller

For over 30 years, Donald Goines has been hailed as the Godfather of African-American Pulp Fiction, selling over 10 million copies of his raw subversive Thrillers in which desperate hustlers live and die by their wits in the urban jungle. Today he is more popular than ever with an eclectic mix of readers introduced to him via hip-hop culture, college literature courses, prison literacy programs and word of mouth. Goines books are fast-paced, with lots of colloquial dialogue and free-wheeling action. The tension never lets up, and graphic violence is omnipresent, as well as a good deal of sex, profanity and drug use. For Goines, Crime is not a riddle that can be solved, and the books are not Mysteries, having more in common with Noir Fiction and Suspense.

Goines lived and died what he wrote. A Detroit pimp, burglar, hustler and heroin addict, he began writing during one of the seven prison sentences he served in his short life. When a fellow inmate introduced him to the stark street writings of Robert "Iceberg Slim" Beck, Goines abandoned his unsuccessful attempts at the Western genre and wrote *Whoreson*, a loosely autobiographical novel about a prostitute's child raised up in the flesh trade, and *Dopefiend*, a sordid chronicle of the descent of two black middle-class girls into the nightmarish world of addiction. Largely ignored by the literary mainstream, Goines quickly became a bestselling author in the underground African-American market, producing 16 novels in 4 years, a feverish pace fueled in part by the demands of his costly drug habit. In 1974, unknown assailants broke into his apartment and murdered Goines and his wife;

David Wright is a librarian and readers' advisor with the Seattle Public Library Fiction Department. He is co-chair of the Public Library Association's Readers' Advisory Committee, a member of the Readers' Advisors of Puget Sound, and reviews fiction for *Booklist* and *Library Journal*.

NoveList/EBSCO Publishing © 2003

Goines was sitting at his typewriter working on *Kenyatta's Last Hit* when the bullets found their mark.

Goines's own story is central to his appeal for many readers, lending authenticity to the street life he describes. Whether they share his background, or are taking a vicarious walk on the wild side, readers know that Goines wrote from first-hand experience, presenting reality as he saw it, free from high-handed moralizing and saccharine sentimentality. The lack of positive role models and uplifting messages, together with the profanity, misogyny and ruthless violence found in these books have made them the subject of controversy, which has in turn fueled their success with independent readers demanding unvarnished truth. For this reason, many readers of Goines also appreciate Noir, Hardboiled, and True Crime writing.

While most of Goines's books are stand-alone titles, they share a common villain: the Ghetto. Goines's pimps and hustlers are denizens of an inner-city Hell where the common currency is flesh, needles, and bullets. In this criminal economy, the only way to rise above the ranks of nameless prey is to become a predator. Yet the skilled players are themselves played by societal forces beyond their control, paying the price of success with their souls and lives. Late in his career, Goines wrote a series of five books featuring his only real hero, Kenyatta, a well-armed black militant who answers the ghetto in the only language it can understand, laying waste to black drug dealers and white racist cops alike. It was the closest Goines ever came to a solution.

Readers new to Goines should start with his earliest and purest books, *Whoreson* and *Dopefiend*, although those looking for a hero would be better advised to try his Kenyatta series, beginning with Crime Partners. Here are some other writers who share Goines's sharp ear for the language of the street, feel for gut-wrenching action, and commitment to confronting America at its worst.

Read-alikes

Robert Beck came to be known as Iceberg Slim during the three decades he spent hustling on Chicago's South Side. Upon retirement, he parlayed this experience into the cult classic *Pimp: The Story of My Life*. In addition to serving as a model for Goines, this unflinching account of ghetto survival rendered in tough, ebullient speech gave rise to a series of dialog-driven, nasty thrillers in which menacing predators and dazzling con artists negotiate the urban jungle with lethal skill. Goines and Slim are both published by Holloway House, home to several authors writing in a similar vein. http://hollowayhousebooks.com/.

Few writers depict the harsh realities of urban decay and pandemic racism so convincingly as Chester Himes. From the scathing anger and despair of his social novels (*The End of a Primitive*, *If He Hollers Let Him Go*) to the manic, headlong action of *Run Man Run* or his Harlem Mysteries with Coffin Ed Johnson and Grave Digger Jones, Himes presents the reader with an unbalanced world seething with racial tension and paranoia. Himes's prison experiences are revealed with shocking candor in *Yesterday Will Make You Cry*. The vividly depicted violence and stark brutality found in some of these books should not pose a problem for fans of Goines.

Clarence Cooper Jr.'s *The Scene* anticipated Slim and Goines in its searing portrayal of Rudy Black, a ruthless pimp and pusher caught in the grip of "The Man" and the needle. The book's painful realism was hard won. Cooper, a boyhood friend of Malcolm X, was a heroin addict who published most of his daring novels of street life and drug abuse from behind bars before dying in obscure poverty. Cooper and many other all-but-forgotten authors of African American pulp fiction were recently revived in W. W. Norton's Old School Books imprint, a series that will reward Goines readers with a host of powerful writers who told it like it was, and still is. http://www.wwnorton.com/osb.

In his gritty thrillers *Stray Dogs, Everybody Smokes in Hell, The Drift*, and *Love Is a Racket*, John Ridley updates African-American noir fiction to the greed-driven chaos of the contemporary West. Like Goines's works, these deeply ironic and insightful tragicomedies focus on a succession of underdogs struggling to come out on top, in a savage world bent on pushing them under. For all their corrosive anger, Ridley's brutal and swift-moving stories are often desperately funny, a trait he shares with other neo-noir writers such as Elmore Leonard and Carl Hiaasen.

Readers who revel in the relentless action and unabashed funkiness of larger-than-life blaxploitation epics such as *Superfly* and *Shaft* will get a real kick out of Gary Phillips. From his raunchy, drug-infused roller coaster rides *The Jook* and *The Perpetrators* to the racially-charged Ivan Monk series and the flashy B-Movie escapades of Las Vegas mob courier Martha Chainey, Phillips's down-and-dirty thrillers leaven their social critique with ample helpings of sex, swift and satisfying violence, and anti-heroes who brim with badass attitude.

BIBLIOGRAPHY

Selected Historical Sources

Carrier, Esther Jane. *Fiction in Public Libraries, 1876–1900.* Lanham, Md.: Scarecrow, 1965.

———. *Fiction in Public Libraries, 1900–1950.* Littleton, Colo.: Libraries Unlimited, 1985.

Chancellor, John, Miriam D. Tompkins, and Hazel I. Medway. *Helping the Reader toward Self-Education.* Chicago: American Library Assn., 1938.

Doud, Margarey. *The Readers' Advisory Service of the St. Louis Public Library.* St. Louis, Mo.: St. Louis Public Library, 1929.

Flexner, Jennie M., and Byron C. Hopkins. *Readers' Advisers at Work: A Survey of Development in the New York Public Library.* New York: American Assn. for Adult Education, 1941.

Flexner, Jennie M., and Sigrid A. Edge. *A Readers' Advisory Service.* New York: American Assn. for Adult Education, 1934.

Foster, Jeannette Howard. "An Approach to Fiction through the Characteristics of Its Readers." *Library Quarterly* 6 (April 1936): 124–74.

Lee, Robert Ellis. *Continuing Education for Adults through the American Public Library, 1833–1964.* Chicago: American Library Assn., 1966.

Lyman, Helen Huguenot. *Readers' Guidance Service in a Small Public Library.* Chicago: American Library Assn., 1962.

Regan, Lee. "Status of Readers' Advisory Service." *RQ* 12 (spring 1973): 227–33.

Shortt, May. "Advisers Anonymous, Arise!" *Ontario Library Review* 59 (May 1965): 81–83.

Selected Contemporary Sources

Baker, Sharon L., and Karen L. Wallace. *The Responsive Public Library: How to Develop and Market a Winning Collection.* 2nd ed. Englewood, Colo.: Libraries Unlimited, 2002.

Balcom, Ted, ed. *Serving Readers*. Fort Atkinson, Wis.: Highsmith, 1997.

Burgin, Robert, ed. *Nonfiction Readers' Advisory*. Westport, Conn.: Libraries Unlimited, 2004.

Fineman, Marcia. *Talking about Books: A Step-by-Step Guide for Participating in a Book Discussion Group*. Rockville, Md.: Talking about Books, 1997.

Jacobson, Rachel W. *The Reading Group Handbook: Everything You Need to Know to Start Your Own Book Club*. Rev. and exp. ed. New York: Hyperion, 1998.

Katz, Bill, ed. *Readers, Reading, and Librarians*. New York: Haworth, 2001.

Langemack, Chapple. *The Booktalker's Bible: How to Talk about the Books You Love to Any Audience*. Westport, Conn.: Libraries Unlimited, 2003.

Moyer, Jessica. "Adult Fiction Reading: A Literature Review of Readers' Advisory Services, Adult Fiction Librarianship, and Fiction Readers." *RUSQ* 44 (spring 2005): 38–47.

Pearlman, Mickey. *What to Read: The Essential Guide for Reading Group Members and Other Book Lovers*. Rev. and updated ed. New York: HarperPerennial, 1999.

Ross, Catherine Sheldrick, Kirsti Nilsen, and Patricia Dewdney. *Conducting the Reference Interview: A How-to-Do-It Manual for Librarians*. New York: Neal-Schuman, 2002.

Shearer, Kenneth D., ed. *Guiding the Reader to the Next Book*. New York: Neal-Schuman, 1996.

Shearer, Kenneth D., and Robert Burgin, eds. *The Readers' Advisor's Companion*. Englewood, Colo.: Libraries Unlimited, 2001.

Smith, Duncan, and Suzanne Mahmoodi. *Talking with Readers: A Workbook for Readers' Advisory*. Ipswich, Mass.: EBSCO, 2000.

Underhill, Paco. *Why We Buy: The Science of Shopping*. New York: Simon & Schuster, 1999.

Websites for Book Discussion Leaders

Amazon.com Book Clubs. http://www.amazon.com/exec/obidos/tg/browse/-/292203/002-9892715-9916804.

Ballantine Reader's Circle. http://www.randomhouse.com/BB/read/.

BookBrowse.com Reading Guides. http://www.bookbrowse.com/bookclubfun/index.cfm.

HarperCollins Reading Guides. http://www.harpercollins.com/readers.asp.

Houghton Mifflin Reading Guides. http://www.houghtonmifflinbooks.com/readers_guides/.

Oprah's Book Club. http://www.oprah.com/books/books_landing.jhtml.

Oxford World Classics. http://www.oup.com/us/collections/owc/reading.room/?view=usa

Penguin Putnam Reading Guides. http://www.penguinputnam.com/static/html/readingguides/index.html.

RandomHouse.com Reading Group Guides. http://www.randomhouse.com/reader_resources/browsetitle/index.pperl.

Reading Group Choices. http://www.readinggroupchoices.com/.

Reading Group Guides. http://www.readinggroupguides.com/.

St. Martin's Press Reading Group Guides. http://www.stmartins.com/smp/rgg.html.

Time Warner Bookmark. http://www.twbookmark.com/books/reading_guides.html.

AUTHOR INDEX

This index includes the fiction and nonfiction authors cited as examples in the text. Subjects and authors of reference sources are listed in the "Subject Index" beginning on page 205.

SUBJECT INDEX

This index includes subjects and authors of reference sources. For authors cited as examples in the text, see the "Author Index" beginning on page 199.

Joyce G. Saricks became literature and audio services coordinator at the Downers Grove (Ill.) Public Library in 1983, when she and Nancy Brown created a readers' advisory service there. She has presented more than one hundred workshops on readers' advisory for public libraries and library systems and has spoken at state, regional, and national library conferences. In addition to two previous editions of this title, she has also written the *Readers' Advisory Guide to Genre Fiction* (ALA, 2001) and is a columnist for *Booklist* as well as a consultant and readalikes author and coordinator for NoveList. Saricks was the 1989 recipient of the Public Library Association's Allie Beth Martin Award, which honors "an extraordinary range and depth of knowledge about books or other library materials and . . . a distinguished ability to share that knowledge." In 2000 she was named Librarian of the Year by the Romance Writers of America. Saricks retired from the Downers Grove Public Library in 2004 to pursue speaking and writing opportunities.

CPSIA information can be obtained at www.ICGtesting.com
Printed in the USA

267979BV00002B/25/P